# THE ITALIAN IN AMERICA:
# THE PROGRESSIVE VIEW,
# 1891-1914

# THE ITALIAN IN AMERICA: THE PROGRESSIVE VIEW, 1891-1914

edited by
Lydio F. Tomasi

1978
CENTER FOR MIGRATION STUDIES
NEW YORK

*The Center for Migration Studies is an educational, nonprofit institute founded in New York in 1964 to encourage and facilitate the study of sociological, demographic, historical, legislative and pastoral aspects of human migration and ethnic group relations. The opinions expressed in this work are those of the authors.*

The Italian in America:
The Progressive View,
1891-1914

First Published 1972
Second Edition 1978

Center for Migration Studies
209 Flagg Place
Staten Island, New York 10304

ISBN 0-913256-03-X
Library of Congress Catalog Card Number: 72-80258
Printed in the United States of America

# Introduction

Between 1880 and 1915, approximately four million immigrants came from Italy to the United States. Yet, despite the numerical magnitude of this movement, it is only in recent years that Italian Americans have begun to acquire a respected status in this country. In fact, those Italian immigrants who arrived just prior to the passage of restrictive laws ending mass immigrations to the U.S., met with only a bitter-sweet experience.

From the founding of the American Republic to 1880 over ten million immigrants were admitted to the United States. In the period from 1880 to the United States' entrance into World War I the volume of immigration doubled. Native Americans became alarmed about "hyphenated Americans". Following the 1880s, prevailing concepts considered the "new" immigrants from southeastern Europe biologically inferior to those of northwestern Europe and that such differences could be observed in specific social characteristics. Those who argued in favor of a restrictionist policy did so not merely because they wished to reduce the total volume of immigration, but because they wished to exclude the new immigrants from the U.S. and to perpetuate the influx of those immigrants who were part of the "old" immigration movement. The national origin of an immigrant was assumed to be a reliable indication of his capacity for assimilation. The Dillingham Commission, created on February 20, 1907, did not use the opportunity afforded it to make an objective study of the problem. The 42 volume report, made public on December 5, 1910, was neither impartial nor scientific, since it began by taking for granted the conclusions that the new immigration was essentially different from the old and less capable of being Americanized. These assumptions were the fundamental premise behind the immigration legislation of 1917-24 and the McCarren-Walter Act of 1952.

The contemporary press debated the various opinions and policies affecting immigration. This can be seen in the discussion of the "Ten Per Cent" Immigration Bill proposed in 1913 by Senator Dillingham, chairman of the late Immigration Commission and author of a previous immigration bill, vetoed by President Taft mostly because of the literacy test. The New York *Sun*, The Indianapolis *News* and the San Francisco *Labor Clarion*, for example, welcomed the new bill providing that the number of aliens of any nationality who may be admitted into the country during a year must not exceed 10 per cent of the number of persons of that nationality resident in the United States. It would have reduced the immigration from southeastern Europe by about 130,000 annually, and the number of aliens coming from northwestern Europe could have been increased by two-thirds. On the other hand, other newspapers such as the Philadelphia *Record*, the New York *Evening Post* and the Philadelphia *Public Ledger* could see no merit in the immigration restrictions proposed by Dillingham.

A magazine which served as a significant clearing house for the current thought and programs of social and settlement workers throughout the United States during the early 20th century was *Charities*. The 39 selections, by nearly as many different authors, reprinted in this volume represent most of what appeared on immigration in general and Italian immigration in particular in *Charities* from 1891 to 1914. They document an important part of American history.

*Charities* was sponsored by The Charity Organization Society of New York. "It is charity in its original meaning of 'love' ", wrote the president of the Society, Robert W. De Forèst, in the first issue of *The Charities Review* in 1891, and "not charity in its debased meaning of 'alms' ". According to De Forest, charity organizations "should not only aim to be beneficent forces and organizing forces, but to be educating forces as well". *Charities* magazine was such a force. Most of the contributors to *Charities* opposed nativism and racism and helped to delay the passage of immigration restriction laws.

*Charities* was started in 1887 as a small leaflet under the name *Lend-a-Hand*. Its purpose was to keep the members of the New York Charity Organization Society in touch with their work. Reflecting on the development of the magazine, its editors noted, "taking up the discussion of other forms of charity work, its pages came gradually to represent the workers in all forms of charitable activity. While its circulation included all of those professionally engaged in philanthropy, the number not so engaged but keenly interested in social progress, grew rapidly. No part of the broad program of social reform has been overlooked." Contributors and editorial writers voiced their views, related their experiences and initiated standards for social progress and legislation. The magazine was involved in such major issues of the period as child labor, tenement conditions, congested districts, crime, the fight against tuberculosis, settlement work, immigration and labor. The first issue of *The Charities Review — A Journal of Practical*

*Sociology*, appeared in November, 1891. With Volume VI, No. 1, January 5, 1901, the magazine was published under the name of *Charities — A Weekly Review of Local and General Philanthropy*. In Volume XV, No. 5, November 4, 1905, it was published under the name of *Charities and the Commons — A Weekly Journal of Philanthropy and Social Advance*. Finally, with Volume XXII, No. 1, April 3, 1909, until its demise in May, 1952, the magazine was published under the more comprehensive title of *The Survey — A Journal of Constructive Philanthropy*.

The writers in *Charities* generally reflected the ambivalent attitude of the progressives toward immigrants. In an editorial in the 1904 "Immigration Number" of *Charities*, which constitutes the bulk of Part I of the Volume, *Jewish Charities* said that the issue enabled "one to see the drift of expert opinion among the trained philanthropists of this city and elsewhere". The writers in *Charities* tried to find some answers to the famous question posed by Jean de Crevécoeur in 1782: "What then is the American, this new man?" This question is still debated by the "new Pluralists" in their search for new meanings of *American-ness* in today's ethnic revival.

John Watrous Knight's "The Working Man and Immigration" echoes the nativistic syndrome of the late 1880s and 1890s, when nearly all of America's internal problems were attributed to the "new" immigrants. Edward T. Devine, general secretary of the Charity Organization Society of New York City, questions the assimilative capacity of the "new" immigrants, while F. H. Ainsworth, secretary of the Immigration League, assumes that immigration is only beneficial for Europe, and Robert DeC. Ward discriminates "desirable" from "undesirable" immigrants to preserve the "future of the American race". On the other hand, Kate Holladay Claghorn, assistant registrar of the New York Tenement House Department, contrasts immigrants to the pauper group and writes, "the Italians, Austrians and Russians who make up the bulk of our immigration today . . . are almost exclusively of that great body of toilers upon whose broad and patient shoulders rests the towering structure of the European states". Relating immigration to household labor, Frances A. Kellor, scores the abuses of intelligence offices.

Gino C. Speranza, a lawyer born in the United States of Italian parents and corresponding secretary for the Society for the Protection of Italian Immigrants, looks at the immigration "problem" from the view of the host society and the "responsibility of the federal government". According to Speranza, "exploitation at docks and on trains and boats; traveling conditions which imperil safety and health; oppression at the hands of the *padroni*, isolation from family life and comforts; frauds on the part of banker, notary, and steamship agent, and misrepresentation at the hands of interpreters and fraudulent lawyers when they violate the laws they do not understand, make 'handicaps' out of immigrants". An area where the state's "educational and assimilative powers" do not reach the immigrants as they should is described by Sarah Wool Moore in her report on the labor camps' schools.

The progressives' agrarian bias shared by some writers of *Charities* explains their efforts to rechannel migration to the countryside, the final repository of American civilization. The immigrants were accused of congesting the cities, while rural areas were short of help. If the main motivation bringing immigrants to America was economic, they could hardly be expected to enter farming which had become the least lucrative of all occupations and was giving rise to the Populist revolt. To resolve the problem of city congestion Eliot Norton, president of the Society for the Protection of Italian Immigrants, and Broughton Brandenburg, proposed the settlement of immigrants in rural areas. Alexander E. Cance, of the Immigration Commission, in his report describes the settlement of the "problem groups": South Italians, Poles, Jews, Portuguese, Bohemians and Japanese.

The Italian immigration to the United States swelled to enormous proportions after 1880. The greatest influx of Italian newcomers occured concurrently with the progressive reformism sweeping the nation during the early 20th century. Shedding light upon this complex relationship was the 1904 "Italian Number" of *Charities* and other articles following this issue which form Part II of the volume. Announcing the "Italian Number", the editors of *Charities* wrote, "the May magazine issue will be dominated by a discussion of the social and economic conditions and benevolent activities of the Italians in this country. This issue will be unique in American periodical literature, and unusual in point of view, from the fact that a majority of the writers will be Italians who have become citizens, or who are residents in this country. The social and benevolent activities among Italian immigrants, their sanitary traditions, their agricultural colonies, and — most important and least understood — their assimilation and the impression made upon them by American institutions, will be written upon by fellow countrymen who have at heart the Americanization of the Italian laborer and the advancement of his children. Somewhat in contrast will be articles on Italian children in American schools and factories, and on the conditions which were left behind in the fatherland, by American writers especially qualified for their task. A few pertinent illustrations will add to the interest of the discussion of the Italian immigrant as he really is. It cannot be doubted that such a program will tend to throw light on the whole tendency of Italian immigration at the present time — a tendency which those well informed hold and differs widely in intent and personnel, no less than in numbers from its early years."

A fundamental assumption of these "fellow-countrymen" and other American writers is that the American creed requires that immigrants become a working part not only of our political and economic but also of our ideological system of life. Gino C. Speranza reversing his earlier liberal approach to immigration, argued that national unity, dependent on racial and cultural homogeneity, was being transformed by ethnic intermixing, and advocated "complete American conformity".

While these writers failed to understand that to build on existing attitudes is wiser than to seek to destroy them, they considered distinctive immigrant organizations as influential contributors rather than obstacles to assimilation. Among the various private organizations was the Society for the Protection of Italian Immigrants, whose activities were frequently reported in *Charities* (Cf. Vol. VIII, 1902, 435; 247-48; Vol. X, 1903, 122-24).

The reader should also remember that starting toward the end of the nineteenth century, Southern Italians contributed about 80 per cent of the entire Italian migration to the United States. Prior to their great migration these Southern Italian masses had been politically, economically, and socially abused. By the time of emigration, the vast majority of the peasantry were still landless, illiterate, and demoralized. Of the four million Southern Italians who entered the United States between 1880 and 1915, 80 per cent declared themselves to be agricultural workers who were accustomed to the most abject poverty and to the narrowest horizons of aspirations. Their condition illuminates their experience in America and the relativity of analysis of their behavior by many "social scientists".

In their discussion of the reasons for the Italian migration to the United States and the effects of that exodus upon Southern Italy, the writers in *Charities* reflect the current assumptions of the American progressives who attributed this exodus to the alleged decadence of Southern Italian society and the seemingly superior socioeconomic progress of the American nation. William E. Davenport, head social worker for the Brooklyn Italian settlement, maintains that the wages of field laborers had increased because the exodus to America had resulted in a scarcity of labor in many sections of Italy. The Italian American Baptist minister Antonio Mangano, in his voluminous articles, holds that poverty was the fundamental cause for the emigration from Southern Italy; to Southern Italians, America was "almost an enchanted country" (Cf. Vol. XIX, 1907-1908, 1475-1486; Vol. XX, 1908, 13-25; 167-179; 323-335).

The tenement life of the Italians in urban America is discussed by Robert A. Woods, a noted settlement house worker, Emily W. Dinwiddie, an inspector for the New York Tenement House Department, Antonio Stella, an Italian American physician, Rocco Brindisi, and Eleanor McMain.

Crime among the Italian newcomers was also a subject for discussion during the progressive era and in *Charities* magazine (Cf. Vol. XXV, 1911, pp. 488-489). Although Robert A. Woods and Gaylord S. White express a fear of excessive criminal activity among the Italian migrants, writers in *Charities* magazine do not profess these attitudes. I. W. Howerth assures his countrymen that the Italians are not a "dangerous" class.

Robert A. Woods and Bertha Hazard, consistent with the progressive view, contend that Italians should be directed into agriculture. Broughton Brandenburg recognizes that most of the Italian newcomers were "willing to do anything else for any rate of pay rather than continue farming" in the New World. Nevertheless, he supports the effort to direct the Italian migration to the rural areas of the nation. Mina C. Ginger, of the Consumer's League of New Jersey, conducted an investigation in 1905 into the substandard living conditions of Italian farm hands in the berry industry of that state. Both she and Emily Fogg Meade maintain that those Italians who owned farms in New Jersey ate better and were in better circumstances than their compatriots in the cities. In 1909, Alice Bennett noted the prosperous condition of Italian farmers in New York State (Cf. Vol. XXI, 1908, pp. 57-60), and in 1911, Alexander E. Cance emphasized the success of the Italian farmers in Wisconsin and the South.

That industrial America at the turn of the century faced a variety of internal problems is well known. Not least of these were the exploitation of labor and capital, strike breaking, anti-union violence, recurrent financial recessions, and a great disparity between the rich and the poor. Italians were part of the great proletarian immigration to the United States. *The Survey* has a report in 1913 on "The Dead Man at Mamaroneck" in connection with the New York, New Haven and Hartford Railway's strike: "It took the killing of one man in the prime of life, a strike sympathizer — a small merchant and property holder, he was of Mamaroneck — and the wounding of half a dozen strikers by local police and New York detective-agency men, to bring to public notice in New York not only the low pay of the Italian 'pick and shovel men' employed in the suburban towns along the Sound, but also the general violation of New York State laws on jobs done under contract for the state and various municipalities." Edith Waller in her poem, "The Italian Workmen of America to Americans", asks that these immigrants be given a chance. Although the prevailing judgment among social scientists has been that Italian Americans are basically conservative and anti-union, there did emerge some exceptional figures who had a decisive influence on Italian American workers. Prominent among them are Arturo Giovannitti, an Abruzzi born poet, editor of an Italian radical newspaper in New York, *Il Proletario*, secretary of the Italian Socialist Federation, and with another Italian American labor leader, Joseph Ettor, one of the Industrial Workers of the World leaders of the 1912 textile strike in Lawrence, Massachusetts, which was the Wobblies' greatest triumph. Mary Brown Sumner analyzes his literary production, and James P. Heaton gives an account of the Salem Trial.

It seems clear from the articles in *Charities* that the gulf separating the Italian immigrants from the American reformers was not bridged in the progressive era. Some of the reformers were aware of "how it feels to be a problem". Others, arguing for a rapid wrenching of the immigrants from their traditional culture, merely caused alienation and social disorganization.

I wish to acknowledge the aid of Sylvano M. Tomasi, C.S., Edward C. Stibili, O. Praem. and Donald Horrigan. I am also indebted to Robert Beech, the librarian of Union Theological Seminary, New York, for his valuable assistance.

L.F.T.

# Contents

# List of Photographs

# I

# The Immigrant:
# His Problem and Ours

Italian iceman.

# 1

# The Working-Man and Immigration[1]

JOHN WATROUS KNIGHT

It seems to be a popular impression, especially among politicians, that those citizens of this American republic who are citizens by adoption and not by inheritance, must necessarily be opposed to any and all change in our immigration laws, more especially if that change be in the nature of a restriction. The "foreign vote" — so called — must be catered to, it must be coddled and humored like a spoiled child; or, perhaps better, it must be handled gingerly as if it were a bomb which an incautious word were likely to explode, dealing political death and destruction to the party of the rash speaker.

It is probably true that a part of this "foreign vote" is at once antagonized by any talk of restricting immigration; but it is also true that this part is of the lowest, most ignorant, and altogether undesirable part of the community. Unfortunately, however, this ignorant, vicious, and undesirable citizen is, thanks to the early fathers of liberty, almost at once the equal at the primaries and at the polls, of the intelligent student of political science, — and is much more likely to be found there.

Some of our Northern Congressmen are undoubtedly dependent on the "foreign vote" for their election, and many others believe themselves to be thus dependent; to such, "immigration" is a bugaboo and little help can be expected from them. They are apt to hold their personal interests so near to them that the welfare of the community at large which lies just beyond, is entirely hidden from their view. They are glad of any opportunities which may be given them to speak for what they are pleased to call the "honest hard working immigrant who seeks a home for himself and his family in the land of freedom", etc., etc. And we may be sure that remarks to this effect

1. *The Charities Review*, Vol. 4, 1895. Pp. 363-375.

are not allowed to fall and die upon barren places, but are carefully reprinted and distributed among the zealous Congressman's foreign constituents.

Even granting, however, that our suppositious Congressman is honest in his zeal for the immigrant, is he correct in his contentions?

What is the character and influence of this foreign element which he represents, and of the immigrants to whom he refers?

Regarding the restriction of immigration, is not this foreign element certainly as much concerned as any other element of the population?

What effect has immigration on wages and on the standard of living set by the American working-man?

Is the "working-man" who shares the Congressman's solicitude in even a larger degree than the foreign voter, interested in immigration?

We would say that though he may not as yet be greatly interested in the subject, he certainly is concerned whether he knows it or not, and he must soon be interested as well.

This is a large subject, but we will consider a few details briefly.

The census of 1890 shows that 37½ per cent of the entire white population of the United States is either foreign born or of foreign parentage, and that all but about 6 per cent of these foreigners are in the Northern and Northwestern States. As about 76 per cent of the entire population is in these same States, this means that very nearly one-half of our Northern population and three-eighths of our entire white population, is either directly foreign or is foreign within one generation.

This very large element can not but have some influence in shaping the affairs, economic and otherwise, of this Nation; and if this influence be not in harmony with American institutions and the American standard of living, the worse for the Nation. When the alien declares his intention of becoming a citizen, "renounces forever all allegiance to any foreign prince or potentate", and swears to support the Constitution of the United States, his point of interest, if he is to be a good citizen, at once changes. He is no longer an Irishman, a German, a Bohemian, but an American. His interests now are in and for this country — his country none the less because it is his by adoption. He is interested in protecting his country and his home from invasion of any sort — as much from a horde of undesirable immigrants, as from the dread cholera or an armed enemy. He is interested in keeping up wages and in keeping down vice and crime, and in promoting the general prosperity and happiness of the community. He is as vitally concerned in all these things as any native born citizen. In fact there should be no distinction, politically or otherwise, between a native born and a foreign born citizen. Both are citizens — Americans — and as such their interests in the welfare of their country are one.

The American working-man, whatever may have been the country of his birth, should be more interested than any other citizen in the matter of immigration, because he is more directly influenced by it and more quickly feels its effects. About 30 per cent of the persons engaged in the manufacturing, mechanical and mining industries in the United States are of foreign birth, and doubtless as many more are of foreign parentage. The policy of this government has been continuously for the past thirty-five years, to protect the American manufacturer directly and the American working-man indirectly, from foreign competition in products. At the same time, it somewhat paradoxically allows the alien laborer to come to this country at will, where he may share all the advantages of the American, and where he will at once be in direct competition with him for the opportunity to work.

Of late years the immigrants who have come here have represented a very different type from those of thirty or forty years ago. They are of a decidedly lower scale in life. They are not used to the American way of living, and they do not seem to care to imitate it. They have no idea of bringing up their families after the American custom. They do not appreciate the institutions of a free land; they care nothing for the public schools, and very little whether their children receive any education at all. They appear to have no desire for the comforts they might easily have, but are content to live in a way that no native American would endure complacently. They have no desire to own a home, to become a part of the community. The object of many of them is merely to save enough money to enable them to return to their old homes where they can live in idleness for the remainder of their lives. To attain this end, each member of the family must contribute his labor, the earnings usually going to a common fund; and in the mean time they live more like cattle than like human beings, with little or no regard for the sanitation or the common decencies of life. As examples of this class may be mentioned the French-Canadians of New England, the Hungarians and Slavs in Pennsylvania and other mining districts, and the Italians in many places. The effect in the labor market of such competition as this is apparent. The axiom that the base metal will drive out the good, is equally true when applied to this class of labor.

To quote Prof. Richmond Mayo-Smith, "the reason these imported laborers can displace the American by taking lower wages, is that they live in a way which it is impossible for the native workman to imitate, and which it would be a misfortune for the civilization of the community if he should".

The census of 1890 shows that 44 per cent of all the foreign born, — not including those of foreign parentage, — live in 124 principal cities of the United States, those cities undoubtedly being where the greater part of the manufacturing of the country is done, where labor is most in demand, where the supply is also greatest, and where competition is most active. The endeavors of most State Bureaus of Immigration, and of most of the laws hitherto passed to facilitate immigration, have been to induce immigrants to take up land from the Government, or to settle in the more sparsely populated sections of the West. In spite of these efforts, however, we find nearly half the foreign born population in 124 certain cities, and in these same cities are 48 per cent of all the Germans in the United States, 56 per cent of all the Irish, 57 per cent of the Poles, 58 per cent of the Russians, 48 per cent of the Bohemians, 58 per cent of the Spaniards, and 59 per cent of the Italians.

While immigration in 1893 was more than double what it was thirty years ago, it has also undergone a very noticeable and significant change in character. From 1820 to 1870, about 50 per cent of the immigrants were from the United Kingdom, while the countries of Southern Europe — Italy, Russia, Poland and Austro-Hungary, — furnished scarcely one-half of 1 per cent. This had increased to 32 per cent of the total immigration in 1890, and 40 per cent in 1892, the following table giving the figures:

| No. of Immigrants decade ending 1870 | 1890 | Years 1891-2 |
|---|---|---|
| Austro-Hungary | 7,608 | 300,817 | 130,887 |
| Bohemia |  | 47,265 | 20,293 |
| Poland | 20,027 | 51,806 | 60,796 |
| Russia | 2,512 | 201,374 | 121,439 |
| Italy | 10,834 | 307,309 | 138,192 |

The total immigration from these countries up to and including 1880, exceeded by only a few thousand that of the single year 1892. It is seen that this immgration has increased from practically nothing in 1870 to two-fifths of total in 1892, and a little investigation may develop some interesting facts regarding these people. It is of importance to the good people of this country to know something about the half million immigrants from these countries who landed on our shores in 1891-2 and of the influences they brought with them.

Immigration from Great Britain and Northern Europe indicates that the families keep well together, the percentage of males and females being nearly equal. The proportion of males is much larger from the countries of Southern Europe, Italy sending the largest proportion of any country, 79.4 per cent of its total number. Italy also sends us the largest percentage of persons past the prime of life.

In spite of the wholesale naturalization carried on at election time about one-third of the foreign born males over 21 years of age have not been naturalized, — are not citizens — and of these, one-third do not speak the English language.

The census of 1890 shows that of the crime committed in the United States by white men and women whose nativity is known, 43.19 per cent is chargeable to native element, and 56.81 per cent to foreign element. Of the white paupers who were inmates of almshouses in the United States in 1890,

41.56 per cent comes of native and 58.44 per cent of foreign parents. The Secretary of State of New York reported in 1887, that there were in county poorhouses in that State, 9,172 native and 9,288 foreign born paupers, and in city poorhouses there were 18,001 native, and 34,167 foreign born paupers.

The question of illiteracy is one of the most important relating to the assimilation of the immigrants to American ideas, and it is one upon which there is least information attainable at this time. Of the native white population of the United States, 8.7 per cent were illiterate in 1880, and 6.2 per cent in 1890; while of the foreign born, 12 per cent were illiterate in 1880, and 13.1 per cent in 1890; showing that the standard of the native element had materially improved, while that of the foreign element had deteriorated.

No statistics of illiteracy of immigrants by nationalities have been kept prior to the year beginning July 1, 1894, but the report of the Superintendent of Immigration for 1893 shows that of the 359,153 immigrants over 15 years of age, 57,897 could not read, 59,582 could not write, and 61,038 could neither read nor write *any* language. In the report for 1892, is given a table of illiteracy in Europe, and while it is by no means conclusive as regards emigration, it may be safely assumed that the immigrants who reach us from these countries would not tend to lower this percentage:

In 1888 in Eng., Scotland & Wales,   8 pr. ct. pop. above 10 yrs. illiterate
In 1886 in Ireland                   21 pr. ct. pop. above 10 yrs. illiterate
In 1886 in Austro-Hungary            41 pr. ct. pop. above 10 yrs. illiterate
In 1886 in Italy (upper)             40 pr. ct. pop. above  6 yrs. illiterate
In 1886 Italy (lower)                72 pr. ct. pop. above  6 yrs. illiterate
In 1886 in Russia                    80 pr. ct. entire pop'ln were illiterate

In commenting upon this subject, the Superintendent says in this same report, "an educational test of an immigrant, if it is confined to the rudimentary branches, is not un-American, for the public school is the most distinctively American institution we have, and an educational test ought to be the most American test". This argument is made the stronger by the fact that it is not proposed in the new immigration or naturalization measures, to require the immigrant to read or write the English language, but merely that of the country from which he comes, or the land of his birth. It is held that with the assistance of the large number of newspapers published in the United States in foreign languages, an immigrant who could read some language, would more readily become familiar with American ideas and purposes. Statistics show that less than 3 per cent of the persons who cannot read at 16 years of age, ever succeed in learning.

No better commentary on the character of the citizens whom we are receiving year by year with open arms, can be given than statistics on occupations. The Bureau of Immigration classifies the occupations as "professional, skilled, miscellaneous, not stated, and without occupation".

These statistics show that one immigrant in 200 had a profession, one in ten was a skilled workman, and the remaining nine-tenths were of "unskilled" or "no occupation". The figures are:

| Occupation of Immigrants, decade 1881-1890 | | Years 1891-2 |
|---|---|---|
| Professional | 27,006 (.005 per cent) | 6,105 (.005 per cent) |
| Skilled | 540,411 (.103 per cent) | 105,171 (.09  per cent) |
| Miscellaneous | 2,079,135 (.396 per cent) | 514,615 (.434 per cent) |
| No occupation | 2,600,061 (.496 per cent) | 557,512 (.471 per cent) |

The class "professional" includes actors, artists, clergymen, lawyers, musicians, physicians, and teachers. The class "skilled" includes all the principal trades, most of which, if not all, are organized into Trades Unions here. The class "miscellaneous" includes, in the order of their number, laborers, farmers, servants, merchants, (mostly peddlers). Much the larger class, nearly one-half of the whole number, is made up of those who have no occupation or who do not state it. Of this number, however, (decade 1881-90) 1,767,284 were females, and 597,715 of the males were under 15 years of age, which leaves 253,062 males who are not even classed as laborers, and who in the words of the Chief of the Bureau of Statistics, "are unskilled and untrained in any vocation, and are probably unprepared to contribute much of industry, experience or ability, to the welfare of the community of which they become a part". Continuing he says, "if the classification by occupation of the males alone for the year 1892 be considered, it will be found that the professional and skilled classes together, contributed 13.03 per cent, the miscellaneous 57.57 per cent, while 29.40 per cent were without any occupation whatever".

About 50,000 skilled and professional workmen came here in 1892, but to this large number of men who at once began seeking a means of subsistance at their several trades, must be added nearly six times as many men physically capable of earning a living, but who have not even the capital of knowledge or ability in any special craft, and whose average cash capital, (as shown by the report which follows,) was $20.09.

In the report of the Superintendent of Immigration for 1892, is given a very interesting table of the amount of money brought by immigrants, which is quoted here in a condensed form:

"The 152,360 immigrants above 20 years of age who arrived at the port of New York during the six months ending June 30, 1892, brought $3,060,908.05, the average being $20.09 per capita.  5,814 immigrants brought more than $100 each, and 146,546 brought less than $100 each. Immigrants from France brought the largest amount of money per capita, the average being $55.67. Switzerland follows next with an average per capita of $44.01. Wales follows close, with an average of $43.06; Germany next with $35.42. Hungary, Italy and Poland brought the lowest average amount of case of any countries contributing to our population. They are within a fraction of the same average per capita, Poland being $12.31, Italy $11.77, and Hungary $11.42. The figures disclose an average per capita from Russian immigrants of $22.10. The immigrants from Russia have the widest variations in financial conditions, of any people who come to our country. Of the 9,639 immigrants who arrived, 333 brought more than $100 each, several of these bringing considerable sums, one bringing $25,000. All these were men conducting a prosperous business in Russia, and were driven from home on account of persecution, and who had converted their large estates into the cash they could secure, and fled the country. The 9,306 Russians who brought less than $100 were nearly all destitute. Very few of them had sufficient money to pay their passage to their destination in the interior of the country; the vast majority of them came on tickets furnished by the 'Baron Hirsch Fund'. The $3,060,908.05 is a very considerable sum of money to be brought into our country by new citizens, but when distributed among 152,360 persons, it becomes an inconsiderable amount. $20.09, the average amount of money per capita, cannot be considered a reasonable amount of money for the average immigrant to commence life with, in a new country."

The census of 1890 places the per capita wealth of the United States at $1,010. If the 152,360 immigrants considered in the foregoing report had brought with them this average instead of the amount they did bring, the wealth of the country would have been increased by $153,883,600, instead of $3,060,908.

There is undoubtedly in the table Occupations, and in the subject of Money Brought by Immigrants, matter worthy of the attention of every citizen, not the least interested of whom is the "laboring man". No one will dispute the fact that, upon the whole, wages have been much higher, and still are higher, in this country than in Europe, and the lot of the working-man is easier here than there. He and his family can live more comfortably and more independently here. Here are free schools for his children, and many advantages easily within their reach, that were never even thought of for himself in the land of his birth. It is easily possible for him to become a land owner. Here he has no military duty to perform; his time is his own for labor, for profit, and for the pursuit of happiness. To a knowledge of these facts is undoubtedly due a large part of our immigration. But who can say how long these privileges will, nay, can continue within his reach, if year by year, from a quarter to a half million men are added by immigration to those already here, and almost — in many cases — fighting for an opportunity to work for their living? The Trades Unions struggle desperately to keep up the scale of wages, without apparently taking into consideration the fact that our already large supply is constantly being augmented by newcomers. The law of supply and demand enters as fully into the question of labor and of wages, as it does into any commodity. Capital naturally avails itself of the abundance of labor, and vice versa, labor of its scarcity. The industries of this country are constantly developing and expanding, but if the status of the working man is to remain the same, *new* work must be found *daily*, sufficient for 901 men, that being the average number of male immigrants landing daily from 1881 to 1892. And this does not take into consideration the natural increase of our own population, which is said to be about 1,500,000 a year. Assuming that one-half of these are males, 2,000 of our own citizens are daily entering the field of labor for the first time. Thus, on the basis of recent immigration, we have nearly 3,000 men, all told, to be provided with *new* work, each day. The conditions that exist today are such that labor is bidding against labor, and the result is almost sure to be a deterioration of the American standard. That standard has been, and, upon the whole, is still high, and the American has the advantage of a good start; but the supply of the baser material is well nigh inexhaustible, and it is always more difficult to raise than lower the level.

A very interesting and valuable report was recently made by Mr. Carroll D. Wright, United States Commissioner of Labor, of an investigation in the slum districts of the cities of New York, Philadelphia, Baltimore, and Chicago, in which the native and foreign born population were compared. The districts canvassed for this report by no means contained the entire slum population of these cities. The population of districts canvassed was, in 1890, 77,386, while from reliable estimates the total slum population of the same cities is about seven times that number. The districts, however, are fairly representative of the city slums, and are thought to be indicative of the conditions existing elsewhere.

| Percentage foreign born in City at large | | In slum districts |
|---|---|---|
| Baltimore | 15.88 per cent of total | 40.21 per cent |
| Philadelphia | 25.74 per cent of total | 60.45 per cent |
| Chicago | 40.98 per cent of total | 57.51 per cent |
| New York | 42.23 per cent of total | 62.58 per cent |

To go back one generation, we find, taking the average of the four cities, that 11.79 per cent of the persons in the slum districts are of native, and 88.21 per cent of foreign parentage — in the case of New York the percentage of foreign parentage rising to 95.23.

Regarding illiteracy, the report shows a great contrast, not only between the city at large and the slum district, but between the native and foreign born in the slums.

Percentage of Illiterates

| In city at large— | | In slum district— | | | |
|---|---|---|---|---|---|
| Baltimore | 9.79 | Native | 8.13 | Foreign | 30.62 |
| Philadelphia | 4.97 | Native | 8.44 | Foreign | 46.61 |
| Chicago | 4.63 | Native | 5.64 | Foreign | 33.86 |
| New York | 7.69 | Native | 7.20 | Foreign | 57.69 |

Of those in the slums who are illiterate, .09 per cent are native and 91 per cent foreign born. The countries of Austro-Hungary, Poland, Russia, and Italy contribute 72.27 per cent of this 91 per cent, Italy alone furnishing nearly one-half. In New York, 79.75 per cent of the foreign born illiterates come from the last named country.

Thus it is seen that while 44 per cent of total foreign born population of the United States was in 124 certain cities, in the slums were from 40 to 62 per cent, that from 30 to 57 per cent of these could neither read nor write, and that nearly 75 per cent of these illiterates came from four countries of Southern Europe.

The smaller number of people required to support a saloon in the slum districts — or the greater number of saloons required to support the people — does not augur too well for the respectability and character of this part of the community.

| Saloons in the city at large | | In the slum district |
|---|---|---|
| Baltimore | 1 saloon to every 228 persons | 1 saloon to 105 persons |
| Philadelphia | 1 saloon to every 870 persons | 1 saloon to 502 persons |
| Chicago | 1 saloon to every 212 persons | 1 saloon to 127 persons |
| New York | 1 saloon to every 200 persons | 1 saloon to 129 persons |

We have now examined some of the more pronounced characteristics of the men who are landing on our welcoming shores by the hundred thousand every year. We find that a large number of them eventually reach some of our charitable or corrective institutions. We find that one-half of them remain in the larger cities, where the supply of labor almost always greatly exceeds the demand. A very large proportion of them, as has been seen, gravitate to the slums; can it be called a case of "natural selection"? These are the men who bring with them $11 per capita as their entrance fee into the land of freedom and plenty which henceforth "owes them a living". These are the men who, in more than half the cases, cannot write their names or read newspapers printed in their native tongue; nine out of ten of whom have no trade or profession, who are "the hewers of wood and drawers of water"; and whose intelligence is measured, in the large majority of cases, by the pick and shovel, and who are, and always will be, aliens in fact and in purpose, as well as in tradition. Superintendent of Immigration Owen was very conservative when he said (Report 1892) that the time had come when the country and not the immigrant should be given the benefit of any doubt in immigration matters.

In many instances this unskilled labor, having mastered the simple operations of industrial machinery, goes into the factories, driving out the more intelligent labor by reason of its willingness to work for lower wages. The French-Canadians are an instance of this class of labor, and in New England they have very largely supplanted the old operatives. They do not, however, take the place of the old inhabitants in the social life and welfare of the community. Several trades, tailoring and boot and show making for example, are now very largely in the hands of foreigners, mostly poor Russian and Polish Jews. Prof. Mayo-Smith, in writing of this subject says in part, "the testimony before the Ford Congressional Committee was that these new arrivals, entirely destitute, ignorant of the language and accustomed to a low style of living, fell at once into the 'sweater' system, with its miserable wages, long hours of work, employment of women and children, and disregard of all the decencies and health requirements of life. In New York it was shown that the wages of sewing women (at best but meagre) had been reduced by the competition of Russian and Polish men who would work for less wages. It is this kind of competition that is unfair to our working classes, and a danger to the community. It is unfair to ask the working man to compete against labor based on a standard of living which we should be unwilling to see him adopt."

France, in 1888, alarmed at the "large and increasing number of foreigners", adopted laws for their registration, which it was hoped would tend to discourage immigration. These foreigners at that time constituted 3 per cent of the total population. Here they constituted, at the same time, about 15 per cent. It should be said that there has been a large decrease in immigration to this country for the fiscal years 1893 and 1894, owing first to cholera, and later to the panic and the business depression here. Still, a large number of immigrants can be better provided for when times are good, factories running, and the industries of the country flourishing, than can a small number when thousands of men already here are out of employment, and are clamoring for work.

Whenever a measure is introduced in Congress looking to an improvement in our immigration or naturalization laws, there is always more or less grandiloquent talk about the "proud name of American citizen", a favorite comparison being that of "Roman citizen" at a time when Rome was mistress of the world. But such speakers seem to think that if the American citizen has now the prestige that his Roman prototype once had, it follows that he always will have it, without regard to changing conditions from within; and they leave us to infer that Roman citizenship could be as easily acquired as can that of America, whereas nothing could be further from the truth. For many years the alien at Rome was outside the pale of the law, and had no rights of life or property; and while these severe measures were modified in course of time it was only at an expense of considerable money or service — usually military — that the alien ever attained the rights of the citizen. And as this privilege increased in value, the difficulty of obtaining it increased also. It is safe to say that a barbarian who appeared at the gates of Rome, ignorant of its customs, its language, its laws, with but $20.09 in the pocket of his tunic, and who asked to be admitted to full citizenship, including eligibility to the Senate, might have counted himself fortunate to have escaped with his life.

Would not American citizenship be more highly prized, if its acquirement involved on the part of the alien some sacrifice of time, money, or labor?

It has been true in the past, and possibly is true still, that men of other nations upon coming to this country have seemd to lose many of their native characteristics, and to have become, henceforth, Americans. This regeneration of all the kindred of the earth into a distinctly new and different type, the *genus Americanus*, has excited the wondering comment of the world. Hitherto the assimilation of this conglomerate mass of nations has been achieved without apparent loss to the health of the body politic; but who can say how near the health of this body may be to the point where it breaks down? Who can say how much longer this assimilation can continue without impairing the present American standard? Indeed, are we so sure that it is not impaired already? Considerably more than one-third — probably two-fifths — of our entire population are foreigners by birth or within one generation. Can we, as a nation have absorbed this immense number of people without its having a very real effect, especially when we remember that statistics show conclusively that these people, in the vast majority of cases, have been far below the standard of what we are glad to believe is that of the American people. We have been strong enough to stand the strain thus far. How long can we continue to stand it?

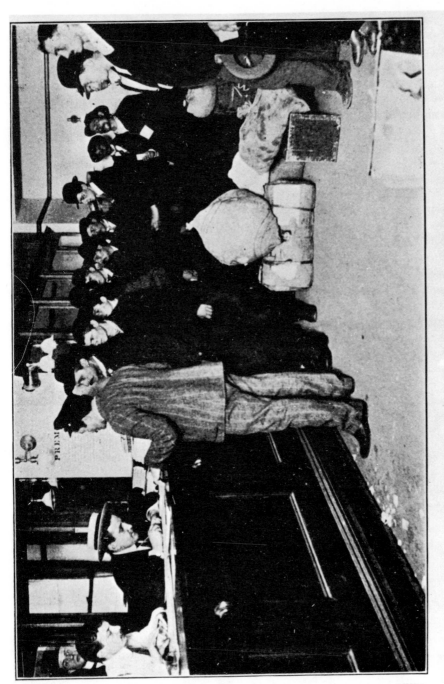

Courtesy of Leslie's Weekly

New Arrivals Registering at the Protection Society's Main Office on Pearl Street.

# 2

# Immigration as a Relief Problem[1]

EDWARD T. DEVINE

The relief problem of the American seaboard cities is greatly affected by
immigration. The immigrant of the twentieth century offers little resemblance
to the colonist of the early days of the republic. The colonist was establishing
new outposts of civilization; he was one who was capable of making his
way in the face of adverse circumstances; he was influenced by some strong
religious or political or economic motive, and felt within himself a daring
and strength of character sufficient to overcome the dangers, the loneliness,
and the privations of the frontier. Colonization is, in short, one of those
differentiating agencies leading to the selection and survival of those who
have initiative and exceptional capacity. Immigration, on the other hand, is
a comparatively easy escape from hard conditions. The immigrant is one
who follows in a path already made easy. He goes where his friends or
relatives have gone, and settles in the spot where they have settled. He yields
to the artifices of transportation agents, or may even be assisted by the
public authorities of his own community to emigrate for his country's good.
Until legal interference is interposed he comes under a contract to work at
occupations and under industrial conditions about which he may be entirely
ignorant, thus lending himself readily to a lowering of the standard both of
living and of wages. He is scarcely conscious even of the handicap of
speaking a foreign language, since he is worked and lodged with others of
his own nationality, and under foremen who can speak to him in his own
language.

The immigrant who goes under tempting circumstances to a place literally
prepared for his arrival, has therefore rather less than the average initiative,
independence and courage, the qualities which are so predominant in the

1. *Charities*, Vol. 12, 1904. Pp. 129-133.

original settlers of a new country. This is, of course, by no means a correct description of all immigrants. There may be little difference between the best immigrant and the best colonist, or even between the majority of immigrants and the majority of colonists. The description applies rather to the marginal colonist and immigrant respectively — to the least efficient class who are nevertheless represented in each in considerable numbers. In the frontier colony the minimun wage-earning capacity and industrial efficiency is necessarily high, in the immigrant it may be very low, and it is with these marginal immigrants that relief agencies have chiefly to deal.

## The Margin of Immigration

The immigration laws of the United States have been amended explicitly, although not yet adequately, to meet this situation. Not only is it made unlawful for lunatics, feeble-minded persons and habitual criminals to enter, but those who are "liable to become public charges" are also excluded, and large discretion is necessarily lodged in officials stationed at the various points of entry, in determining whether particular persons are or are not included in this category. The possession of a stipulated sum of money, or positive assurance from a friend or relative, apparently worthy of confidence, are regarded as evidence of eligibility for admission. No such test, however, can effectively bar out all, or even any large proportion, who are on the brink of dependence, and as a matter of fact many immigrants do become public charges, either in their own person or through the commitment of their children to public institutions, within a few years of their arrival. While the former practice of deporting public dependents as an economical means of getting rid of the burden of their financial support may have been discontinued there is said to have grown up in recent years in its place a very systematic commercial substitute which operates in precisely the same manner, so far as its effect on the stream of inefficient immigration is concerned. An agency at Bremen and other points of embarkation, with offices in many parts of central and southeastern Europe on consideration of what appears to the emigrant to be a moderate charge, say ten dollars, in addition to the ordinary steamship passage, contracts to relieve those who apply to it of the risks and incidental expenses of their journey. This payment is understood to guarantee in effect a safe landing at the point of destination. In case of failure to pass successfully the ordeal of scrutiny by the immigration authorities, the steamship company is required under the law to return its passenger to the place from which he sailed, while the agency to whom the fee has been paid meets likewise the expense of the return to his original starting point. There may be occasional loss on individuals thus rejected, but, of course, in the large proportion of cases the fee represents a large margin of profit, and the net earnings of the commercial undertaking are said to be very considerable, averaging perhaps one-half of the fee charged. The assisted ocean passage and the ready employment on arrival, to which reference have been made, although they serve to attract less efficient and intelligent laborers, are not to be had for nothing. By excessively long hours; by overcrowded unsanitary tenements, and by insufficient wages, the immigrant returns full measure of payment for his escape from the necessity for independence and initial hardships. Initial obstacles have been removed only that the remainder of his days be exploited to his injury. The liberty which he has bartered he may regain by suffering and toil for himself or for his children, but there will be many who fail, and it is to meet these failures that the relief policy must be framed. The widows and infant children left behind by those who have died from consumption or who have been killed in factories; the shiftless, intemperate men and women whose lives have been sapped by their premature employment as children; ineffective workers who are so because they are illiterate and untrained; the sick and disabled whose relatives are in distant lands and are poor, these, and other types of dependents are increased in number and their natural resources for relief are fewer because of immigration.

### Absence of Family Ties

Recognition of the family, even in its collateral branches, and the placing of burdens upon those who are thier blood kindred is one of the first principles of organized relief. When, however, all inquiries run quickly to the ocean's edge, the chances of any effective recognition of family responsibility are greatly lessened. A vague statement that one's parents or other kindred in Syria, in Poland, in Southern Italy or in Ireland have all that they can do to support themselves, is not easily disproved, even if it is not always true. Correspondence with relief agencies throughout the European continent is difficult, and even when it has been established, is often inconclusive because of the different points of view and the differences in language, customs and standards. When one has lost employment and has but a few acquaintances, and these perhaps hastily formed, it is, of course, more difficult for him to give those evidences of character and fitness which would be available in his native land, but which are not readily imported among the immigrant's assets. It is beyond reasonable expectation also, that when one has through old age or infirmity become a public charge, there should be quite the same degree of tenderness and consideration for an immigrant as the same individual might have experienced in a similar adverse fate in the home of his ancestors.

I am not apologizing for any indifference to the necessities of those who are in distress, but pointing out that absence from those upon whom they have the strongest claim for the offices prompted by ties of kindred and of intimate association through generations, is a deprivation of that for which there is no ready substitute. This, however, increases rather than lessens the responsibility of those who in public or in private charities administer relief. Those who have been in the country but a short time may wisely be returned to their homes, but others who may remain after the lapse of years essentially immigrants, may be in distress and it may be possible to relieve them, or necessary to support them in their dependent condition. It is not by withholding relief from individuals or from families who may be wisely aided, that the evil consequences of unrestricted immigration are to be met. The strengthening of existing laws, an additional clause excluding illiterate adults, and by providing more efficient means for the deportation of those who have been admitted through misrepresentation or fraud is advisable, and the uniform and equitable administration of existing laws is essential, and in addition voluntary agencies and private citizens may wisely counteract, at the sources of emigration the misinformation which has been persistently spread abroad. Definite measures are now taken, for example, in Ireland to check emigration, and these are supported by representative Irishmen whose devotion to the interests of the Irish people, both at home and in America, is unquestionable.

### Labor Which is not Socially "Cheap"

The arguments in favor of unrestricted immigration are that cheap labor is needed in the building of railways and in many other undertakings in which the directive intelligence can be separated from the physical labor required; and that any practical test such as ability to read or write, possession of a given sum of money, or even a certificate of good character from the place of departure will operate to exclude many who nevertheless under new conditions, in a new land, might prove to be very useful and entirely self-supporting citizens.

While it is true that cheap labor may be made profitable from the employer's point of view, it does not follow that those who are considering the interests of the community as a whole can look with favor upon it. The superintendent of a mill, which had within a few years replaced efficient, but highly paid American laborers by Hungarians, analyzed the results of the change in conversation with the author as follows: The new laborers could do less work in a given time, but they were willing to work at less wages, and they were willing to work more hours in the week. Being less efficient and having less initiative it had been necessary to increase the number of foremen and to pay them somewhat higher wages, holding them responsible to a greater extent than before for the correction of mistakes and for driving the men under them at their maximum capacity. As the men worked for longer hours the machinery was idle for a smaller part of the time and the total product was increased at less expense. This illustration is not presented as typical. In many instances the product would doubtless be diminished rather than increased by such a substitution, and the cost increased so that the net result would be a diminution of profits. Within reasonable limits the general principle is that high-priced labor is economic labor, the condition being that it shall be as intelligent, as trustworthy and as efficient as it is well-paid. Nevertheless the exploitation of cheap labor, as is illustrated in the instance above cited, is not infrequent, and whether in the long run it is disastrous or beneficial in a given industry, there is no doubt that for individuals in charge of particular times, it will offer an opportunity for pecuniary profit and that such an opportunity will be seized. With the consequences to the industry in the long run, the employer of the moment may have little concern. The effect of utilizing underpaid immigrant labor under conditions which, in order to afford a living at all, makes excessive demands upon adult men, and leads irresistibly to the employment of women and children, is directly to increase the number who sooner or later require relief. To produce stray instances or even a goodly number of persons who have struggled through such adverse conditions without becoming dependent upon others, is not to offer evidence to the contrary. The plain tendency is to augment the number of those who break down prematurely; of those who in advanced years have made no provision for their own maintenance; of the children whose support must be supplied by others than their own parents, and of those who, meeting with unexpected misfortune of any kind, have no resources except the generosity of strangers.

## The Burden at the Seaboard

It is, of course, ports of entry, and preeminently the city of New York, that suffer most from the effects of undesirable immigration. Those who have even normal wage-earning capacity, and who do not require the presence of a number of their own nationality about them, may push on to the interior cities and towns, or may find employment at farm labor. Those who remain behind comprise the most and the least ambitious. For the man who can really succeed, there are, perhaps, greater rewards in the greater cities, but those who are least efficient and capable remain, not because it is to their advantage, but because it is easier. They do not know, and they have no means of finding out, what opportunities would be open to them elsewhere, and they shrink from a venture which might prove fatal. Their instinct leads them not to repeat the original mistake of cutting loose from friends and acquaintances, even if these are of but slight value as compared with the more than lifelong ties which have been severed by their removal from their original home. The conditions which arise in the seaboard cities

from every augmenting immigration, call for some revision of the principles
of settlement and of transportation.

The principles relating to settlement inherited from the English Poor Law,
and applied with many modifications in the various states, is that so far as
public relief is concerned dependent persons are to be aided in the communities
in which they have had a permanent residence, and that if they become
dependent elsewhere they may be legitimately returned to the place in
which they last had a permanent residence. However necessary or expedient
it may be to limit public relief to those who have a settlement established
through long-continued residence, it is clearly unwise to adopt the same
principle in the administration of private relief, and then to apply it both in
public and in private in such a way as to lessen the distribution of the
immigrant population throughout the entire country.

## A Question of Assimilating Capacity

The argument for liberal immigration laws is based upon the assimilating
powers of the American people. If immigrant colonies, however, are
established at the very point of entry the opportunities for assimilation are
greatly diminished. The inducement for those who speak a different language
to acquire knowledge of English is lessened, and there are fewer occupations
open to those who are required in any event to learn some new means of
livelihood. Many of those who are still admitted should be excluded by
more stringent laws, and there should also be developed systematic plans
for distributing them to the places where there is need of the labor which
they can perform, or if necessary to colonies established for the purpose of
affording them a home and employment, and an opportunity to make a
start under favorable conditions. A temporary landing in New York City,
and the spending of a few months in a desperate attempt to gain a footing is
not in any real sense to establish a residence. When one who has had this
experience becomes, through loss of employment and inability to find
anything to do, dependent, it may be advisable to aid him and impracticable
for exceptional reasons to return him to his native country, but the general
principle that dependent persons are to be aided where they have a settlement
ought not to debar the giving of aid in transportation to some other place
where the conditions are known to be less unfavorable. It is not the general
condition of the market for labor that determines the matter, but the limited
demand for the excessive supply of the class of unskilled immigrants, or
immigrants whose skill lies in a direction for which there is no demand. In so
far as relief is required the responsibility for it rests undoubtedly upon the
community in which the person has become dependent, or the one from
which he has come. Those who remain dependent immediately upon transfer
to some other place should be returned at the expense of those who have

sent them away. Transportation to other places should not be resorted to merely as a means of lessening the demand for relief. Only in so far as there is a reasonable prospect of actual employment in the new community, or a transfer of the burden to those upon whom the dependent person has an immediate personal claim, is the resort to transportation justified, and even this is justified only as a remedy for an insufferable condition created by immigration and the congestion of an abnormal number of the least efficient immigrants in the cities of their first arrival.

Either the number to be admitted must be greatly reduced or the burden of assimilation must be far more widely distributed, and in truth there is need of both remedies.

"The newly rich set against the shadows of their former selves reject the newly arrived immigrant." A cartoon by J. Keppler, 1893.

# 3

# Are We Shouldering Europe's Burden?[1]

F. H. AINSWORTH[2]

In no other city of the United States, perhaps, is there so close a relation between the alien population and the recipients of charity, in one form or another, as exists in New York. The cause of this is not very difficult to understand if we refer to the report of the commissioner-general of immigration for the past fiscal year. There it will be seen that of 857,046 aliens who arrived during that period 254,665 were destined to New York State! Among these were 91,774 South Italians; 50,945 Hebrews; 16,018 Poles; 15,491 Germans and 12,711 Scandinavians. How many of these remained in this city I have no means of knowing, but those who frequent the parts of the city occupied by these peoples could probably give some interesting testimony in this respect.

For the financial condition of the different immigrants reference is made to the report of the United States Industrial Commission for the year 1900. On page 284 it is stated that South Italians bring an average of $8.84 per capita; Hebrews $8.67 per capita; Poles $9.94 per capita; Germans $28.53 per capita and Scandinavians $16.65 per capita. Just fancy an American landing in St. Petersburg with one suit of clothes and nine or ten dollars in money. This will give some idea of the people who come to New York in large numbers and of their inability to withstand sickness or lack of work.

Next, attention is invited to the reports of some of the private hospitals, as an illustration of the origin of many of those who seek free treatment. On page 50 of the report of the Lying-in Society for the year ending September

30, 1902, it is stated that 2,595 outdoor patients were treated. Of this number 1,449 were Russians; 390 Austrians; 315 natives of the United States; or, in other words, only about twelve per cent of those treated were of American birth. This hospital has a reported deficit of $88,477.63 at the present time. In the Presbyterian Hospital, according to the last report, 3,026 patients were treated, of whom 1,417 were born in foreign countries. Of the total number of those who received treatment, 68 per cent were so cared for without charge. Applying this to the foreign-born it would indicate that 963 received free treatment. What percentage of these were aliens is not indicated, but it may be safely stated that a very considerable number of them were not citizens. This hospital has a deficit of $58,504.88 for the period covered by the report. On the other hand, however, an inspection of the subscription list fails to disclose any considerable sum *donated by aliens* resident in this city.

The foregoing statistics have been referred to as suggesting this question: "Is not a very large sum of money expended in public and private charity upon individuals from European countries whose causes of indigency originated before they came to this community?" And, also, this question has a direct bearing upon the subject: "If no alien who had lived in this country less than five years should have been the recipient of free treatment in our private hospitals, would the large deficit that is reported exist?" I firmly believe that our charitable citizens are supporting not only the legitimate needy and suffering of this community, but also a very considerable number of aliens. It is not intended in any way to reflect upon those who administer the funds of the various institutions, for they are bound to render aid where it is needed, but the bulk of immigration to this country lands at the port of New York, and those who are unfortunate, unsuccessful, or indolent, either stay there or return as soon as they feel the need of aid.

Referring to the present laws, William Williams, Commissioner of Immigration at the Port of New York, says: "But these laws do not reach a large body of immigrants who, while not of this class (*i.e.,* those now excluded), are yet generally undesirable, because unintelligent, of low vitality, of poor physique, able to perform only the cheapest kind of manual labor, *desirious of locating in cities*", etc. (the italics are mine).

The present situation is, then, that not only are the contributors to our great charitable institutions called upon to support those who have some claim to assistance, based on the fact that they took some part in the progress of the city by their labor or industry while prosperous, but are burdened with a horde of aliens who have produced nothing here and whose only interest is to be maintained in their affliction or indigence.

Is it not time the immigration of such be made impossible?

# 4

# Immigration and Dependence[1]

KATE HOLLADAY CLAGHORN[2]

The popular idea of the relation of immigration to the problem of dependence was well expressed in a recent newspaper picture which showed, to illustrate the evils of immigration, a vast ocean steamer, the stern touching the European shore, the bow, the American shore. Into this, on the European side poured a vast throng of people, winding down from the poorhouses of Europe; from it, on the American side, the throng reappeared, to take up the straight road to the poorhouses of America.

It is not difficult to show the crudity and falsity of this presentation. In many important respects, indeed, the foreign immigrant is the very anti-type of the pauper. The Italians, Austrians and Russians who make up the bulk of our immigration to-day, are, even less than the English, Irish and German immigrants of sixty years ago, when we had not the strict immigration laws of the present, drawn from European poorhouses. They are almost exclusively of that great body of toilers upon whose broad and patient shoulders rests the towering structure of the European states. Their very presence here shows the desire for bettering one's condition and the energy to set about it that is so characteristically a lack in the true pauper.

In age, sex and family relationships the immigrant group is again in direct contrast to the pauper group. The pauper population is predominantly composed of the old, and of the very young. The immigrant group is predominantly composed of young adults, with males in the majority — a class most able and most likely to take care of itself.

1. *Charities*, Vol. 12, 1904. Pp. 135-137.
2.Assistant Registrar, New York Tenement House Department

This circumstance, by the way, shows the unpractical character of one at least of the popular remedies proposed for the evils of immigration, the exclusion of those past middle life. The New York Board of Trade the other day recommended "the exclusion of aliens of sixty years of age or over, who are not financially able to provide for themselves, or have no children or other relatives here who are willing to protect them". Of the 850,000 and more immigrants who arrived during the year 1903, only about 40,000 were 45 years of age or over. Had all of these been excluded, without regard to their personal means, or family connections, we should still have had over 800,000 immigrants, while if the Board of Trade rule had been followed, it is safe to say that not more than one-tenth of the 40,000 could have been excluded.

Considering the volume of immigration, it is obvious that the great mass of our immigrants are absorbed in the industries of the country with surprising rapidity and completeness. The very movement of immigration, indeed, seems to show an apparently automatic adjustment of labor supply to labor demand. Not only does the tide of immigration rise and fall with periods of industrial prosperity and depression, but a return current, not shown in immigration statistics, is set up in dull times, carrying back thousands and thousands of foreigners to their old homes, to remain there until there is a renewed demand for labor, and thus relieving this country of the burden of their support during periods of unemployment.

In contrast again to the pauper type, the difficulties into which the foreign immigrant does fall after arrival here are mostly of a temporary nature. It is pressure of adverse circumstances rather than deep-seated defects of character that occasions the need for relief among our foreign population. This fact in itself makes the burden more tolerable to us. There is a distinct satisfaction felt in starting the wayfarer along the first steps of an upward road that is replaced by a feeling of dragging discouragement when the effort must be exerted to make the true pauper retrace the downward road he has traveled for so long.

When all is said, however, it is still possible for the advocates of severe restriction of immigration to point to facts that are patent to all; that by far the greater proportion of both public and private charity is expended upon foreigners, and that the slums of our great cities, with their overcrowded and unsanitary tenements, and other attendant evils, are the "foreign quarters".

The simple and natural explanation of all this, and one at the same time not at all discreditable to the immigrant, is the true starting point for the discussion of the good or evil of immigration, so far as it affects the problem of dependence, at least. Our foreign population furnishes the greater part of our dependent population, because foreigners constitute the greater part of those economic classes from which dependents in any country are drawn, while the native-born are for the most part found in those economic classes that do not furnish dependents.

Foreign immigrants on their arrival here, enter the class of unskilled workers, casually employed, or regularly employed at a rate of wages that does not allow for expenses of illness or other accident; or they enter the class of skilled workers who, with higher wages, are yet subject to periods of unemployment. The native-born population, on the other hand, is almost exclusively found in the higher grades, as owners of land, in commerce, in the professions, and, in general, as officers in the great industrial army in which the foreigners are privates.

The discussion, then, should turn on the question whether, without the immigrants, we could have an industrial organization without these lower, dependent-producing grades, or even with considerable elevation of their general level.

This is far too large a question even to be taken up within the present limits. There is not, indeed, any body of authentic material bearing on this point to which one can go for direct proof on one side or the other. It can only be suggested here that all statements as to what form of industrial organization we should have had if left to ourselves, are purely conjectural. There is certainly no analogy in civilized history to show that with the present utilization of resources, our industrial organization would be substantially different. The two European countries of perhaps the highest industrial development and the best racial stocks, England and Germany, have the same economic classes and the same problems of dependence that we have, and until lately, no appreciable "foreign element" to account for them.

It may further be suggested that the low standard of life brought here by the immigrant, that leads him to accept, on first arrival, a low place in the industrial scale, raises itself more easily than many suppose. The individual change and movement in tenement quarters, the tenacious pursuit of higher wages in strikes, and the general desire on the part of immigrant parents that their children, at least, shall enter a higher economic grade, are some of the indications of this.

Perhaps, after all, if a race distinction is to be made, we native-born Americans should rather congratulate ourselves that the foreigners have come among us to enter so freely and willingly the lower industrial grades, than try to shut them out, with the chance of being obliged to occupy those lower grades ourselves. And perhaps we should feel that as we are now as a class occupying so favorable an industrial position, we can well afford to pay the bill for damages incurred by those who are less fortunately placed.

Mrs. Motto and family making flowers in tenement, 302 Mott St., top floor, December 1911.

# 5

# The Immigration Problem
# Its Present Status and Its Relation
# to the American Race of the Future[1]

ROBERT DeC. WARD

The immigration question is at once one of the most important and one of
the most perplexing problems before the American people. It is important
because it concerns, in the most intimate way, not only the present welfare
of all our citizens, but the welfare and the character of the citizens of future
generations. It is perplexing because of the variety of the interests which are
involved in any discussion of it. So complex a problem does not lend itself
readily to brief consideration. If we would consider it at all, we must confine
ourselves to one or two aspects of it alone. It is my purpose to discuss this
question in some of its broader aspects, in the light of the conditions which
have developed as recently as during the last two years, and to include also
some consideration of the immigration of future years and of its relation to
the American race which is to live on after we are gone. I shall have
something to say, in closing, on the question of the further restriction of
immigration, and I assume, at once, without attempting to argue the matter,
that my readers are agreed that every nation has the undoubted *right* to
restrict or to prohibit immigration, if it sees fit. The sentimental predisposition of hospitality and of fraternity in favor of *absolute* freedom of
immigration to this country — a feeling which used to be universal, as it was
traditional — has of late years very largely, I may even say almost entirely,
disappeared, in the face of the changed conditions of immigration, which
have made it plain that a departure from this traditional policy is not only in
the highest degree expedient, but even absolutely necessary for the welfare
of the country and for the preservation of its standards of citizenship and of
character. Our fathers were undoubtedly right when they openly welcomed
the sturdy immigrants from northern Europe. Shall we say that we are

1. *Charities*, Vol. 12, 1904. Pp. 138-151.

wrong if we believe in maintaining American standards of living, and in selecting, to some slight extent, if we may, the elements which are to make up the American race of the future?

In such a consideration of the immigration problem as that before us at the moment, there is no need of wearying ourselves with a lengthy examination of statistics of immigration. During the ten years, 1880-1890, immigration amounted to five and a quarter millions, or over one-third of the total immigration from 1820 to 1890. At its maximum, over one per cent was added to the population of the United States in a single year, and the average during the period 1886 to 1896 was 435,000 a year. Between 1890 and 1900, owing to the period of industrial depression which came in that decade, the numbers fell to somewhat over three and a half millions. There has always been a close relation between the number of alien arrivals in this country and the general state of business here. Periods of financial depression are soon followed by a smaller immigration, and periods of industrial activity bring in much greater numbers. Immigration has thus come to us in great waves during prosperous times, with a falling off in the intervals of financial crises, but, on the whole, *each wave during prosperity is higher than the last*. When a period of depression sets in, to the already large numbers of our own unemployed there are added thousands of immigrants with no occupation or skill. Our skilled workmen are thus deprived of the opportunities to tide them over until better times, and our unskilled labor is reduced to a starvation basis through being underbid by immigrants who are willing to live in a way utterly incompatible with American habits and character. In times of ordinary business activity the same results are produced, though in a less degree.

It is perfectly true that there has been a great demand for labor during the past two or three years, but if our material growth can only be secured through a degradation of our citizenship, is such material growth an altogether desirable thing?

You often hear it said by persons who are but mildly interested in the immigration problem, or who wish to be non-committal, that immigration regulates itself by falling off during periods of depression. It should be noted, however, very carefully, that in times of depression the falling off is largely of the most skilled and industrious races, whereas the unskilled laborers are the last to be affected. This will be increasingly true in the future, because so large a part of our present immigration is artificially stimulated, and does not come directly in obedience to economic laws of supply and demand.

Since 1898, there has been a very rapid increase in the numbers of our immigrants. In 1899, we received 311,715; in 1900, 448,572; in 1901, 487,918; in 1902, 648,743, and in 1903, 939,830, an increase of nearly 300,000 over 1902.

*The Present Exodus From Southeastern Europe*

With continued business prosperity; with an ever-increasing facility of transportation, and with a widening sphere of the steamship agent's influence, there is every reason to expect a still larger immigration during the current fiscal year, and in a few years, as the number and size of steamships increase still further, we may easily have two million newcomers every year. In fact, unless some action is taken by this country to prevent it, the tide will flow on so long "as there is any difference of economic level between our own population and that of the most degraded communities abroad", as the late Gen. Francis A. Walker put it.

No one who notices, even in the most casual way, the faces of the people he sees on the streets and in the cars, need be told that a most striking and fundamental change has taken place in the nationalities of our immigrants during the last fifteen or twenty years. A few years ago practically all of our immigrants were from northern and western Europe, that is, they were more or less closely allied to us racially, historically, socially, industrially and politically. They were largely the same elements which had recently made up the English race. As experience has shown, they found little difficulty in assimilating with the American people, and what is more, they were as a whole eager to become assimilated. They intermarried among themselves and with the older American stock, which was akin to the English. Now, however, the majority of the newcomers are from southern and eastern Europe, and they are coming in rapidly increasing numbers from Asia. These people are alien to us, in race (at least, within reasonably modern times), in language, in social, political and industrial ideas and inheritances. Their standards of living are very different from ours. They have a very high percentage of illiteracy. (In 1903, for example, there were among the southern and eastern Europeans over fourteen years of age about forty per cent of illiterates.) And most of them are unskilled laborers. In 1869, immigrants from Austria-Hungary, Italy, Poland and Russia were about one-hundredth of the number from the United Kingdom, France, Germany and Scandinavia; in 1880, about one-tenth; in 1894, nearly equal to it; in 1903 three times as great. In 1903, Great Britain and Ireland sent us about 70,000 immigrants; Germany 40,000 and Scandinavia about 70,000, whereas Austria-Hungary sent us 206,000; Russia, 136,000 and Italy 230,000. Unless all signs fail, this startling change in nationality is destined to continue, and to become much more marked in the future, Asiatic races of which we have perhaps as yet hardly heard, playing a more and more conspicuous part in the years to come.

*The Causes of the Change*

As regards the immigration from northern and western Europe at the present time, and for aught that we can now see, for the future, there is no need for concern on our part. This immigration seems for the present to have attained a fair balance between supply of and demand for skilled labor in this country. It may be considered fairly normal immigration. It is chiefly made up of persons who come to join, relatives on this side; is on the whole intelligent, desirable and easily assimilable. When times are not good here, such immigrants are usually advised by their friends in the United States not to come over. It is the large immigration from southern and eastern Europe that at the moment concerns us much more closely. Concerning this immigration it should be most emphatically stated that no one should object to the coming of the better classes of Italians, Austrians and Russians, even in fairly large numbers, but the point is that such better elements do not, as a rule, come.

What causes have operated to bring about this radical change in our immigration? There are many, and among them may be mentioned:

(1) The prosperity of our country, and the opportunity for improved conditions of work and of living here.

(2) Oppression on account of race or religion in parts of Europe and of Asia.

(3) The ease and the cheapness of getting here.

(4) The activity of steamship agents.


*Artificial Stimulation by Steamship Agents*

There are many other causes, as well, such as the "assisting" of persons to emigrate from Europe by persons already here, etc., but it must suffice us to confine our attention to but two aspects of this question, *viz.*, the artificial stimulation of emigration by the steamship companies' agents, and the increase in our alien arrivals because of oppression in Europe. I choose these two causes because they are among the most potent factors in the problem at this moment. The number and the size of Atlantic steamers increase every year, and the sailings are being rapidly extended to ports with which we had but little, or even no, direct communication a few years ago. Thus, we have all seen a very rapid development of passenger steamship service from New York and Boston to the Italian, African, Austrian and Asian ports of the Mediterranean. Every such extension means more immigrants. Many have noticed the increase in the number of Italians in Boston since the Dominion steamers began to run between Boston and the Mediterranean, and it is not an altogether gratifying piece of news to read that the White Star Line, in its new Boston-Mediterranean service, is to put on large ships and have frequent and regular sailings; nor is it pleasant to be told that the Cunard Line, which is fighting the International Mercantile Marine, is to compete for a share of the emigrant traffic from the Mediterranean by putting on steamers between New York and Mediterranean ports. This move on the part of the Cunard Line means probably at least 25,000 more immigrants a year from southern Europe, Africa and Asia. The fight for immigrants in the Mediterranean, between the Hamburg-American, North German Lloyd, International Mercantile Marine and now the Cunard companies, simply means that thousands of persons, who have perhaps never even thought of leaving their old world homes, will come to us under the stimulus of the steamship agent's power of persuasion. The recent establishment of a new line of steamers between New York and Odessa is distinctly a move to increase the emigration of Russian Jews from that port, and that it will have that effect no one can fail to see. There is absolutely no doubt that a large part of our present immigration is thus artificially stimulated. During the past summer, an agent of the treasury department made an investigation of this matter in Europe, and found that the steamship companies have secret paid agents or solicitors to drum up steerage passengers. Among these paid agents there are school-teachers, postmasters, notaries and even priests, peasants and peddlers. In this way, there is little difficulty in filling the steerages, and the people who fill them are among the poorest, most ignorant, most degraded of their communities. Human beings make profitable freight. A man takes up less room than a grand piano, or than most pieces of machinery. His steerage passage money far more than pays for his food and for the agent's commission. Thus is our country to-day being largely populated, not by people who have been impelled to come because of their own aspirations, but who have come practically because they were forced to. Foreign steamship companies, aided by large employers of labor here, are importing human beings like cattle, absolutely regardless of the welfare of the country, or of the people who are brought. The kind of immigration here referred to has been described as "Pipe Line Immigration" by one writer (Gen. Walker), and as a more and more thorough "drainage" of the inland regions of Europe by another (James Bryce). A very different type of character was demanded fifty years ago, when our immigrants came by sailing vessels, enduring a long, hard voyage, and paying a high passage rate. The large emigration, back to Europe, which has crowded the steerages of outgoing steamers during the weeks preceding Christmas, is an annually recurring movement, which always attracts attention in our newspapers. This return does not, in any way, affect the general proposition before us. The people who go back, spend the holidays and the winter in their old homes; leave the money they have earned here, and come back in the spring, bringing their relatives and friends with them. This emigration, and the subsequent return to this country, increases when we have prosperous times here, and when these people can afford to go home.

*Oppressions: Racial Antipathy*

As regards the causes which, apart from the artificial stimulus just spoken of, induce immigration, a word or two may be said of oppression, resulting from racial antipathy, as in the case of the Jews in Russia and Roumania, for example, or from burdens of excessive taxation and landlordism, as in Italy. Jewish emigration from Russia first became noticeable about twenty years ago (1882) when the "May Laws" were promulgated. These laws brought about the reenforcement of former regulations concerning the Jews, and since that time more and more restrictions have been placed upon the Russian Jews until life has become almost, or wholly, unendurable for many of them. Among these restrictions may be mentioned the requirement that with the exception of a few favored classes, all of the Jews shall reside within the Pale, and even within the towns of the Pale; that they shall not own, lease or even manage, land; that they shall only engage in specified occupations, chiefly small trading and peddling; that only a certain small percentage shall be allowed to attend schools and universities, and so on. In times of want the Jews have even often failed to receive government aid. Under these conditions of life, crowded into the towns and cities, and engaged in a desperate struggle for existence, hundreds of thousands of Russian Jews have emigrated to the United States, the Hirsh Fund having aided many of the poorest to come. There is no evidence that these oppressive restrictive measures are to be relaxed, but one thing is certain: that the way to bring the Russian Government to a proper attitude towards its Hebrew subjects is *not to make it easier for these subjects to leave Russia and come to the United States.* We shall not benefit the world at large by providing the safety-valve for Jewish discontent in Russia. We shall do the best for our fellow men everywhere if we, together with the other civilized nations, bring pressure to bear upon the Czar in such ways as shall cause him to relax the harsh measures already alluded to, and thus to allow Russian Jews the privileges which other Russians enjoy. These thoughts are prompted by the results of the Kishineff Massacre of this last summer. We all remember the horrible shock which the world felt when the news of this massacre came. Americans were perhaps more horrorstruck than any other people, and our Jewish fellow citizens, and many others, responded at once by sending considerable sums of money to the unhappy Jews in Russia. Such philanthropy, natural and in some respects praiseworthy as it is, has had one inevitable consequence: it has enabled a very great many of the poorest Russian Jews to come to this country. The question is, of course, a very delicate one to handle, but while it is clear on the one hand that man should help his fellow man in distress, it is also just as clear that we have a Jewish slum problem in this country which we ought not, in justice to our Jewish fellow citizens in the slums, and to ourselves, to aggravate any further.

Russia is only too glad to have its Jewish population removed in this way by philanthropic Americans, and indeed it seems to me not unlikely that other massacres may be precipitated by the fact that the massacre of a few Jews means the incoming of many American dollars; and the incoming of many American dollars means the emigration of many more Russian Jews. It is an easy way to solve a very perplexing problem, is it not, if one is not overscrupulous in shedding a little Jewish blood? This Jewish emigration from Russia to the United States is growing every day, and will continue to grow. Even now we read in our papers that some Jews living in America are seriously considering bringing all the Jews within the Russian Pale to this country. The widespread lack of employment in Russia at this moment is causing a very rapid increase in the emigration of Jews to the United States. From Austria-Hungary and from Roumania will come thousands more. In fact, there is no doubt that, if things continue as they are in Europe, and if we continue our present immigration policy, this country will be the Zion of the world's Jews, and perhaps before the present century is half over, the majority of the Jews in the world will be living in the United States. There are now less than 200,000 Jews in Great Britain; in the United States there are over a million. Yet in England the present Parliament is likely to pass a bill of considerable stringency against alien immigrants, the special classes to be legislated against being Polish and Russian Jews. The London *Times* of August 26, 1903, said:

> Even looked at with friendly eyes, they (*i.e.*, the Jewish immigrants) are not exactly the stuff out of which the best citizens are made.

And Major W. Evans Gordon, M.P., member of the Royal Commission on Alien Immigration (1903) has said:[2]

> A large part of the recruiting ground of our aliens (again having reference to the Jews) cannot be expected to produce any of the qualifications of good citizenship.

### Oppression: Economic

Oppression not racial, but economic, is behind the enormous Italian immigration which we are now receiving (230,000 last year). Excessive taxation of the necessaries of life and a non-resident landlord class are evils in Southern Italy which have made life at home too hard for the Italian peasants. Doubtless also the 7,000 steamship agents scattered throughout Italy have succeeded in persuading many thousands to come who would otherwise have remained at home. The Italians who are now coming are very largely peasants, and are generally illiterate. A woman who has lived much in Italy, and is prejudiced in favor of Italians, told me, after she had

2. *World's Work*, April, 1903, p. 3,281.

carefully observed the steerage passengers on the steamer on which she sailed from Naples to Boston, that they were about the kind of people you see in the slums of Naples.

*The Slum of the American City: A Foreign Product*

No argument is necessary to convince any American that the hope of this country lies in the assimilation of our foreign-born population. We want these aliens to become Americans with us; to love and to preserve our institutions; to speak our language; to live, so far as possible, up to American standards of living; to contribute to the well-being of society. But this most necessary process of assimilation, which is of such vital importance to national unity, is becoming increasingly difficult every day because of the wide gulf which separates the majority of our latest immigrants from ourselves; and furthermore, and very largely, because so many of these immigrants are illiterate and because of their unfortunate, albeit perfectly natural, tendency to settle in communities of their own in our large cities. In a very valuable special report of the United States Commissioner of Labor, issued a few years ago, it was shown that persons of foreign birth or parentage form seventy-seven per cent of the total population of the slum districts in Baltimore, ninety per cent in Chicago, ninety-one per cent in Philadelphia, and ninety-five per cent in New York. Further, southeastern Europe has furnished three times as many inhabitants as northwestern Europe to the slums of Baltimore, nineteen times as many to the slums of New York, twenty times as many to the slums of Chicago, seventy-one times as many to the slums of Philadelphia. The slums of our large cities are thus chiefly a foreign product and a product of the countries which have sent us rapidly increasing numbers of immigrants during recent years. Of the slum inhabitants of the above-mentioned cities the average illiteracy was, for those from northwestern Europe, twenty-five per hundred; for those from southwestern Europe, fifty-four per hundred; for native Americans, seven per hundred. In this connection it is worth noting that Dr. Shively has estimated that 23,000 tuberculous immigrants were landed in New York in 1902, and has pointed out the impossibility of making these persons take proper care of themselves because they cannot read the directions printed in almost all known tongues and distributed throughout the city. Our recent immigrants have also brought us other diseases, many of them almost unknown in this country before.

It is one of the most striking facts that so much of our present immigration does not distribute itself over the country districts of the West and South, but remains to increase the congestion in a few states. In 1902, nearly sixty-eight per cent of the total immigration was destined for the four states of Illinois, Massachusetts, New York and Pennsylvania, and during the period from 1890 to 1900, eighty per cent of the whole increase of foreign-born was concentrated in the North Atlantic States (New England, New York, New Jersey, and Pennsylvania). This steady drifting of so many thousands yearly into our city slums enormously increases the competition among those already living in these slums, and makes it harder and harder for the new, as well as the older, immigrants to earn a living. Thus, in the twenty-seventh annual report of the United Hebrew Charities of New York (1901) we read that:

A condition of chronic poverty is developing in the Jewish community of New York that is appalling in its immensity. Forty-five per cent of our applicants, representing between 20,000 and 25,000 human beings, have been in the United States over five years; have been given the opportunities for economic and industrial improvement whch this country affords, yet notwithstanding have not managed to reach a position of economic independence. . . . It is unnecessary to introduce to this audience the causes that underlie these conditions. The horrible congestion in which so many of our coreligionists live, the squalor and filth, the lack of air and sunlight, the absence frequently of even the most common decencies, are too well known to require repetition at this writing. Even more pronounced are the results accruing from these conditions: the vice and crime, the irreligiousness, lack of self-restraint, indifference to social conventions, indulgence of the most degraded and perverted appetites, which are daily growing more pronounced and more offensive. . . . The problem of the care of the Jewish poor in the city of New York is essentially the problem of the immigrant, and as such it passes beyond merely local lines.


## The "Ghettoes"

It is, of course, perfectly true that the more prosperous Jews are public-spirited citizens and are very liberal in contributing toward the care of their poor; that the majority of the Jews have prospered; that they have a very small criminal record; that they do not commit serious assaults; that they are peaceable citizens as a class; that they are usually eager to become educated; that they are brilliant students; and that their family life is in the main wholesome. But the congestion of so many thousands in our Ghettoes produces a condition which is far from being beneficial to those concerned. A recent writer (Roger Mitchell) has put the case thus plainly:[3]

The fact that this (immigration) has been stimulated by pressure from behind rather than by a demand in the industrial market here has tended to make it possible not only for the movement to override or evade our immigration laws, but also to get beyond the control of the philanthropic organizations which have the best interests of the immigrants at heart. The tendency of the Hebrews to prosper

3. *Popular Science Monthly*, February, 1903, p. 341.

diminishes as they congregate together, and, quite apart from the matter of physical disabilities, there is a proportion above which they are unable to thrive in any given city or town. These conditions have already been realized in certain localities here.

The picture drawn above by Jews of their own people in one large city, is but one view of what is more or less — and it will be more and more — true of other foreign quarters in other cities.

Dr. F. A. Bushee, who has recently made a very careful study of "The Ethnic Factors in the Population of Boston", finds that:

The present immigration of southern Italians brings a large superfluous population of hot-headed men who are fit only for unskilled labor, and the presence of these men has reacted on the Irish making their employment less steady.... Italian immigration represents little money and very poor social conditions. The high rate of infant mortality among the Italians indicates small physical stability.

## The "Little Italys"

As they come they are not bad material, although they are poor and ignorant, but:

There is every reason to believe that the Italians, if allowed to continue their present mode of life, will develop a large number of delinquents and dependents, and will form extensive permanent slums.

The Jews, to a considerable extent, hold themselves aloof, socially and religiously, from their fellow men, and thus are with difficulty assimilated, and the Italians, in the opinion of a settlement worker is one of our large cities, "have thus far made little progress toward assimilation".

## Distribute the Desirable; Keep Out the Undesirable

In the "Little Italys", the "Little Syrias", the "Little Armenias", etc., we find increasingly difficult and burdensome problems of public and private charity, of police, of education, of religious training, of public health. If these people could be scattered throughout the country, the evil effects of their crowding into particular sections would be diminished, but no one can suggest any practicable scheme for doing this on a sufficiently large scale to be useful, even with enormous expense. In most cases where this has actually been tried it has proved a failure. What is more, the various states, when asked a few years ago by the Immigration Investigating Commission what nationalities of immigrants they desired, in only two cases expressed any desire for Slav, Latin, Asiatic, or Jewish settlers and both of these cases related to Italian farmers with money, intending to become permanent residents. In spite of the enormous immigration of 1903, the demand for farm laborers in the West and South has been even more imperative than in the past, because most of the incoming immigrants settled in the East. Even at this moment a movement is on foot in the South to have the immigration laws so amended as to admit coolie labor from Asia to work in the cotton and rice fields. In his last annual report the commissioner-general of immigration strongly recommends the establishment of bureaus of information, through which immigrants may be directed to the states where they are most needed, so that the present congestion may be relieved. There are, however, two sides to this matter of distribution. The easier we make it for every undesirable immigrant to find work — and it is chiefly the undesirable ones that are crowded into our cities — the more we shall induce others to come; and further, the more we scatter our recent immigrants, the more widely do we spread the evils which result from exposing our own people to competition with the lower classes of foreigners. I think we must agree with President Roosevelt, who, in his message to Congress noted the need of distributing the *desirable* immigrants throughout the country and of keeping out the *undesirable* ones altogether. Most writers on this question have emphasized the need of scattering the undesirable, who, as President Roosevelt points out, should not be admitted at all. Besides the fact that our recent immigrants naturally tend to remain where most of their fellow-countrymen are, there is the additional fact that the majority of the newcomers have but little money. The average amount of money brought by each immigrant during the last five years was about $16. In the report of the United States Industrial Commission, it is shown that the amount of money brought by immigrants from northern and western Europe averages considerably greater than that brought by those from other countries.

It is unnecessary to multiply the illustrations which might be given of the conditions of life of many of our recent immigrants, and of the burdens, financial and otherwise, which they bring upon our communities. If further illustrations are sought they may be found among the foreign-born miners of Pennsylvania, some of whom, we have been told, live in rickety, miserable shanties unfit for a well-bred dog to live in; and among the people who were discovered in New York "contentedly living in the midst of the filth that dripped from the garbage-dumps". The Italians, we learn from Dr. Bushee, "herd together persistently, and as they are increasing rapidly, they form objectionable permanent slums....The conditions are aggravated by an excess of unskilled laborers — single men who are idle a large part of the time. The result thus far has been a high rate of infant mortality, an excess of serious crime among the men, and an increase of drunkenness and sexual depravity. In other words, the Italians show the beginnings of a degenerate class....They are a simple peasant class who respond readily to their environment; if allowed to continue in unwholesome conditions we may be sure that the next generation will bring forth a crop of dependents, delinquents, and defectives to fill up our public institutions."

*The Cost of the Undesirable Alien*

There is no "Know-Nothingism" in the feeling that the unlimited immigration of the races who are now coming to us in such large numbers should, in some wise way, be regulated. Those who come into direct contact with our slum population realize that the difficulties of assmiliation are steadily increasing; that there are more and more unabsorbed foreigners in our midst; that the life of our foreign-born, as well as of our native-born, is made harder because of the ever-increasing competiton caused by the newer immigrants. It is pretty clear that we are not properly assimilating our foreign population when we hear (August 5, 1903) that a judge in New York State recently rejected the naturalization papers of sixty persons, on the ground that "when a man has been in this country five years and is unable to speak our language...he is not fit to be admitted to citizenship". Or, to take another case, when we find that in the factories of the Empire State there are young men and women of seventeen, eighteen and twenty, who have lived in this country since they were four or five, and who can neither understand nor speak English. It must, moreover, never be forgotten that, even if we succeed in raising all these unabsorbed foreigners up to something like our own level, there is an inexhaustible supply behind, which will always be tending to pull down what we have raised, and which, in turn, we shall have to try to raise up. And then there is the financial burden. A writer in the Brooklyn *Eagle* has recently held that the total cost of caring for the poor of New York State is over $24,000,000 a year, and, as the foreign-born are estimated at at least one-half, it means $12,000,000 annually for their support. Godwin Brown, an expert on lunacy statistics, says that one-half of the inmates of the insane asylums of new York are foreign-born, and predicts that in ten years the alien insane will cost the United States $50,000,000 a year. This leaves out of account the cost of maintaining charitable homes for children, one-half of whom, in New York, are born of foreign parents, this item being $10,000,000 a year. The economic and the social burdens of this new immigration are already formidable enough. In a few years they will become insupportable, if the present condition of things is allowed to continue. A recent thorough study of the New York City public schools, by Miss Adele Marie Shaw,[4] leads to the conclusion that the only remedies for the conditions there existing are "the restriction of immigration, and a vast increase in expenditure — larger than any yet dreamed of". "With eighty-five per cent of its population foreign or of foreign parentage", says Miss Shaw, "its salvation dependent upon the conversion of a daily arriving cityful of Russians, Turks, Austro-Hungarians, Sicilians, Greeks, Arabs, into good Americans.... the city has a problem of popular education that is

4. *World's Work*, December, 1903.

staggering." And "unless legislation dams the encroaching flood, more babies will be brought here and more babies will be born here than ever before".

It is clear that if we would do the best for our country, and for those immigrants who have recently come, and who are as yet unassimilated, we cannot continue to receive an annual immigration of 1,000,000 souls. In this matter we cannot, of course, consider ourselves alone, but we must take account of what is best for those who come and also for those who remain in their Old World homes. If this immigration were of distinct benefit to the immigrants themselves, and also to their fellow-countrymen whom they left at home, we might be ready to suffer inconvenience and to undergo additional expense ourselves for the sake of conferring these benefits. But the case is not so. It is increasingly true that many of the newer comers are not very much the gainers themselves; that they make conditions harder in the slums for those already here, and that their leaving home does not help those who are left behind. Arnold White has recently shown that, in spite of the enormous emigration from the Pale, conditions there are steadily growing worse. The same is true in a general way of Italy. Even in the case of Finland, from which we receive many desirable immigrants, a recent writer tells us that those who are left behind "are literally suffering from physical, intellectual, and moral starvation. There is left nothing to refresh, fertilize, and energize the nation's vitality". As General Walker put it, in his characteristically plain language:[5] "All the good the United States could do by offering indiscriminate hospitality to a few millions more of European peasants, whose places at home will, within another generation be filled by others as miserable as themselves, would not compensate for any permanent injury done to our republic. Our highest duty to charity and to humanity is to make this great experiment here of free laws and educated labor, the most triumphant success that can possibly be obtained. In this we shall do far more for Europe than by allowing its city slums, and its vast stagnant reservoirs of degraded peasantry, to be drained off upon our soil."

*The Economic Problem — A Far-Reaching One*

Although we probably all believe that the evils of immigration are confined to a few cities, chiefly in the East, it is well for us to know that the standards of living of our American farmers in the Middle West are seriously threatened by the competition of foreigners. Prof. T. N. Carver, who spent his summer studying the economic and social conditions of the great corn belt, says that the leading problem now confronting the corn region is that brought about by the constant arrival of foreigners with a comparatively low

5. *Discussions in Economics and Statistics.*

standard of living, who are able to supersede the first settlers, since, by living at a lower cost, they can afford to expend more for land and improvements than people having a higher standard of living. For this reason the future racial and sociological conditions of the corn belt are somewhat uncertain.[6]

Before leaving the economic side of the question, I should like to quote briefly from the last annual report of the commissioner of immigration at the Port of New York, in which the present status of the problem is very clearly set forth:

It is as irrelevant as it is misleading to assert that, because immigration in the past has been a source of greatness to the country, and because the great building and other industrial operations now going on in the United States require labor, therefore immigration should not be further restricted. Past immigration was good because most of it was of the right kind and went to the right place. Capital cannot, and it would not if it could, employ much of the alien material that annually passes through Ellis Island, and thereafter chooses to settle in the crowded tenement districts of New York. Let it be again plainly stated that these remarks are not directed against all immigration; that the great debt which this country owes to immigration in the past is cheerfully acknowledged; and that the strong, intelligent emigrant, of which class many are still coming here, is as welcome to-day as ever he was.

A strict execution of our present laws makes it possible to keep out what may be termed the worst element of Europe (paupers, diseased persons, and those likely to become public charges), and to this extent these laws are most valuable. Without a proper execution of the same it is safe to say that thousands of additional aliens would have come here last year. But these laws do not reach a large body of immigrants who, while not of this class, are yet generally undesirable, because unintelligent, of low vitality, of poor physique, able to perform only the cheapest kind of manual labor, desirous of locating almost exclusively in the cities, by their competition tending to reduce the standard of living of the American wageworker, and unfitted mentally or morally for good citizenship. It would be quite impossible to accurately state what proportion of last year's immigration should be classed as "undesirable". I believe that at least 200,000 (and probably more) aliens came here who, although they may be able to earn a living, yet are not wanted, will be of no benefit to the country, and will, on the contrary, be a detriment, because their presence will tend to lower our standards; and if these 200,000 persons could have been induced to stay at home, nobody, not even those clamoring for more labor, would have missed them. Their coming has been of benefit chiefly, if not only, to the transportation companies which brought them here.

## The Question A Racial One Also

Most of the discussions of the immigration problem in the past have been concerned with its economic side. The question is, however, a racial as well

6. *World's Work*, December, 1903.

as — I myself believe even more than — an economic one. With an easy-going, laissez-faire spirit we have said to ourselves: "Yes, truly, we are receiving an enormous lot of foreigners — Jews, "Dagoes", Poles, Syrians — but they will all be assimilated and become part of our old Anglo-Saxon, American stock. The old American stock is, and will always be, very greatly in excess, and these foreigners will not affect the future of the country or of the race. Don't let us worry. It will settle itself." Within a few years, however, and chiefly within a year or two, a radical change has been taking place in the view of the problem which is being taken by thinking men and women. People are coming to see that we have spent too much time studying the economic sides of the question. There is a racial side which is even more important than all the economic aspects put together.

President Eliot did much to set people thinking on this question when he showed, in his annual report for 1901 and 1902, that of the graduates of seven Harvard classes in the 1870s, twenty-eight per cent are unmarried, and those who are married average only two surviving children. President Roosevelt, at about the same time, attracted considerable attention to the general subject of the American birth-rate by his use of the term "racial suicide", which has since often been quoted. Following along the same lines as those suggested in President Eliot's investigation, Professor Thorndike, in the *Popular Science Monthly* for May, 1903, discussed the question of the low birth-rate as shown by statistics from Wesleyan University, New York University and Middlebury College. His results in general confirmed those of President Eliot — to the effect that the birth-rate among college graduates, at least in the East, is too low to keep up their numbers. A very exhaustive study of the statistics of Massachusetts from 1885 to 1897, by R. R. Kuczynski, published in the *Quarterly Journal of Economics* for November, 1901, and February, 1902, has shown that the proportion of persons married among the natives is much smaller than among the foreign-born; that the proportion of childless married women is much greater among the natives than among the foreign-born; that the birth-rate among married women of child-bearing age is much larger among the foreign-born, and that the marriage rate is decreasing among the natives and increasing among the foreigners. Mr. Kuczynski concludes: "It is probable that the native population cannot hold its own. It seems to be dying out." Dr. Bushee, in his investigation of *The Ethnic Factors in the Population of Boston*, likewise comes to the conclusion that the native whites are failing to keep up their numbers on account of their low birth-rate. Statistics, therefore, "put the whole native population of Massachusetts in the same position as college graduates, and the question accordingly seems to be one of the upper class, or of the older part of the population, and not simply a question of the educated classes". The size of families is, of course, determined by the interaction of many diverse causes. Among them late marriages; the increase

of luxury; higher ideals of education for children; the longing for freedom
from household cares; greater prudence; interests of women outside the
home, and, indeed, actual racial infertility, have all been urged as contributing causes. As to race sterility, cases of animals which are bred for special
purposes and which become sterile, are known, and it has been urged that
selection for our civilization may have the same result. However this may
be, one cause of a lowering birth-rate has been suggested which seems
reasonable, potent, and of increasing importance. I refer to the effect of
foreign immigration. This point was first brought out by Gen. Francis A.
Walker, as a result of his studies as superintendent of two United States
censuses. General Walker showed that, contrary to the usual belief, foreigners
did not come here in the past because Americans despised manual labor, but
that Americans gave up manual labor because they did not wish to be so
closely associated with the less intellgient and less progressive foreigners. In
his *Discussions of Economics*,[7] he wrote:

> The American shrank from the industrial competition thus thrust upon him. He
> was unwilling himself to engage in the lowest kind of day labor with these new elements
> of population; he was even more unwilling to bring sons and daughters into the world
> to enter into that competition.... The great fact protrudes through all the subsequent
> history of our population that the more rapidly foreigners came into the United
> States, the smaller was the rate of increase, not merely among the native population,
> but throughout the population of the country as a whole, including the foreigners....
> If the foregoing views are true, or contain any considerable degree of truth, foreign
> immigration into this country has, from the time it assumed large proportions,
> amounted not to a re-enforcement of our population, but to a replacement of native
> by foreign stock.

## The Displacing of Native Americans

Thus, it has come about that Americans have not married, or, if they have
married, they have not been willing to increase the size of their families until
they have had the means to enable their children to withdraw from
competition with the lower classes of foreigners. As lower and more degraded
immigrants come, it is to be expected that this process will apply to a larger
portion of the people already here. Possibly we may feel that General
Walker went too far in his view of this matter, nevertheless the United
States Industrial Commission, which has made one of the most thorough
studies of immigration ever undertaken, said in its report, p. 277: "It is a
hasty assumption which holds that immigration during the nineteenth
century has increased the total population".

7. Vol. II, pp. 417-426.

Dr. Bushee has called attention to this law of population which was formulated by Dumont to the effect that population increases inversely with "social capillarity". The stronger the competition, the greater the effort to maintain and raise the standard of living and the social position; the greater the effort, the greater the voluntary check to population. In large cities, the rearing of large families, sometimes even marriage at all, may become inconsistent with the maintenance of American standards of living in the keen competition which prevails on all sides. Competition is much more serious in its consequences when it is due to the immigration of races which are able and content to live under wholly inferior conditions. It is the desire to live above the social stratum of the recent Jewish, Italian and Hungarian immigrants that operates to keep the native American from marrying or from having large families. On the other hand, while the native American white population is apparently destined to decline, the foreign elements are increasing very rapidly, not by immigration alone, but by their own natural high birth-rates. In Boston, it appears that "all the foreign-born groups show a high natural increase. . . . (and) on the whole, the most recently immigrating nationalities have the highest birth-rates". The same thing is true for Massachusetts, and probably also elsewhere, where social conditions are similar. The foreigners who compete with the natives do not dread the lowering of the social standard nearly as much as do the natives, and hence the check on population does not operate in the same way in their case. Among the families of our newest immigrants, children are born with reckless regularity, the birth-rate being very high among the Jews and Italians. Furthermore, the Jews have extraordinary vitality. Although poor, and living under miserable conditions, the mortality of both children and adults is very low. Probably long generations in the Ghettoes of Europe have fitted them for their present conditions of life. It is likely that in a few generations the birth-rates of many of our more recently immigrating races will fall somewhat, for this has been the case with our older immigrants, the Germans and the Irish, for example. The Jewish birth-rate, however, will probably never fall as low as that for the other nationalities; because it has not done so in other countries. The Russian Jews are now surpassing all the other nationalities in their natural rate of increase. The birth-rate in Italy, also, is much higher than that in Ireland. In the second generation of Jews and Italians there is an increase of the death-rate, but the balance remains on the side of a rapid increase of population by excess of births over deaths. As regards second generations of immigrants in general, we may assume that, as Dr. Bushee has pointed out, "the second generation of those nationalities which tend to congregate in the slums shows a deterioration over the first". "With other nationalities, who are increasing less rapidly, and who live in more healthful surroundings, the second generation appears to have made an improvement over the first."

The question before us is, therefore, a race question. Slav, Italian, Jew, not discouraged by the problem of maintaining high standards of living with many children, are replacing native Americans. The highest stratum is gradually being eliminated in the course of natural selection, because of the external pressure on the American stock.

## The Forming of a Race of Unknown Value

There can, then, be absolutely no doubt that the recent change in the races of our immigrants will profoundly affect the character of the future American race. What the resulting physical and mental changes will be, Prof. Franklin H. Giddings, of Columbia, and Gustave Michaud have recently told us.[8] The ethnic composition of an average immigrant has radically changed during the past few years, the Baltic and the Alpine stocks giving way to the Mediterranean. The dilution of the energetic Baltic blood, which, "combined with the conditions peculiar to a new country", has made us "preeminently an energetic, practical people, above all an industrial and political people", will, according to Mr. Giddings, inevitably cause a decline of this American push. The increasing proportion of Alpine and Mediterranean blood will "soften the emotional nature, but it will quicken the poetic and artistic nature. We shall be a more versatile, a more plastic people, gentler in our thoughts and feelings because of the Alpine strain; livelier and brighter, with a higher power to enjoy the beautiful things of life", because of the Latin blood. "We may doubtless learn courtesy from many an Italian; virtue from many a Slav; family loyalty from many a Jew; the beauty and the refining influence of music from many a Hungarian." Turning to the physical side it is clear that the average stature will be reduced and that the skull will become broader and shorter. He would, indeed, be a hopeless pessimist who should maintain that this racial change will have *naught* but undesirable effects, mental and physical, upon the future American race. We probably need less nervous energy and push; we shall undoubtedly benefit by a quickening of our artistic and poetic nature; we shall probably not be injured by an infusion of some of the "conservative and contemplative stock which comes from eastern Europe". The good qualities of the new races we may need; their defects we should be willing to do without. Yet, when all is said regarding the benefits which we may, or even must, derive from these new elements in the blood of our race, are we not, as it were, giving away to the philosophy of despair? Are we not, most of us, fairly well satisfied with the characteristics, mental and physical, of the old American stock? Do we not love American traits as they are? May we not be rather reckless in

8. *Century*, March, 1903; *International Quarterly*, June-September, 1903.

assuming that everything will settle itself for the best? It may be that the American race of the future is to be a far better race in every respect than the old one. But we should remember that, as it has been put by a recent writer, "in forming a race of unknown value, there is being sacrificed a race of acknowledged superiority in originality and enterprise".

## Past Legislation

Such are the conditions of the immigration problem at this moment, and such are some of the effects of immigration in the future. It remains only to refer briefly to the question of legislation. In order to understand the present situation, it is necessary to look back and see what has been accomplished along the lines of the proper restriction of immigration. The first general immigration act was passed in 1882 and fixed the head tax at fifty cents; the contract labor acts in 1885 and 1887; another general act in 1891; an administrative act in 1893; the head tax raised to one dollar in 1895; a general codifying act in 1903, raising the head tax to two dollars. Immigration legislation may be divided into two parts — that defining what classes of immigrants shall be excluded, and that providing the machinery whereby the exclusion is accomplished.

Let us here consider the excluded classes. (1) The act of 1862 prohibited the importation of "coolie" labor from oriental countries, and was, therefore, broader than the later "Chinese Exclusion Acts", which have always been considered as distinct from "immigration acts", and which have superseded the coolie provisions. The act of 1875 added convicts (except those guilty of political offences), and women imported for immoral purposes. The act of 1882 added lunatics, idiots, persons unable to care for themselves without becoming public charges. The act of 1885 implied, and the act of 1887 expressly added contract laborers. The act of 1891 added paupers, persons suffering from loathsome or dangerous contagious diseases, polygamists, "assisted" immigrants (i.e., those whose passage has been paid for by others unless they show affirmatively that they are otherwise admissible). The act of 1903 added epileptics, persons who have been insane within five years previous, professional beggars, anarchists, or persons who believe in or advocate the overthrow by force or violence of the government of the United States or of all government or of all forms of law, or the assassination of public officials, persons attempting to bring in women for purposes of prostitution, and persons deported within a year previous as being contract laborers.

## The Educational Test

The act of March 3, 1903, which adds somewhat to the classes of persons whom we wish to exclude, and contains certain other provisions regarding administration, is practically futile as far as a further restriction of immigration is concerned. It is evident, on the face of it, that the casual inspection of the incoming aliens on the dock can but seldom detect polygamists, or professional beggars, or anarchists, or convicts, or paupers. Except in exaggerated cases it is also impossible to detect idiots, or insane, or persons suffering from contagious diseases. For this reason, the number actually debarred has averaged only a fraction of one per cent. As to further legislation, I myself am a firm believer in the educational test — that an adult immigrant shall, with exceptions in favor of wife and minor children and parents or grandparents, be able to read a few lines in his own language. This test has had the united support of the great majority of students of the immigration problem, not because illiteracy *necessarily* means that an immigrant will prove a bad citizen, but because the measure will be practical in keeping out some of the nationalities who have been shown to be generally undesirable because of ignorance, lack of occupation and of resources, tendency to crowd into slums, and the like. As Commissioner-General Sargent has said:

This requirement, whatever arguments or illustrations may be used to establish the contrary position, will furnish alien residents of a character less likely to become burdens on public or private charity. Otherwise it must follow that rudimentary education is a handicap in the struggle for existence.

Evidently, the races which are destined most profoundly to alter the character of the future American race would be most affected by an educational test. I believe that if the educational test bill which passed Congress in 1896 had become law, there would now be little need of discussing the immigration problem. It is not likely, however, that an illiteracy test bill will pass Congress this session, although President Roosevelt is heartily in favor of such a measure. Those of us who believe in some further regulation of immigrant travel to the United States should stand together in support of whatever reasonable legislation may be proposed. It is certain that the steamship companies will fight it, whatever it be.

A last word: Our immigration is changing rapidly in character. Our people are being exposed to a competition unheard of in the past. A new race is being produced, perhaps better, perhaps worse, than the old. We have an opportunity which few nations enjoy of practising artificial selection in the choice of the blood which shall go into the new race. Is it not well to take advantage of this opportunity? Shall we not, at least, try to keep within some sort of reasonable limits the infusion of new blood, concerning whose ultimate effects the wisest of us know so little?

# 6

# Immigration and Household Labor: A Study of Sinister Social Conditions[1]

FRANCES A. KELLOR [2]

Immigration, the intelligence office and household labor are factors which almost any householder who employs servants knows, are very closely related. In any further restriction of immigration, the effect upon the home and the servant problem will have to be considered.

New York City has in the neighborhood of 300 intelligence offices which supply chiefly domestic servants; one-third of these depend almost entirely upon the foreign-born, or American-born children of foreign parents for their supply, while another third depend quite entirely upon "green" girls or new arrivals — girls who have never been in this country and know little or no English. There is at present enough of such a supply to give at least a fair and in many instances a very good remuneration to these offices.

The supply of servants in New York, owing to competition, more attractive features of other occupations, and social obscurity and limitations in time and privileges in household work, is far inferior to the demands. One thing is inevitable. Unless conditions are improved so they will correspond more nearly with other trades, the American home cannot depend upon American labor. Indeed, it does not now, for the only hope of a *continued* supply comes from the immigrant class. This is especially true for general housework, for only the less desirable girls and new arrivals will go willingly into this work, which is less skilled than that of the waitress, maid, cook, etc., is heavier work and not so well paid. This supply is especially desirable from the standpoint of the employer. Although the immigrant so frequently

1. *Charities*, Vol. 12, 1904. Pp. 151-152.
2. Fellow College Settlements' Association.

lacks training, she is strong, asks few privileges, is content with lower wages and long hours, and has no consciousness of a social stigma attaching to her work.

But between the householder and the immigrant stands the intelligence office, which is both a blessing and a curse. To understand this demand for immigrants for households, glance at the methods of some of these offices. They cannot begin to meet the demand normally, so they import girls. They have agents who induce the girls to come over here upon the most extravagant promises; they prepay their passage, and they enter into collusion with boarding-houses to supply them with girls. Upon inquiries during the summer at agencies we were told "the proprietor is abroad getting a supply of girls for the winter". The immigration authorities refuse to release girls directly to these agencies, but they will give them to responsible relatives and friends, so the office has an army of enlisters who pose as such and secure the girls.

Even though such offices in an untold measure rob and defraud and extort money from these poor immigrants, they are still public servants, for they do bring the employer into contact with the employee, and because they know the language, customs, and habits.

But some offices are not wholly for the employers' interest. A conservative estimate shows that in New York alone they send some 10,000 or more a year into prostitution, thus depriving households of valuable help, for many go blindly and unwillingly. Their hold upon girls who know only their language is such that, once placed, they leave at the request of the office and are placed over again, thus increasing the fees of the office. They pilfer and rob homes and bring their plunder to the office to be disposed of, because the office treats them well and pays them. The office initiates them in deceit, lying, and fraud, so that when the home gets them they are no longer simple peasant girls, ready to work and honest, but instilled with all sorts of impossible ideas. One poor Jewish girl left place after place because an office which had imported her, told her the streets were "lined with gold", and she still hoped to find it.

These offices run lodging-houses and are often in tenements. When the girls come from the dirty, unsanitary, crowded, immoral conditions in which they have been kept until the office gets ready to place them, they may go into homes diseased and germ-laden and moral lepers. Employers who patronize better offices turn aside, feeling it is not their problem. It is their problem, for after awhile the girl learns the language, gets experience, and if she does not get into a disreputable house she gets into a better office and the employer gets, a "rounder" — intemperate, dishonest, inefficient, and impertinent — whose first step was the intelligence office which trained her.

This is only a pen picture of the vast system which honeycombs employment of immigrant women in household labor in New York.

The Irish, German and English immigrants no longer arrive in such great numbers, for these have no such elaborate systems. The statistics of female steerage passengers show that for 1903 there were: Swedes, 16,220; Austro-Hungarians, 58,027; Russians, 43,158, and of Germans only 15,225, Irish, 19,334, and English, 10,626. The offices which control these first three classes are those which have in largest measure such methods as have been given.

Anxious householders ask are there no remedies for such a condition, for they realize that this great source — the only source of supply for general housework girls — cannot be cut off and diverted. Yes, there are remedies — there is the free employment agency, but so long as it cannot speak the language of these immigrants, and has such a small appropriation that it cannot employ competent agents, it cannot compete with "native" offices. Then there are immigrant homes, doing a vast amount of good. These have missionaries at Ellis Island and they save and train many girls, but they do not cooperate with each other but are, rather, rivals. Even when these homes take girls in, the agencies employ spies or send out runners, who try to get hold of them.

What is needed is co-operation. An organization acting as a clearing-house which by efficient business methods can wrest this supply from these disreputable offices and place them in good positions. It must understand their methods and worst them by equally efficient but honest ones. Single-handed, these immigrant homes have been struggling with the problem for years, but the writer believes only an efficient business organization on a clearing-house plan, ready to give unsparingly in co-operation with all honest agencies and equally ready to expose every dastardly fraud and diversion of labor into ruinous channels, would meet the need. These offices combine, they exchange girls, they co-operate with boarding houses and relatives where these immigrants lodge, they actually pay boarding-houses fifty cents or one dollar each for every girl they send; they work shipping companies to furnish transportation and then get this back with interest from the girls when they get them positions. These methods must be thoroughly understood, and only a combination understanding them can meet the combine which is operating them.

Italian Swiss Colony.

# 7

# The Need of a General Plan for Settling Immigrants Outside the Great Cities[1]

ELIOT NORTON[2]

There is a very large immigration into this country, chiefly composed of very poor people. For various reasons the numbers of these poor people are likely to show no material decrease during the next ten years. This alone calls up the question whether the immigration should be restricted in any way. Inasmuch as the larger part of these immigrants are Europeans and are conceivably capable of being decent citizens, there is no probability that a general exclusion law directed against all immigrants or against all of any particular race or tribe could or will be passed. Hence any and all restrictions will be directed against the individual, which is the nature of the laws of the United States now in operation.

These laws when properly administered would and do exclude the greater number of those immigrants who are undesirable judged from their personal qualifications. Some additional requirements might be made, but none that have been suggested are so conclusively advisable as to win any great amount of support. This is conspicuously true of what is known as the reading test, which can only have been suggested by some persons wholly unfamiliar with immigrants.

## Administration of Present Laws

Some changes might well be made in the administration of the present laws which would tend to reduce the number of mistakes made. But even if the present laws were extended in their scope and very carefully adminis-

1. *Charities*, Vol. 12, 1904. Pp. 152-154.
2. President of the Society for the Protection of Italian Immigrants.

tered, yet so long as they are directed to the exclusion of individuals for reasonable personal objections, it is quite certain that the number excluded will be relatively very small to the numbers admitted and the latter will be absolutely very large. Hence it becomes important to consider whether this large continuing immigration brings with it possible dangers and actual losses to this country, and if it does how these dangers can be counteracted and these losses, injuries and evils remedied.

On these questions there is a great deal more prejudice and sentiment than actual knowledge expressed. The sentiment may be entirely correct, but as a basis for action it is unreliable because insufficiently founded upon facts. Thus some people would not hesitate to express the view that the vast hordes of Italian laborers coming here constitute "a menace", whatever that may mean. Such people, before recommending any action to be taken upon the strength of their belief, sentiment or prejudice, should first answer the question whether these Italian laborers are doing necessary and valuable work in this country and how this work can be done if they should in any manner be restricted from coming.

There is, however, at least one evil connected with the large immigration to this country which is not a matter of prejudice or sentiment and which can be readily demonstrated. This is that far too many immigrants settle in our cities both for their good and for the welfare of the cities and of the country. This is particularly true of such a city as New York where large numbers of immigrants land. While it is very difficult to remedy this evil by getting people who have already settled in the cities to move away, still much can be done, as has already been done among the Jews, to get those who are not successful or who are dissatisfied to move away and be established in the country. But a great deal can be done with actual immigrants who have not formed definite plans or associations and who would settle in the cities from mere accident. Such immigrants would for the most part be willing to settle in the country if they were sure of meeting others from their country, if they were provided with the means of getting to the place deemed advisable and agreeable to settle in, and if they could be secured a livelihood until the land which would be their means of livelihood became productive.

With different races of immigrants different arrangements would have to be adopted, but these would differ only in detail. A general plan of getting immigrants to settle out of the cities would not be very difficult to institute if the money necessary for its operation were provided.

### Settlement Away from Large Cities

Of course, no plan would be warranted or effective unless it involved having considerable amount of preliminary work done among prospective immigrants before they started for this country. That such a plan could be made effective the work now being done among the Jews shows, as does also the experience of the officers of the Society for the Protection of Italian Immigrants. For had this society sufficient means it could have placed, upon farms, in the last eighteen months, not less than 10,000 Italians who have now more or less permanently settled themselves in New York and other cities. That such an enterprise would be of very great value to the immigrant and to this country cannot be doubted. Its advantages over the settling of the immigrant cities are too plain for discussion.

In view of the fact that a general restriction of immigration cannot be put in force and that consequently very large numbers of immigrants will come to this country, plans for the advantageous settling of the immigrant where he will do most good to himself, his family and the country, have not received the attention they deserve. It is natural that in the past, with our enormous unsettled country and small uncrowded cities, we should have been indifferent to where the immigrant went. But now there is real objection to his settling in particular localities, and his doing so, apart from all other objections, results in a charge upon the community which will grow greater and greater as time goes on. It is, therefore, becoming really necessary that attention be paid to where the immigrant settles. Perhaps it may be necessary for laws to be passed to prevent him from settling in certain places. Certainly no effort should be spared to get him of his own will to settle away from the cities. Where he settles is a far more important question than the mere fact of his coming here.

The Padrone. *Leslie's Weekly*, August 11, 1888.

# 8

# Paternalism and the Immigrant[1]

BROUGHTON BRANDENBURG [2]

In the next twelve months Congress is going to rehabilitate our immigration system, and in all probability it will be many years before the many varying interests urging reform will be united again sufficiently in opinion and backed by public alarm and anxiety, so that it behooves all true lovers of their country to consider well the steps to be taken. Everybody but the immigrant having been consulted, the affairs of the immigrant in the new world are to be cobbled into shape. If mistakes are not to be made before Congress is through then considerable enlightenment of that body must occur, for from some recent expressions, I can understand why the governments of Europe are confident that they will suffer no ill effects from our effort to gulp their surplus millions.

There are just three great tasks in this immigration problem. The first is to select healthy honest immigrants capable of making their own living. The possession of a few dollars more or less or the ability to read and write a language they will not use here does not matter.

The second is to safeguard the selection and the immigrant in transit, for in other times and places I have shown the devilish ingenuity with which Europeans evade American laws and the mulctings, hardships, and brutalities the immigrant undergoes. I underwent them myself, to learn the truth.

The third is to prevent the congestion of the immigrants on the Atlantic seaboard and scatter them where they will do the most good.

It is of this third labor of Hercules that the most is to be said in this article for it has been conclusively proven that the facts as to whether an immigrant

1. *Charities*, Vol. 13, 1905. Pp. 432-436.        2. Author of *Imported Americans*.

is fit or not to come to the United States are obtainable only in the village of his residence abroad and that by visiting inspectors. It is a gigantic, inhuman crime that the fourteen thousand people to whom it was necessary to deny admission to the United States last year were ever allowed to sell their property, give up their work and ruin themselves in a futile effort to get into the promised land. No tongue can tell their sufferings. They should never have been allowed to leave home. But if we have done a great wrong we have been grievously treated in our turn. When in only one commune in Austria 180 of 270 criminals released last year from an overcrowded prison were sent at once to the United States, according to Special Inspector Marcus Braun's report, how many other thousands total of cutthroats told our officials they were honest and walked in unhindered?

Commissioner Sargent has proposed that every immigrant be compelled to bring a certificate of his character from the local authorities. This would merely make the graft of the communal offices that much fatter. Some of the consuls have thought it best that the immigrants be compelled to appear before them and obtain certificates. When it is a notorious though shameful fact that too many of our consuls are men appointed as a reward for political services to get them away from trouble-making at home, it is to be imagined what beautiful uniformity would be obtained. Incidentally if there were to be any certainty that the immigrant's statements to the consul about himself were true, it would be necessary to send inspectors to the villages to check up the information from the communal records. So, why not send men to the villages in the first place? Also, in Russia and one or two minor countries, the applicants would not be allowed to travel to the consular seats. Another great advantage of visiting inspectors would be that by sending agents to Danish, German, Belgian, French, Scotch and English villages from which there is no immigration at present, a very desirable movement could be incited, because families who have something to lose by coming to America will not now risk being debarred. If sure of admittance they would come.

## The Task of Distribution

But the first and the second tasks are complicated in no such way as is the third. There the only thing that the several thousand earnest people who are agitating concerning immigration distribution know in common is that there are too many immigrants in the cities. All have other fragmentary bits of intimate knowledge and on these they base their projects. Some of these projects can only be excused on the grounds of ignorance on the part of the perpetrators, and those grounds must need be extensive to afford adequate excuse.

Having, after years of study of the complex situations of mixed life on both sides of the ocean, no real project to offer beyond one slight suggestion, what I may say since it will only be of conditions will be the entire truth as I have seen it, for nothing will be withheld to prevent a theory's destruction nor will anything be adduced merely to support one.

The immigration of the next year will be the largest movement of human beings from any one continent to another the world has ever seen. It will run far over the million mark. Ever since Roosevelt's election more than two hundred thousand re-patriated Italians have been celebrating in their home towns with fiestas, processions, speeches and fireworks. They are assisted by those who hope to come and all will voyage to America if possible. My correspondents report over eighty meetings of rejoicing over the victory in Southern Italy since November 18. But new immigration of the Iberic race will drop and the Slavic and Hebrew surge ahead once more. These two are the most important in considering distribution. The two forces driving them are first, economic and social pressure in Russia due to the war; and second, the increasing prosperity in America. Societies are operating all over the continent to succor the Poles and Jews pouring over the Russian border and ship them to their already burdened countrymen in the United States. Slavs of all the national divisions are even now buying tens of thousands of tickets to send home to relatives to come over this spring in time for the grand rush of summer work.

There we have roughly the motives for migration. Not once in a hundred times is it an initial, uninfluenced move on the part of a whole family to take up residence in a new and better country. Among the Italians, Greeks, Hungarians, Poles, etc., the hardy laborer comes first and wins a foothold and then sends for the remainder of the family. Therefore the mass of the immigrants have a fixed destination very firmly decided upon by circumstances before they ever leave home and any information bureau established at this end of the line to endeavor to induce them to go some place else would be a waste of words and printed matter. If the immigrants are to be influenced in their destination it must be done before they leave home, for they are going where their friends are and their friends are where they can get work and the places where they can get work are in the industrial centers and the industrial centers are in the congested sections. There has been no difficulty in getting abundant immigrants into Colorado, in fact, too many touched with socialism and anarchistic venom as the recent troubles showed, for there are mines in Colorado to employ them. As for the Jew, he goes where his relatives are or where the charitable society that is getting him out of Europe sends him, and the society is certainly not going to pay fare farther than New York.

The Scandinavian distributes himself. The German is too speedily assimilated to be dangerous or burdensome wherever he goes, except in Milwaukee, Chicago, St. Louis, Cincinnati or Pittsburgh where the generation of anarchy, "saengerbunds" and breweries have offset each other. The Irishman has been displaced as a laborer by the Iberian and the Slav and is readily distributed by the employment agencies into domestic service. Two-thirds of the present Irish immigration goes at once to domestic service.

That narrows the distribution problem down to the Jews, the Slavs and the Iberians.

### The Jewish Immigration

There are 600,000 Jews in the State of New York alone, nearly all of these in the City of New York, and the 75,000 men, women and children who support the mass of the others are engaged in the tailoring trades. If the approximate 550,000 Jews in New York City are to be distributed over the country, are the tailoring industries which have centered and maintained them in New York to be distributed with them, or are they to have no work? Russia has committed a multitude of murders and worse deeds to make farmers out of her Jews. In three years the removal committee of the United Hebrew Charities has succeeded in removing from the city to the country but an average of 4,250 persons per year while as many fresh immigrants have arrived in the city in one week. The difficulty has been not a matter of funds or places for families, but of willingness of the families to go. If the struggling, sometimes starving Jews of New York refuse to go to the country under the persuasion of their own leaders what good will it do to endeaver to effect inducement by railroad land-settling advertisements and pamphlets? One-eighth of all the Jews in the world are in the United States and yet there is but a handful outside the cities and eighty-six per cent are in cities of over 25,000. By what process is the Jew to be induced to take up a rural residence where he can get support only from the soil and that if he will dig it out with a hoe?

### The Italians

On the other hand, the Italian presents the farmer ready made, but the situation is even more difficult, for though nine-tenths of the Italians who come to the United States have followed agricultural pursuits, they are willing to do anything else for any rate of pay rather than continue farming. In Southern Italy from which the mass of immigrants come, there is no considerable industry except farming, and men who are naturally gifted for other pursuits must do work in the soil to live; therefore each overburdened peasant has come to look on the soil as his master and he as its slave, and when they come to the United States nothing is farther out of the range of their expectations than to take up rural life. They are sick of the soil. There are three classes in Italy which as designated here have an influence on the immigrant's aspirations; the aristocracy, the "employed" class, and the peasants. The peasant who comes here and gets a job dodging blasts in a railroad cut writes home proudly that he has risen to the employed class. If on a railroad, best of all; but if in a trench, still very good.

And again, the Italians are expert farmers and irrigators in their own crops — grapes, figs, tomatoes, pears, apricots, berries, cabbages, hemp, beans, cotton, silk, etc., but compared with our agricultural processes, their work is all done in miniature. The spade takes the place of the plow in all Southern Italy. If a large colony of Italians were put down, let us say in southern Georgia, a few years would see merely a reproduction of the tiny gardens, elaborated, channeled and watered, which they have known at home. They would not be able to compete with the American farmer who produces on a larger plan, all other things being equal. This offsets the greatest inducement which could be held out to immigrants to go west and south; that is, ownership of their own land.

Lastly there is another phase of the immigrant's attitude which not one of the busy men who are planning to distribute him seems to have considered and that is the intention of the immigrant when he leaves his home. He only hopes to come to the United States for two or three years, get as good a job as possible, save as much as possible, and get home again where he can get the most possible for his money. He has very little thought of remaining unless it is too hot at home for him or some relative is already firmly established in the United States. The idea of taking up a farm and buying stock and tools is the last idea that would be acceptable; and as for becoming a hired man at eighteen dollars a month and his board, there is no chance of inducing him to do that as long as he can live in the city for $2.50 a week and earn thirty-three dollars a month at day labor. Also, if he would go where farm labor is needed he must pay from ten dollars to twenty dollars railroad fare. Add to this the naturally gregarious instincts of the Italian brought about by the landowners, compelling the peasants for generations to live in villages, and one can understand why the Italians do not and will not go west to the open lands.

In Westchester County, N. Y., and on up into Connecticut some of the Italian families, living in the villages to be near the railroad, quarry or factory work, have taken up abandoned farms or bits of waste land, turned small streams from their channels, and done wondrous things in the gardening way. The most fruitful gardens I have ever seen in the United States are some little patches on rocky soil just north of Mamaroneck, N. Y. They would put an American or German gardener to shame, but the occupants do not depend on them for maintenance. These gardens merely show what can be done.

*Two Ways of Appeal*

There are two ways of appealing to the natural keenness of the Italian mind under these circumstances and overcoming some of these prejudices and misunderstandings. If the Italian can be shown that it is much to his advantage to go to the country instead of living miserably in the city, he will go there. If the advantage cannot be shown he will not go there nor can he readily be forced to go. Already he is distrustful because he has been so egregiously lied to by the railroad immigration bureaus, land companies and others. The new colonization experiments which have been tried and failed, such as the one at New Palermo, Ala., have been discussed and rediscussed with bitterness among the Italians in the city colonies. One of the ways is to appeal directly to the class of Italians who have made money and are going home in the fall. Give them literature to take back with them and let that literature be prepared by persons who understand their wants. Every illustrated American souvenir book is passed from hand to hand in the villages. Instead of investing their savings in Italy the returned immigrants may come back the next spring and invest them in western or southern land. The interests which make money from the immigrants understand just how to direct incitation. If a few hundred such investors prosper the remainder will be easy.

A second way would be to use the power of the padrone banker. The padrone bankers direct two-thirds of the stream of Italian immigration. They supply the railroads, the mines and the factories with the contract labor. If a demand for three thousand farm laborers in South Dakota were placed in the hands of any padrone to-morrow the men would be in Dakota at work in April.

The reader must not be confused by the statements that the immigrant goes where his relatives already are and that he goes where the padrone sends him. The padrone secures his fresh men through their relatives already under his thumb.

*The Slavs*

Of the Slavs nearly the same things are to be said as of the Italians, only that a far larger number of Slavs who come to the United States are miners or factory workers before they leave home and there is not quite the same tendency to return home, especially among those who come from regions of political oppression. On the whole, they are far less mobile than the Italians.

In recapitulation I would strongly enforce the fact of the feeling among the Italians, Greeks, Hungarians, Montenegrins and several of the Slav divisions of being here for but a little while, the prejudices against the soil, the present improper presentation of any advantages that country life may possess, and the folly of attempting to divert the immigrant after he makes up his mind to immigrate, for when he does that he knows where he is going, he cannot be diverted en route and when he reaches his destination it is too late.

Compulsory diversion to certain states would be high-handed, but effective. Suasion must begin very early and be conducted very patiently by men who understand what the immigrant wants and are in sympathy with him. The prospects are, though, that a very great deal of time, money, and enthusiasm are about to be wasted.

Ortolano family, Vineland, New Jersey.

# 9

# Immigrant Rural Communities[1]

Alexander E. Cance[2]

Something like one-fourth of all male breadwinners of foreign parentage in the United States were engaged in agricultural pursuits in 1900. Although by far the greater part were of the older immigration, who came from northern Europe and settled in the middle West years ago, among them are a not inconsiderable number of recent immigrants from southern and southeastern Europe who have established themselves on the land. The races under consideration by the Immigration Commission were chiefly Italians, Hebrews, Poles, Bohemians and Portuguese; and most of these were settled rather recently in more or less sharply defined rural communities.

The inhabitant of the upper Mississippi Valley is well acquainted with immigrant farmers, and a township of Scandanavians, Germans or Bohemians excites no comment and invites no comparisons. There the foreigners, long settled in rural districts, have become thoroughly American, have so completely lost themselves in the rural population, that they retain very few of their distinctive race characteristics. In the East and South, however, and in the instance of certain recent colonies elsewhere, the foreign rural group, composed of Italians, Poles or Hebrews, is still an object of curiosity. Not only are the foreigners on the land infrequent, but they have yet to prove their fitness for agricultural pursuits — for country life.

More than 150 rural groups or parishes of these more or less recent and

---

1. *The Survey*, Vol. 25, 1911. Pp. 587-595.
2. In charge of Report on Recent Immigrants in Agriculture United States Immigration Commission. The author has quoted freely from his reports written for the commission.

agriculturally doubtful races were visited by the commission — groups representing many different forms of agriculture in nineteen states chiefly along the Atlantic and Gulf coasts, where many incipient settlements have sprung up recently. A smaller number are established in the middle West. Nearly all of these groups are racially homogeneous, but not only are they engaged in a variety of agricultural sub-industries, but the conditions of soil, climate and method of settlement are so diverse, that generalizations are difficult and the most satisfactory procedure is a monographic study by community groups.

As a farmer or permanent farm laborer, the immigrant becomes a real element in such rural communities. There is a second way in which the incoming foreigner may come into contact with the soil, but without gaining other than a casual economic interest in rural pursuits, as a seasonal agricultural laborer who lives in the city and works for a few months yearly usually in the fruit or vegetable districts.

This class of laborers is usually composed of foreign-born persons, who work in gangs and who are recruited outside the neighborhood in which they find employment. They are employed for short seasons only, frequently on piece work; ordinarily men, women and children work together; often they follow a regular itinerary, leaving the cities in the spring and returning in the autumn. Thousands are employed every year in all parts of the United States where specialized crops, for whose culture a relatively large amount of hand labor is essential, are produced. Of the seven groups of "black" Portuguese, Poles, Belgians, Sicilians, Japanese and Indians studied by the commission, only the south Italian berry pickers of New Jersey can be considered.

One who has seen a train load of incoming foreigners unloaded at some water-tank railway station in the Northwest, with children, food, bags, bedding and belongings dumped in a promiscuous heap at their feet, has a good replica of the unloading of a carload of Italian berry pickers at Hammonton or Port Norris, N. J. at the beginning of the picking season. Great bales of bedding; old trunks, barrels and boxes of clothing; bags of Italian bread, macaroni, peas and cheese; clanging bundles of metal cooking utensils; occasionally a stove and frequently a number of baby carriages; finally a huddle of children and confused parents await the great wains that drive up and carry them off by the wagon load — luggage, babies, baby carriages and all — to their four or five weeks' sojourn on some berry farm.

These berry pickers are largely Sicilians or Calabrians from the vicinity between South Fifth and South Fifteenth Streets, along Christian and Fitzwater Streets, Philadelphia, and some from Camden; and a canvass of the Hammonton district led to the conclusion that 2,500 to 3,000 pickers — with numerous infant children — were employed in 1909.

They follow a regular itinerary. During the winter most may be found in cheap tenements, the children at school, the men picking rags, sweeping or working on streets and railroads, at odd jobs and in various unskilled occupations, the women in box factories, machine tailoring establishments, or home "tailor work". In various ways they earn a hand to mouth existence until the *padrone* rounds them up about the middle of May and they remove to the strawberry fields of South Jersey, taking the entire family and most of their worldly goods.

The strawberry season over, towards the end of June they are shipped northward, to Hammonton, for example, to pick blackberries; after blackberries come raspberries, which bring the season to nearly August. Some of the families then return to the cities, but perhaps a fourth of them scatter over the country to gather huckleberries, or find work in the tomato, pepper or cucumber fields, or harvest sweet potatoes until the cranberry season begins. The last stage is the cranberry bog, after which the entire remaining company moves back to winter quarters about October 10.

The work is all done by the piece, and since most of the tasks are easily within the strength and intelligence of the women, and children from ten to fourteen years of age, the family becomes the earning unit. The wages received are not unremunerative, and because of the exceedingly low cost of living and the many hands, family earnings for the season frequently reach $200 to $500 or sometimes more, sufficient to enable them to live in comparative comfort until "picking" begins again.

Housing conditions are in general unsatisfactory. Small berry growers, especially Italian, seldom make adequate provision for the sanitary housing of labor gangs. Barns, granaries, old outbuildings of various sorts, stable lofts, and in one instance a condemned school house, are some of the makeshifts utilized. The houses especially erected for laborers are frequently little better. Most of them are constructed with a view to economy of space. Ventilation is not adequate. Often there is overcrowding; sometimes entire families occupy bunks about six feet by eight or sometimes six feet square. In a number of instances privacy or the separation of sexes is secured only by a curtain, shawl, or some article of clothing thrown over a cord stretched across the room or shed.

The berry grower (employer) furnishes well water, straw for filling the box-like bunks, and wood for fuel. In a number of instances toilet facilities were found to be insufficient, and the growers had refused to provide mosquito netting for the windows or any form of lamp or lantern. Few growers take any pains to maintain sanitary quarters, and in consequence the barracks were in many instances deplorably filthy. The chief defense made by the grower is the usual one that the pickers will not preserve or appreciate sanitary quarters, even if provided; and furthermore, that for a short season of six weeks better quarters require too great expenditure of capital, especially for occupation by gangs of laborers who do not care for better.

In standard of living, Americanization, initiative, resourcefulness, progressive spirit, civic and personal respect, and general moral tone, the Italian berry picker is far behind the land owning Sicilian for whom he labors. The contrast at Hammonton and Vineland is strikingly manifest. Many of the Hammonton farmers were previously itinerant berry pickers, and the colony continues to draw a few recruits from their ranks, but fewer now than formerly. With many south Italians this seasonal labor is apparently a permanent occupation, and its bearing on the second generation calls for consideration.

The moral effect of the miscellaneous housing and the unconventional life — even where two-story buildings were provided to segregate the sexes — cannot, to put it mildly, be good. School authorities assert that the itinerary breaks in on the school year with very detrimental results educationally. Certain medical and hygienic experts declare with conviction that exposure to rain, cold and malarial atmospheres are provocative of fevers and tuberculosis, and that neither the water supply nor the surroundings are conducive to physical well-being. But the attention of the lay observer is first drawn to the babies, largely left to the care of some small sister, fighting the swarming flies and sweltering in the hot sun. The insects, the exposure, and the heat cannot be good for the little ones, and after one has seen little tots, not two years old, eating green cucumbers *ad libitum*, skins and all, unrebuked, he trembles for the coming race.

It is but fair to state that the housing and other conditions of the New Jersey berry pickers are worse than in the canning factory gangs in New York or in many gangs of sugar beet laborers or cranberry pickers; and on the whole the circumstances in agricultural employment are more satisfactory than those surrounding Italian contract labor gangs on railway and other construction work, so far as the men are concerned.

There is little doubt that conditions would be improved speedily were it possible for the labor groups to organize and so acquire strength to make unanimous and specific demands of their employers. Occasionally a gang does strike for certain improvements, and nearly every betterment has come about as the result of such local strikes. When the labor supply is short local ameliorations are frequent, but much remains to be done, and in New Jersey at any rate there is immediate opportunity for correction and remedial legislation.

Of the forty or more Italian communities visited in thirteen states, the oldest and largest groups are the berry and truck growers on the pine barrens of New Jersey, some of them the land owners for whom these picking gangs labor during the harvests. Both north and south Italians are landowners at Vineland, and Hammonton is one of the most promising south Italian settlements east of the Rocky mountains. In origin and development both are typically unassisted colonies, whose progress has been continuous since the seventies and whose numbers have been augmented chiefly from abroad. These groups number perhaps 1,200 families of Italian origin, and here veritably the "magic of property" has "turned sand into gold". The hundreds of little berry farms, vineyards, or sweet potato or pepper fields which make these Italian communities real oases in a waste of sand and low-land, bear unmistakable testimony to the ability of the much-maligned south Italian to create wealth and to make progress materially, morally and politically under rural conditions.

At Vineland the original immigration set in from northern Italy, but more recently a large number of Sicilians and other south Italians have come in. Several stages of material progress are clearly delineated. The first arrivals have passed well beyond the experimental and pioneer stages and many of them are pointed out as the most substantial citizens in the community. They are prosperous, influential and intelligent farmers and proprietors. Others are just emerging from ignorance and debt — just getting the upper hand of the virgin sand or muck upon which they settled — just rising above the line of subsistence farming. These men are preparing to build better, spend more freely, "labor more abundantly". Still others are yet in the dependent class — day laborers in factories, ditches or berry fields, on the highways or railroads. They own little homes with small acreages on which their wives and children are endeavoring to support the household, while the husbands work for wages to pay for the house and land. One by one they are abandoning the dependent occupations and joining the ranks of the farmers.

There is a fourth class, the American-born Italian, who represents the new Italian farmer, born on the soil he cultivates. He is the progressive farmer who dares to try new machinery, new equipment, new varieties and new methods. He subscribes to an agricultural paper and belongs to a farmers' co-operative society.

At Hammonton the principal industry is small fruit growing, which has now become highly specialized and is subject to sharp competition. Beyond a comfortable living, little material return can be expected. Near Vineland, with some exceptions and limitations, the situation is decidedly encouraging. It is the region of the grape, the peach tree and the sweet potato vine; the Italians have added peppers to the list of staple products and most farmers have a small berry patch. It is a region of small farms, built on sand, cultivated by owners and made valuable by hard and unremitting toil. Whatever wealth the rural Italians of New Jersey possess has been well earned, and nearly every home, beautiful or unattractive, cheap or substantial, is a home built by the owner's own hands, the product of his own labor; all are home makers in "Little Italy", — there are no parasites and no leisure class.

The Italians of Vineland, in the large, purchased new, uncleared, unoccupied lands, cleared them and made them productive. Not far from Vineland is the later Italian settlement, begun at Newfield and Malaga about

twenty years ago. Economically considered it has a very different significance.

At an early day Malaga was a flourishing village and the surrounding
country was populated by prosperous Jerseymen, who lived partly on their
cereal crops, poultry and fruit, partly on the products of the forest, —
timber, staves, hoop poles and inferior lumber. But the vanishing timber,
the increasing poverty of the soil, the removal of the mills, the depressed
condition of agriculture, and the exodus of the young people made farming
in the late eighties a precarious industry. When the first Italians came in
1889 they found deserted farms and a warm welcome. "Everybody wanted
to sell", said the first comer; "no one was making any money and nothing
was raised for the market."

The south Italians took hold of the abandoned farms, hit upon a new
industry — pepper raising — and developed it, and for the time being at any
rate saved the region to agriculture. Only the fittest of the American farmers
who have reorganized their farming have been able to survive. The ingress
of the Italians and the exodus of Jerseymen continues, and careful observers
feel that in time the countryside will be entirely Italian. By sheer hard labor,
the co-operation and field work of wife and children, dogged perseverance
and cheap living, the imitative Italian has been able to out-compete his more
intelligent American neighbor. On the tax roll of the township ninety-four
names of Italian property owners appear, part of them farm owners, part of
them share tenants.

In New England, especially near Providence, south Italians have been
engaged in truck and vegetable farming for many years. As market gardening
has increased in importance, the Providence settlement has been augmented
by defections from the industrial population in the vicinity. An entirely
different type of colony has developed within recent years at South
Glastonbury, Conn., where peach growing on land comparatively sterile
and recently forest-covered is the chief occupation of eighty families of
north Italians. It is the one successful foreign settlement studied in the "hill
towns" of New England.

The Italian settlements in New York are in the western part of the state in
a rather well defined area, most of them along the line of the Erie Canal
from Madison to Orleans county. The south Italian colony at Canastota is
typical. Fifty-four families have engaged successfully in truck farming, chiefly
because of the available supply of muck land, admirably adapted to certain
vegetables after being cleared and drained at a great expenditure of hard
labor. American owners were unwilling to undertake the clearing, hence the
land was purchased cheaply; and since an Italian raised his first crop of
onions in 1897 the farm settlement, now called Onion Town, has grown
slowly but steadily.

Economically it is significant that there has been no displacement of the old agricultural population; that the Italian has developed new land — otherwise commercially unproductive — and a new agricultural industry, and that he has found this rival rural occupation more remunerative than his former employment on railroads or canal. Farms are small, improved land is valued at $150 to $200 an acre, and a number who are not able to purchase have rented land on shares and little houses in Canastota or Onion Town. But few continue as tenants; to most tenancy is simply a temporary condition or stepping stone to land ownership.

From the standpoint of community development, it is significant that while there has been no colonization, the settlers for the most dwell together in a rural village, and thus escape the isolation of country life, and especially during the winter enjoy the companionship of their kind. Two considerations have made this settlement possible — the peculiar quality of the available land and the opportunities afforded for wage-earning at irregular intervals until the immigrant is able to make a living and a surplus from his farm.

Italian farming in the South covers a wide range of products, widely diversified soils and climatic conditions, several forms of land tenure, and various systems of culture. The north Italians among the mountains of western North Carolina practice a self-sufficing, diversified agriculture. In southeastern Louisiana and in the coastal plain belt of Alabama, the south Italian truckers and small fruit growers are doing exceptionally well on the light sandy soils, when they succeed in marketing their products in a satisfactory manner. In the "Delta" both north and south Italian cotton tenants are teaching the cotton growers how valuable careful cultivation, kitchen gardens, and small store accounts may be to the cotton "share hand". In the Ozarks Italians from the Sunnyside group have taken up new land, planted orchards, and become successful apple and peach growers. It is plain that the Italian farmer has been profoundly influenced by his environment. His farming has been directed and his agricultural methods taught him by his new neighbors. He has not been uniformly successful, but his economy stands out in contrast to the more or less shiftless, thriftless southern methods, much more conspicuously than Italian agriculture in Wisconsin or New Jersey.

Italian immigration to the South has been in part stimulated by the cotton and sugar-cane planters, who, dissatisfied with Negro labor, alarmed at the increasing scarcity of every sort of farm labor, and desirous of settling acceptable farmers on the immense tracts of unimproved land, have for years been striving to turn the tide of immigration southward. Instances are cited of plantation owners, who advanced the passage money for the transportation of groups of Italian families and settled them on their cotton plantations. The total immigration induced in this way is not significant, except as it forms nuclei around which gather subsequent immigrants to the United States. Sunnyside colony, originating in the importation of 100 or more families from northern Italy in the nineties', is the mother of several rural settlements.

A number of colonies, notably in Texas and Louisiana, seem to have originated in the purchase of a few acres of land by some Italian farm laborer who, arriving practically without money at a southern port of entry, sought employment on some neighboring plantation.

One of the most notable examples of this method of settlement is the south Italian group of strawberry growers at Independence, La. Independence began to be known as a strawberry center about 1890, about the time the first Italian came with his family from New Orleans to pick berries and remained to purchase a few acres of land. A second family followed in the autumn; these two waxed enthusiastic over the possibilities of berry culture and urged their friends and relatives to join them; more Italian berry pickers came and many remained; now there are perhaps 250 Sicilian small farmers in the neighborhood.

Much of the purchased land was lowland, more or less swampy and covered with a heavy forest growth. A large number who were not able to pay thirty to fifty dollars an acre for land operated a few acres on shares; the owner furnishing the land, preparing it for cultivation, providing one-half of the fertilizer and berry boxes, and paying one-half the cost of picking; after picking, the berries were equally divided between landowner and grower. The Italians without capital found this form of tenure satisfactory, and many of them in two or three years saved enough to purchase five or ten acres.

The holdings are small, the homes, in consequence, have the appearance of a straggling rural village and the community spirit is strong. It is not a homelike village, and in the poorly constructed, rude frame, two- or three-room cabins are few evidences of prosperity or comfort. But their farms are well tilled, their berries are excellent and yield well, and thanks to their organized marketing the returns are fairly remunerative. School waits upon the berry field, but interest in education is increasing. There is little civic spirit, and of 350 adult males not twenty are voters. They have had no adequate Italian leadership, and their American neighbors have apparently given little or no attention to the development of a wholesome social or civic interest in the foreigners.

A very important economic feature is a co-operative marketing association with a membership of more than 200 Italian growers, organized two years ago. The Independence berries go to Chicago and neighboring cities; formerly they were shipped to commission merchants by individual growers. The results were unsatisfactory, sometimes ruinous. Prices were low, handling charges high, and complaints of unjust dealing innumerable. In the crisis the Italians got together, organized a selling association, hired an inspector and a selling agent, and notified the commission houses to come to Independence for their berries. At present all berries are sold to platform buyers f.o.b. Independence. The expenses of management in 1909 were about two cents per twenty-four-pint crate.

During the spring of 1910 the association sold $357,639 worth of berries for its members.

Ability to co-operate is characteristic of Italian farmers who are engaged in highly specialized forms of agriculture. They may not have a strong class consciousness, but they are racially homogeneous, and a community consciousness is readily developed. Moreover, some at least have some knowledge of co-operative organization in Italy. In ability to work together they are far in advance of the native southern farmers.

Some few colonies have been promoted either by some Italian leader or philanthropist or by land companies, honest or dishonest. Some of the exploited colonies failed utterly and none, except Valdese and the St. Helena, N.C., settlements, seems to have prospered. The St. Helena colony is apparently one of the most successful colonizing ventures recently undertaken in the South.[3] Two large elements in this success are the thrifty character of the colonists and the fact that nearly all are immediately from farms in northern Italy. But the exceptional leadership offered at St. Helena, the opportunity to earn a livelihood while paying for his land, assurance of landed proprietorship by mere capitalization of his energy and enterprise, and the companionship of his fellows, all have proved unique elements of appeal to the home and property loving foreigner.

Among Italians, not many skilled workers in the trades or industries, here or abroad, have moved to farms, and comparatively few who have found permanent unskilled work in the industries, after landing, have engaged later in agricultural pursuits. But, notably in Texas, the building of railroads has brought in a number of south Italians, chiefly Sicilians, some few of whom have become either tenants or truckers, or independent proprietors of small market gardens. It may be asserted confidently that there has been no marked shift of Italians from industrial pursuits or from city employments to farms in the southern states. In Missouri and Arkansas, indeed, many Italian farmers supplement their incomes by labor in the coal mines during the winter; otherwise the colonies are purely agricultural.

This brief characterization of Italian settlements sets forth the diverse conditions and circumstances incident to the settlement of immigrant rural communities. In the large, the history of the founding of Polish settlements differs little from the Italian record. The goal of early Polish immigration was northern Illinois and Wisconsin. After 1885 the stream of Slavic immigration set in very strongly, and Polish rural colonies began to dot the prairies of Minnesota and the Dakotas as well as the Lake States. Unlike the

3. *The Survey*, November 6, 1909.

early peasants who came directly from Europe in search of cheap land and homes of their own, a large percentage of these men are day laborers who have been engaged in the mines, steel mills, quarries or urban industrial pursuits, and who are attracted to farms by advertisements in Polish papers or the solicitation of Polish land agents. They settle in small groups, their location is directed, they bring more money than the arrivals directly from abroad, and when they are fairly dealt with they make more rapid progress than the earlier immigration.

Hebrew agricultural colonies are interesting from many points of view. Most of the Hebrew farmers are in New York, New Jersey and southern New England, within easy reach of large commercial centers. Practically all of them were established on the land directly or indirectly by the aid or influence of a Jewish immigrant aid society of some sort. Practically all of the colonies have received artificial support by means of subsidized clothing or other factories, or by loans or virtual gifts from trust funds or philanthropists. A very large percentage of the 1,000 or more Hebrew farmers in New England and in Sullivan and Ulster counties, N.Y. practice what may be designated summer boarder agriculture, — since the soil is sterile, the topography rough, hilly, or even mountainous, and the principal part of the farm income comes from boarding summer visitors.

Other Hebrew farmers in New England are landowners, who depend to a greater or less extent on some outside enterprise — peddling, cattle buying, junk dealing, — for the greater part of their incomes, or who are speculators in real estate rather than permanent, simon-pure farmers. Excepting the recent settlements near Ellington and Hartford, Conn., where agricultural conditions are favorable, comparatively few Jewish farmers in New England may be called successful.

The colony or group of colonies near Vineland, N.J., presents Hebrew agriculture in America at its best. Of the several colonies of Hebrews studied none shows greater apparent material prosperity, a more general dependence on agriculture for a livelihood, a more intelligent, resourceful husbandry or a more wholesome community life, educationally, socially, or politically, in a large sense. There is no doubt that a great deal of material encouragement has been given; that many of the social and educational enterprises were conceived, organized, and supported by leaders without the community, and that co-operative business associations and marketing facilities were promoted by leaders who do not live in the settlements; but once established the colonists have entered into all these enterprises with some degree of interest and are beginning to support them. To all appearances the colonies near Vineland, N.J., are permanently established on the basis of a commercial agriculture adapted to the soil, climate and demands of the market.

The study of the several Jewish settlements emphasized these facts at least: that the Hebrew is not adapted by training or tradition to make a pioneer farmer; that to win success he should start with some capital on improved land; that settlement in groups of sufficient size to maintain a synagogue is almost essential; that those who are likely to succeed are either those who have been farmers abroad or who have had some successful experience in agriculture in the United States previous to permanent settlement.

Limits of space forbid even a mention of the Portuguese, Bohemian or Japanese settlements investigated. Indeed, any summarized account is lamentably deficient, in that it cannot portray the intensely interesting human factors, imperfectly delineated in the monographic reports of the commission, and so significant to the student of rural social science. Only a brief word can be presented regarding the effect of rural life socially and politically on the Italians — the immigrant group to which this paper has of necessity been limited.

Ownership of the land he operates is one significant factor in the social and civic progress of the rural Italian in New England, New Jersey and Wisconsin. The prestige incidental to landed proprietorship, as well as the financial responsibility of an owner, sets the farmer far above the day laborer. Not only is he independent, taking orders from no one, but he is a member of the body politic. He is stimulated to industry, for his cast returns are in a measure proportioned to his exertions. The variety of knowledge of crops, fertilizers, markets and public affairs and the familiarity with a number of occupations necessary to agricultural success educate and develop the newcomer very rapidly.

Interest in taxation, good roads, public improvements and expenses for public schools is a stepping stone to wider civic interest. The foreigner's first interest in suffrage is self-interest; but it is better than no interest at all. On the other side there is the deadening effect of isolation by foreign groups, of segregation in the open country, both on the community and the individual members. Where the Italians are intermingled with an equal number of American farmers, they assimilate rather rapidly; where there is rural segregation of large groups Americanization is a slower process than in the city.

It is certain that the settled farmers live better than the itinerant seasonal Italian laborers. Progress in language and in literacy is slower in segregated rural settlements than in cities, but more rapid among Italians than among Poles in some of the large rural settlements visited. Farm labor keeps children out of school, and lack of opportunity for intercourse with English-speaking people explains the persistence of the Italian tongue, even to the second generation in isolated districts. At Independence, La., for example, the school year closes in March to permit the children to pick strawberries. In the Mississippi Delta region, of fifty Italians interviewed between ten and twenty years of age, only twelve were able to read or write English. In some of the segregated outlying communities of Vineland, Italian is almost universally spoken, since every farmer for miles around is of Italian origin.

Adherence to the Roman Catholic faith is practically universal, but the rural Italian is less a churchman than the urban Italian. Language and church affiliations are obstacles to intermingling and inter-marriage with Americans, but there is more social commingling with the better people in the country than in the city, and more where the proportion of Italians in the total rural population is small. Compared with the progress made by north European immigrants on western farms, the Italian's progress in Americanization has been slower; compared with many rural Poles, his advance has been quite as rapid. Fusion in the case of both races (Poles and south Italians) takes place in the third generation.

The quarrelsome, suspicious, mendacious Italian, so frequently heard about in labor gangs where numerous adult males live together, is infrequently found in rural communities; very rarely among landowners. The rural Sicilian is ordinarily peaceable, quiet, law-abiding, and more easily controlled than the south Italian day laborer, according to all accounts of employers and officers of justice. Quick temper and indulgence in liquor are at the root of most of the disorders that arise in established Sicilian settlements. The north Italians seem to be fully as law-abiding as the other Teutonic races.

Progress in citizenship is less rapid among the south Italians than among those from the northern provinces of Italy, ordinarily; but leadership and live local issues touching property owners have much to do with the number of naturalized citizens. Voting is not the all-important test of Americanization, but in the town meeting of Hammonton, N.J., a vote argues more civic intelligence than in Christian Street, Philadelphia. There is a noticeable cleavage along racial rather than party lines, but the country Italian in the North becomes a citizen sooner and votes more independently than the Italian in industry.

The rural Italian is still concerned with his material subsistence. He has a cheap frame house because he is not able to pay for a better one. Little about the house denotes leisure or higher living. Books, papers, and music, rocking-chairs, or hammocks, or swings find no place until the Italian is materially prosperous. His buildings and grounds do not compare favorably with his American neighbors, except in a few localities where the second generation is operating the farms; but the houses are comfortably large for even large families; there is no overcrowding in the ordinary sense, and the houses, excepting those of recent arrivals, are fairly clean and comfortable. In some old localities living conditions are as satisfactory as in any homes in the neighborhood.

All in all, the rural community has had a salutary effect on the Italians, especially those from the southern provinces of Italy. It has frequently taken an ignorant, abject, unskilled, dependent, foreign laborer and made of him a shrewd, self-respecting, independent farmer and citizen. His returns in material welfare are not great, but he lives comfortably and accumulates a small property. Where Italians have been established for some time in comparatively large groups in the open country, they suffer little by comparison with other foreign farmers in the locality, and second generation farmers are frequently not less progressive than Americans.

More than those in the North, the southern colonies reflect the influence of leaders or the want of them in their growth, economic characteristics, social progress, and institutions. The economic progress of the new colony at St. Helena, N.C., is due to oversight of a colonization company, that not only looks after the social welfare of the Italians, but oversees and gives expert advice with regard to planting, cultivating and marketing. The leaders, though not Italian, have been alert to meet the difficulties and to remove the obstacles that meet the newcomer, ignorant both of language, farm practice and methods of marketing produce. They have urged citizenship and provided a church and a school. Under this kindly tutelage the Italians have progressed rapidly. As a rather striking contrast, compare the independent spirit, the desire for ownership, the political and social progress of the Tontitown Italians with the progress along similar lines made by the Italians at Sunnyside, both originally from the same locality in Italy. Sunnyside, originated, as already noted, in the importation of a group of a hundred colonist families from Italy fifteen years ago, to the cotton region of the "Delta". Tontitown, a settlement of seventy families in the hills of Arkansas was founded by deserters from Sunnyside, and is therefore the younger colony. Albeit, the land is naturally less productive, every farmer is an owner, while at Sunnyside all the immigrants are either "croppers" or renters.

In the South the absence of socializing factors in some districts has tended to make foreign settlements so many unassimilated lumps in the body politic. Wise leaders, either Americans or Americanized Italians, ownership of property, compulsory education, and instruction in the duties of citizenship are all fruitful and powerful influences in the development of foreign rural groups.

Edwina Memorial Free Kindergarten, ca. 1905.

# 10

# The Teaching of Foreigners[1]

SARAH WOOL MOORE

"Education is a vital part of other problems and the state needs a system of education for its aliens."

During the last five years the Society for Italian Immigrants, New York, has carried on night classes among the non-English-speaking adults of several labor camps.

At Aspinwall, Pa., where the filtration plant for the city of Pittsburgh was under construction, a substantial one-story building, well lighted, well heated and convenient, was put up by the company expressly for the evening school, and after serving its term faithfully, passed with the camp, at the completion of the work in 1909; west of Pittsburgh at Ambridge, where the plant of the American Bridge Company is located, a suitable building was hired and a school was maintained for three years when a local committee took charge.

In New York state, schools have been operated at Wappinger's Falls, Stoneco and the Ashokan Dam with more or less success; the efforts of the society are now concentrated on the camp of Ashokan Dam, where the main reservoir of New York's new water supply is being built and where the company has also erected a commodious schoolhouse. When running at full force this school has 200 men on its rolls, many of whom attend alternate weeks as the duty of night-shift work permits. In summer about forty children attend the kindergarten. The practicability of school work among adult foreigners in immigrant camps has been recognized by Pennsylvania and New Jersey. Pennsylvania has passed an act authorizing school boards to establish and maintain these schools wherever called for by petition of

1. *The Survey*, Vol. 24, 1910. Pp. 387-392.

twenty applicants.[2] The New Jersey plan is to execute this trust and duty through a commission.

It is a formidable task to learn a new language and the working man should have at least all the help which a practiced student requires and enjoys. With a proper system of instruction studied out, simplified, unified and made a branch of state education, this great mass of inert and helpless ignorance which threatens to obstruct all intelligent self-government will disintegrate and become the material of organized political life. The cost may be set over against the good citizenship of these aliens. A movement to improve the quality of a nation's citizenship is worthy of the name statesmanship. Maurice says: "The peculiarity of a great people is the power of turning external advantages (or disadvantages if you will) to account, of converting them from impediments into tools".

The state is slow to commit itself to plans involving cost and risk which have not previously been tested and found workable. Trade schools, kindergartens, practically every kind of institution has been launched by private enterprise and later on adopted by the state. This we confidently except will be the history of the labor camp schools initiated by the Society for Italian Immigrants and successfully carried on in Pennsylvania and New York.

The program of the proposed bureau of industries and immigration recommended by Governor Hughes and now under consideration by the New York Legislature, uncovers a very great educational field which will best be taken care of through a system of evening schools. Such a system, in communication and co-operation with school authorities and in conjunction with the state commissioner of education, might very profitably be operated by its own supervisor, have its own corps of trained teachers and its own training school for teachers, where elements of the principal immigrant languages — Polish for example in Buffalo, Italian in Albany — could have a place on the curriculum.

A text-book revisory committee would be very necessary. Its task would involve much consultation and thought. There should be an assembling and a comparison of facts and opinions from Maine to California. The school

2. The plan for state operation of evening camp schools in Pennsylvania as embodied in an act passed in the session of 1907, was briefly as follows: On the written application of at least twenty adults including foreigners, located temporarily or permanently within the boundaries of a school district, the petition being accompanied by a statement declaring intention of using said school privilege, the district school board shall provide a suitable location for the school and engage teachers to instruct its pupils. The school board may either use such schoolhouses as shall be convenient, or erect other buildings portable or permanent for the purpose. In sparsely settled country districts two or more school districts may unite in the establishment, support and maintenance of these schools. This provision is compulsory only such years as a state appropriation is voted to provide for the bulk of the necessary expense. A certain percentage of the school expense and also a measure of local supervision and responsibility thus devolve upon the district or districts in which the camp is located.

boards of Hibbing, Minn.; of Chicago, Pittsburgh, Lowell and Boston would be able to contribute valuable points. The adult immigrant student must be supplied with tools; he is now using toys. A committee of three highly competent persons, each to have the choice of a working partner in the state, and of one advisory member outside the state might effectively dispose of this matter of revision which is of capital importance.

The camp inspectors of the new bureau, in addition to other duties, might be expected to find locations for school buildings and teachers' quarters; compare the schools of different camps, thus securing a measure of uniformity; introduce good points made in one school into another; report at headquarters facilities helpful in one place or lacking in another and bring needed good cheer to teachers and pupils.

Beginning with the Ashokan Dam camp school, where the nightly attendance averages fifty pupils, this educational department of the general bureau might project schools, one by one, into the labor camps along the lines of the Barge Canal and the New York City water supply constructions, making them especially strong at points relatively permanent as, presumably, at the great locks, the Delta reservoir, the siphon extremities on either bank of the Hudson, the basins and the Bronx.

In the organization and installation of this polyglot institution — schools in camps — the object of which is to familiarize foreign laborers with what English they need and to give them an intelligent appreciation of the duties and privileges of the citizenship to which they are eligible the state will not expect to evoke from the void a ready-made practicable system; but it may reasonably presume that, conditions being made favorable, the seed-corn with its irrepressible life-necessity, being planted and watered, growth, evolution and finally results corresponding to the promise will follow.

There will be nearly everything to learn as it goes along and yet some pointers are already set up along the road which undoubtedly may be of use.

The schoolhouse for a moving camp may perhaps be a transformed freight car or a portable building but "most any old country schoolhouse" which may chance to be conveniently near the camp will not be suitable.

Schoolrooms, as at present arranged, are as little adapted to the convenience and comfort of the adult as are school text books. Here again we are trying to make the child's wardrobe fit the man. Whether in city or camp, school-quarters for the adult should be of the reading-room type and conversation should be a stated feature of the course. The ordinary recitation room open for evening classes, with its individual desks screwed to the floor, admits of no grading, no grouping, no pantomime rehearsal of verbs, no impromptu "socials", no flexibility or freedom of program.

Our commodious school-shanty with its open rafters is, at the beginning, forty or fifty feet long by eighteen wide, and soon a wing is added. Under the high horizontal window sashes a continuous blackboard surrounds the walls. The furniture consists of benches or chairs and removable table-tops eleven feet long and two and a half feet wide, supported on horses. A platform at one end of the room and running shelves for books over the blackboards are a necessity. Here one teacher may take care of thirty or forty men in two well-defined grades, if each class, grouped about its long table, has its work planned so that it can go forward while the teacher is busy at the other table. Beginners, without regard to nationality, occupy the wing and have a special teacher.

If a family camp, as soon as possible, facing south or east there should be a sunny kindergarten[3] extension. These three rooms thrown together make a fine assembly or social hall.

In one corner stands a neat, shelved box containing fifty or one hundred volumes loaned by the State Library at Albany. On its top are piled a dozen or two games to be enjoyed Saturday evenings.

The working man likes his school quarters in the heart of his living quarters and of the same homely pattern; he likes to have his regular teacher, his own seat and his own book and he desires ardently what every language student desires, to have exact equivalents for the names of such things as cannot be represented graphically, as, time, distance, value, exchange, wages, debt, savings. He is equally eager to get hold of the English word for objects which may be graphically represented, not doll and kite — however, but subway, tunnel, hoist, steam drill — the implements of a man.

Text books must be the staff of teacher as well as pupil, for few available teachers are at present masters of any of the immigrant languages. They can communicate their instructions only in English and in pantomime, from which perhaps one-half of the pupils may gather profit. What of the other half? Then, too, primary text books insult the intelligence of men who are not infants because they are learning to talk. Already mature and at the prime of brawn and brain and nervous force they have transferred themselves from one to another family of nations and are eager for the English which will express the life they are living.

How is it now? In most night schools for adult foreigners no better way is found than to start up in the evening the machinery of the morning suitable only for children. The inevitable result is discouragement and disgust.

A system must be adopted or devised which with unswerving directness will put the immigrant in possession of the six or eight hundred words which he needs to understand and desires to use. A book entirely English should be prepared, giving at the head of each page numbered cuts of related objects, as, for instance, those composing a kit of carpenters' tools or miners'

---

3. Camp children of school age should also be provided for unless the nearest public school is within walking distance.

implements, and below on the same page, the correspondingly numbered English name for each. "John what is No. 16?" Not only John, but every man in the class searches for cut sixteen and recognizes it as a familiar acquaintance before he finds sixteen in the text below and hears, clearly pronounced by the teacher, its English name. The class repeats the name in concert and individually. This drill must give definite information and give it simultaneously to Finn, Russian, Bohemian, Pole or Italian.

But words capable of graphic representation will not constitute more than an eighth of the number which must be mastered and a committee on revision of text books, which would exercise an important function in the proposed bureau of industry and immigration, would do well to select a suitable series out of existing books, eliminate infantile subjects, expressions and illustrations, and introduce in the most simple and gradually progressive phraseology a man's conversation. From primer to third reader the vocabulary should grow by accretion and use — a constant repetition of the ground passed over, a gradual addition of substantives and words of action, quality and relation. As these new words are introduced their equivalents in, let us say, Finnish, should be interlined, and at the back of the book be it primer or more advanced reader an alphabetical vocabulary Finnish-English and English-Finnish should be subjoined.

With such simple but sufficient tools to work with, the troubled perplexity would pass out of many Finnish eyes, many Finnish brows would clear and

## ENGLISH-ITALIAN LANGUAGE BOOK
### LESSON FIFTH
**The Blacksmith and the Horse-Shoer**
**Il Fabbro e il Maniscalco**

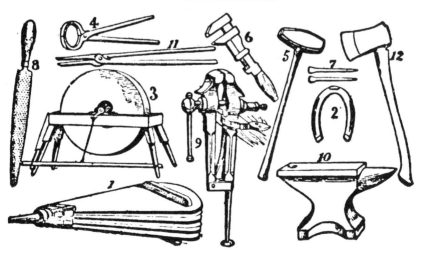

simultaneous enlightenment would come to Pole, Italian, Greek — each man being furnished with a reader identical as to English text and differing from the others only in its interlined interpretations into his own tongue. Excellent text books already exist, but they presuppose a knowledge of our speech which only a few possess.[4]

The evolution of the right teacher is a problem. The kind needed will be attracted to the work — experienced, devoted, capable, reliable and human. Theoretically a man should be the teacher in a labor camp but the Society for Italian Immigrants has had better success in sending women out by pairs or trios, and however forbidding the surroundings, no woman has suffered any discourtesy.

A teacher must expect inconvenience and difficulty. His preparation should include the principles of settlement work and knowledge of one or more foreign languages; for the efficiency of a camp school is not at its highest unless the language of the campers has been mastered by at least one of the teachers.

The problem of full and regular attendance depends largely upon the administrative ability of the principal. If kept busy and gaining a little headway each man says, "Tomorrow I will be here sure". But, it is difficult! Kinsmen and *paesani* from the same village troop in by squads. The beginners' class is suddenly swelled by eleven or twelve additions. Alas for the teacher! The pupils are glad to have mistakes corrected but the teacher must not chide or make invidious comparisons or praise too much, for jealousy is easily aroused. Though so gregarious there is a strange "apartness" between *paesani* of different Italian towns — they do not know or want to know each other's names or numbers or abodes, but that gradually wears off. It is wise to make changes in the order of school exercises without previous announcement. The pupils dislike innovations and the very thing you think will please them most, may work the other way. Each wants his own seat, his own book, his own accustomed turn, though all like a certain variety in the program and not too much time devoted to one thing. Plenty of talk, plenty of repetition, rehearsal of work-orders, concert reading, work on blackboard, phonic drill, free translation and practice in the use of a dictionary, and simple dialogues improvised by the teacher which are rehearsed with great gusto and sympathetically applauded by the school.

Then there is the problem of the pupil, often tired and sleepy, often set back with a new class of starters, often experiencing a most undesired change of teachers, puzzled and at sea but resolute to make the acquaintance

---

4. Chancellor's *Language and Reading for Evening Schools.* Harrington's I and II *Book for Non-English Speaking People.* O'Brien's *English for Foreigners.* Robert's *Lesson Leaves — English for New Americans.* Richman and Wallack's *Good Citizenship.* Howard's *American History, Government and Institutions.*

of his new surroundings, he will smile up at you and say, "Bye and bye", when that is almost the total of his English. Then, the pitiful "out of a job" cases who are "fired" because they consider their work too dangerous and because wages are not scaled up in proportion to risk. "I am willing to work", said one. "I must work, I can't afford not to work but I am not willing to be killed." The pathetic illiterates, young men as well as old, who delightedly practice writing their own names and read at sight words of two letters and often make astonishing progress. The intelligent looking newcomers "dumb as horses", Greeks, Slavs, Ruthenians, Croatians, Bulgarians, Russians, Finns — one can only set before them the array of dictionaries available and make them pick out the words "school", "country", "age", "arrive", etc. — words for which there is no object illustration in sight. Often one of the group will be able to act as interpreter of this or that language.

Night-school attendance seems to be more variable and uncertain in small cities where counter-attractions exist than in camps. Two characteristic though extreme instances are Sharpsburg, Pa., and Newburgh, N.Y. In both cases a petition asking for a school was circulated among the Italians by men who had been members of neighboring camp schools. The school board of Sharpsburg agreed to do as requested, but on account of building operations deferred the matter a year. An evening school was then announced. It was kept open for three successive weeks and not a soul came.

In Newburgh the petition for a school was carried to the Young Men's Christian Association and the secretary writes:

We sent out letters to the men who had signed the petition and urged that they meet on a certain night. About fifteen came. Dr. Peter Roberts was here and taught the first class. The pupils were enthusiastic. It was decided that each man pay the tuition fee of one dollar for his ten lessons to cover the necessary expenses of the class. This they heartily agreed to. That was the last I have seen of any of them for they never came back. Then we had another group of Italians styling themselves the better class. They came three times and were most enthusiastic as long as the class was free and then when we suggested the payment of a dollar it was unanimously suggested by them that we wait until the next lesson. That was the last of them.

Comment is needless. The Italian is nothing if not "unexpected".

In the camp schools of the Society for Italian Immigrants the fee of five cents an evening was given cheerfully and the teachers were invariably reminded of the basket ceremony when it was accidentally forgotten. The Society ordered its discontinuance on the ground that camp schools should be conducted on the same basis as free public schools.

The problem of funds is always acute. It is a perpetual gamble or more properly, the work is pushed on with an inner assurance that, being important and necessary, resources will become available when the pressing need arrives, and until now this faith has been justified though the uncertainty ahead interferes with the best results and makes it all seem temporary, *and it is temporary until the state takes hold.*

In numbers benefited, do schools for non-English speaking laborers pay for the cost of maintaining them?

In Ambridge, Pa., out of 150 Italian laborers, there was an average school attendance of twenty; at the Ashokan Dam there is an average attendance of fifty each evening in a camp of 1,800 to 2,000 laborers. The schools do not pay, and they do. Full explanation of this paradox would fill a volume, but one reason for the negative result is the make-shift character of school apparatus as already described.

The beer wagon problem belongs to the social side of camp school work. Employers say that without beer no considerable number of foreign laborers could be induced to live in camp. The settlement worker's influence will at least modify conditions and cause mothers to refrain from feeding beer and even whiskey to their babes. More than once tots have come to kindergarten drunk, and a series of tragic shootings and knifings, as common among the Slavs and colored people as among the Italians, has, in each case been preceded by too much drink.

Should religion be excluded from school work among adult foreigners? This work is religious because it is fulfilling the golden rule of "Do unto others", etc., and the royal law, "Thou shalt love thy neighbor as thyself". The question of dogma should not be touched. Our pupils are mainly Roman Catholic and we have on our shelves a number of copies of the Pope's Gospels in Italian, the admirable edition issued by the *Pia Società di San Girolamo* in Rome. Sometimes this book is taken down and read, sometimes passages are translated from it into English: "Does not burn us the heart perhaps while along the street he was talking us and was interpreter us the Scripture?" "The Son of Man is boss of the Sabbath", "Jesù the save-man of the world."

The state and country will prosper as we treat with justice, fairness and friendliness the new Americans as they arrive.

# 11

# Handicaps in America[1]

Gino C. Speranza

When the subject of "immigration" comes up for discussion, either in casual talk at table, or in the more serious magazine articles, the discussion is almost invariably confined to the question, "Should the admission of foreigners be restricted or not".

The immigrant is called "a problem" by those who stop to think of him at all, and if his presence in this country is deemed tolerable, it is only in his capacity of workman — a negotiable asset on the troubled balance sheet of capital and labor. Rarely is he thought of as a possible citizen, whose children, with the passing of a few years, will be an inherent part of the strength, or weakness, honor or dishonor of the nation.

Whose business is it to know how the stranger fares, what influence he is giving out, what feeling he is acquiring toward the new country through the forces in it with which he is in contact — often forces of malignity, greed, or indifference?

There is a singular gap in the chain of responsibility for the immigrant, — for our alien population.

Congress, through the Bureau of Immigration, has the right to say who shall be admitted to the country and to decide how many may come in at any time. In the same governing body is vested the right to send out of the country any foreigner who is shown to be a striking menace or an undeniable burden, — the type of immigrant who has brought into our current speech the memorable phrase "undesirable citizen". Even though this power is in the federal government, the state in some cases must find the delinquent person and establish the charges against him.

With these purely technical and legislative relationships the "responsibility"

1. *The Survey*, Vol. 23, 1910. Pp. 465-472.

of the federal government ends; the real, human, moral, mental, *actual* responsibility is upon the state; primarily and overwhelmingly upon the State of New York. A few facts and figures from the census and the reports of investigators, will show the extent of this responsibility.

In 1908 there were about a half million aliens within the state boundaries, who had been here less than five years.

Three-fifths of all immigrants to this country are set down on the New York docks, and in a recent investigation one-sixth of the arriving army expressed the intention of remaining in New York.

The census of 1905 showed many significant figures regarding the aliens then within the state, *e.g.* 1,004,320 had been here for periods of from one year upwards. In ten counties seven per cent of the population were aliens; in four counties over six per cent, and in seven counties five per cent.

So different from our native population, in race, customs, habit of thought and way of living — this mass of "foreigners", fed into the state from the federal government's hopper at Ellis Island, must be assimilated by the state. It is within this boundary that the greater numbers of the alien people make their homes, settle their families, find work, seek recreation and become a vital part, with their human influence, for better or worse, of the neighborhood, town or city which has become their harbor.

To fail to reckon with this power in its play on industrial, social and political conditions now existing in the state, would mean to omit from consideration a potent influence in all these phases of the life of the state.

It may be urged that this mass of people shares the protection and opportunities for industry, education, comfort and pleasure, which is available to any dweller within the province of organized government. This is true, speaking loosely; but a careful diagnosis of the case of the immigrant shows that for him, in the greater part of his relationship with the community, it is not true.

He cannot avail himself of benefits that are beyond his reach, nor of protection that is outside his knowledge. The wires of communication are down — between "the state" and the immigrant with his needs at the other end of the line.

The character of the contemporary and newest industries in our country calls for physical strength; bodily labor. To whom do we look to dig the ditches for our great waterways, to trench and drill for the treasures of our mines, and to labor with the strength of oxen in the midst of blast furnaces where the native products are being made into world supplies? A few cold figures — "statistics concerning immigrants" — show a great part of the answer.

In 1907, seventy-two per cent of all immigrants were men — eighty-nine per cent were above the age of fourteen and the nationalities that made up almost all the lists were the sturdy ones: Italians, Russians, Poles, and

Hungarians. Between these peoples and our native-born there is the silent gap of an alien speech; strange customs — unmeaning to the newfound neighbor but in many instances the mystic ritual of life to him who practices it; and toward government, the peasant's sense, sometimes the serf's fear, as against the American citizen's freedom in "the free city of his birth".

The forces at work for assimilation are not of a character which will best serve the state, or protect and develop the energy, power and spirit of the immigrant. They are in the hands of those who have been aliens themselves. There are Jewish, Hungarian, Austrian immigrant homes — but no American homes — for the coming Americans.

It may be well to remind our readers just here that we are in no sense entering a plea for a class of dependents or deficients in natural power or faculty; quite the contrary, for in the great majority of cases the newcomers take care of themselves with remarkable success in the face of great difficulties.

Some of these difficulties are inevitable — as the difference in language; but most of them, and unquestionably the greatest are superimposed by the greed and inhumanity of persons whose prey the immigrant has become — the petty and grand offenders who range in size and power from the shrewd thug on the dock, who extorts the stranger's few dollars on pretense of service to be rendered, to the big steamship company which locks him in the filthy hold of a boat and transports him, from New York to Fall River, for example, in conditions of distress and hardship unbelievable.

That the conditions are different for the foreigner and the American of the same general status is only too apparent to any one who has followed the trail of both. We speak from the actual cases which have come to the knowledge of the State Immigration Commission of 1908 and 1909. In the first place the American has cost the country several hundred dollars (and rightly so) before he has arrived at the age and capacity of a producer in the field of labor. The other with his full grown strength (all we seem to want of him) is handed over ready made by the older civilizations.

The American entering a new town or city arrives at a railway station, and in the language common to all, can inquire his way to a lodging, judge of or bargain for a fair charge for the same, and can rebuff and deal with any intrusion or molestation that may come his way.

The immigrant arrives at the Battery.[2] He is immediately and violently besieged on all sides by tricksters and thieves in the persons of porters, hackmen, "runners" for employment agencies, many of whom speak his language. They profess friendliness and advise him about his lodgings, employment, transportation to his destination and the many things in which

2. In 1907 the number of immigrants landed was 364,544, and in 1908 the number was 241,343. For 1910 the steamship companies are anticipating immigrants in unprecedented numbers.

he needs help. Licensed city porters wear badges and pretend thereby to be city officials, and get large fees for taking the mute stranger and his bundles to a lodging or agency. A case is known of an immigrant to whom five dollars was charged for a five-cent elevated ticket, which was represented to be a "railroad ticket".

The loss of such amounts of money is a serious matter to a man without employment and the road to dependence, and deportation may be short if work is not immediately obtained.

The American laborer traveling from one place to another rides in the usual typical day-coach, pays a through fare to his destination, knows when and where to get off, and shares all the privileges of service, short of drawing room cars or special sleepers. If there is no dining car the train makes a short stop for lunch. The same is true of boat travel.

In an investigation of traveling conditions made by Commissioner Watchorn, and which the New York State Commission of Immigration found in 1909 had not been materially changed, it was shown that on some lines first-class rates were charged to immigrants for inferior cars; that smokers were used, containing no separate toilet facilities for men and women and no wash rooms. These coaches were crowded with men, women and children. No adequate stops were made to obtain food and no milk could be obtained *en route* for the babies. Lunch boxes can be bought at Ellis Island but there are no bottles or other receptacles to be had in which milk can be taken away. The mothers do not know the length of the journey they are to take from Ellis Island to their destination, nor how or where to get milk to take with them. In some instances much delay is experienced in sending off immigrant trains, and journeys are made across the state and even to Chicago on local trains. No choice of service or road is given to the travelers, who are made to use the worst cars and often to take a very indirect and long journey over a road to which they are assigned by general agreement among the respresentatives of the nine big companies, who have a system of "balancing the passenger business".

The situation on the docks and in the boats both of the coastwise steamers and of the night Hudson River boats is similar.[3] Conditions vary: some better, some worse.

The steerage quarters on the boats are sometimes in the hold and the hatchway is locked after the immigrants are put inside. In some of these quarters there are no sleeping accommodations though the journey is invariably made at night. On one boat no provision whatever is made for sleeping. The passengers sleep among the freight bundles. In the boats where

3. In the six months ending June 30, 1908, 9,701 aliens left New York City by way of coastwise boats. Over 25,000 left on the Hudson River boats in the section described. Ninety per cent of these were aliens.

bunks are provided they are dirty and overcrowded. The difference in fare is rarely more than twenty-five or fifty cents between the quarters in the freight section of the boat and the general passenger quarters. For this difference the American gets fresh air, freedom, a promenade deck, saloon, music and access to the restaurant. The passengers in the hold are not allowed to buy food on most of the boats, and on one trip an investigator saw a porter charge five cents for every drink of water taken. Even when they are able to pay, aliens are not informed of, nor encouraged to use first-class accommodations.

It often happens that immigrants, ready and waiting at docks to return to their native countries, are prevented from sailing because the steerage quarters in the boat for which they hold tickets are already overcrowded. In this predicament and in the frequent accidents of lost tickets and lost baggage there is no one to help except in the cases in which immigrant societies (private and philanthropic concerns) keep a man or two on the docks. These men render such services as they can and obtain protection for their countrymen. On many docks no provision for help is made, and the foreigner must shift for himself amidst the impatience of officials and steamship employees who speak only English. The extent of confusion in the outgoing traffic can be judged by the fact that in 1908, 714,828 aliens returned to their foreign homes mostly through the port of New York.

The hardships encountered in transportation are but a rough introduction to the road the alien has ahead of him. If he has enough to buy the chance to work, he applies to an employment agent. Often the employment agent has been instrumental in bringing him to this country, and he is taken with his baggage, directly to the agent from the steamer. Many of the agents are *padroni* who apparently take the place of a friend or relative of the American looking for work. But the unchecked opportunities for the indulgence of greed have made the *padrone* one of the most unfortunate elements in the life of the alien. The exorbitant fees charged for putting him at work and the large and continuous profits obtained for supplying him with the necessities of life are the source of a spectacular revenue to the *padrone*, his countryman, who has preceded him in residence here, but a few years. Through this *padrone* system the alien may be sent to unsanitary labor camps, the life of which is pictured elsewhere. He may also be sent as a strike-breaker or sent without his knowledge into industries wherein his wages do not enable him to maintain a decent standard of living.

If he escapes the *padrone* and goes to an immigrant agency on his own initiative, he often encounters unforeseen abuses. An Italian carpenter came to the commission a while ago (he had seen a notice of it in a newspaper) to apply for help in the following case:

He had left his tools in his trunk at an agency while he went out to look for work. On his return he found that the agency had been sold "with all its contents" including quantities of baggage belonging to immigrants. The purchaser, who continued in the employment business at the house, refused to give the Italian his tools, and he had not been able to take up his work for two months before he came to the commission. The commissioner's representative talked the matter over with the new owner of the agency (who spoke no English) and persuaded her to give up the tools to their owner.

When the immigrant has found work and a lodging place and the prospect is looking better to him, his next thought is to communicate with his family or friends in the old country; to share his savings and perhaps to bring his family here. The typical method of setting about this process puts him into a labyrinth of difficulties and dangers of which he has never dreamed. In the same circumstances the American writes his own letter and gets his money order or registers his letter, or writes his family to come and goes to the train to meet them. The foreigner can do nothing so simple as this. There has sprung up to meet his peculiar situation "the immigrant bank", a flourishing and extensive enterprise. In 1908 records were obtained of more than five hundred such banks in New York City, and eighty-eight in other cities of the first and second class.

According to the testimony of one large banking house in New York, it had one thousand correspondents scattered throughout the state. Their business was to solicit the savings of immigrants. Fifty-six bonded bankers transmitted over sixteen million dollars in 1907. This represented but twenty-five per cent of the total amount transmitted. The greater part of this money is in amounts of a few dollars each. The deposit business done by these banks is also very large. In 1907 two and one-half million dollars was received on deposit, and in 1908 one and three-quarter millions. Much of the money sent to the people at home by the immigrant does not reach them. There is no guarantee whatever to the immigrant that his savings will reach his family, and in cases of fraud the banker pleads delay and unavoidable loss in transmitting, and waives all responsibility. The money passes through many hands: the correspondent, the banker, often the express office, and the foreign representative who may mail the remittance from the port on the other side to the town or home of the waiting relatives. In case of loss how can the alien isolated in the labor camp, or isolated among his fellows, prove that the money did not arrive while his witness is across the ocean?

There is no regulation of these banks by the State Banking Department. Every bank under the Banking Department in 1907 which suspended business paid its depositors in full. Twenty-five immigrant banks which failed had money of immigrants amounting to a million and one-half dollars ($1,459,295.01). In 1909 the commission found that the assets of these banks amounted to but $295,331.13 and but $500 had been repaid by the bonding companies, though each banker was bonded for $15,000. 12,279 claimants lost their money through these banks. The size of the average claim was fifty-five dollars, but a great number of the claims were around twenty dollars. Anyone familiar with the pay and the work of the day laborer on public works in our tunnels and ditches, and in places of danger, can best realize what these losses mean to the workman and to the family across the water, depending on the earnings and their safe transmission.

The immigrant bank is a curious institution. It not only undertakes to care for the savings of the immigrant but it acts as a social center and place of appeal in many emergencies. The banker maintains a postoffice where mail can be called for or from which it can be forwarded. It sells steamship tickets and is the office of the notary public who prepares legal documents, performs legal services and helps the foreigner obtain citizenship papers.

One of the most profitable mediums of revenue to the vampires of immigrant ignorance is the sale of worthless steamship tickets. As soon as the immigrant has taken a foothold here and begins to plan to bring his family or brother or sister or parents to his new-found home, he becomes fair game for the bogus ticket seller.

The steamship companies have authorized agents in the foreign quarters of the city who are empowered to conduct a legitimate ticket selling business, but around these centers, both within their knowledge and outside it, many other agents and peddlers have sprung up who reap a livelihood from the sale of worthless pieces of paper purporting to be steamship tickets.

One of the authorized agents, a man of long experience in the business, who had offices in Manhattan, Brooklyn and the Bronx does a business amounting to over three hundred thousand dollars a year. He testified in a recent investigation that "there are about fifteen authorized agents on the East Side, and eight not authorized but doing business in offices and getting their tickets from authorized agents; that there are probably from five to six thousand, and certainly three thousand runners or peddlers in New York City, who sell tickets outside of offices".

The steamship companies have a technical rule in regard to furnishing tickets to peddlers, but it is not only not enforced but the traffic of the peddlers is secretly encouraged by the steamship companies. Another authorized agent testified that twenty per cent of his business consisted of the sale of tickets to peddlers. These peddlers sell steamship tickets from pushcarts, in tenements, and in small groceries and other shops.

A typical case of a defrauded man is given in the following testimony:

I agreed to purchase from the firm of A and B two steamship tickets for passage from Antwerp to New York for the sum of ninety dollars and to pay twenty dollars down and two dollars each week until the ninety dollars should be paid. I paid the twenty dollars and received an order which I sent to my sister and her husband in Russia. Upon receipt of this they started at once for Antwerp. When they presented the order they were told that it was no good. My sister and her husband were stranded and were obliged to beg. As soon as they wrote me these facts I went to the agents and they demanded an additional ten dollars to have the original order stopped and agreed to give me another order. This second order I sent to my sister and it likewise was no good. As soon as I learned this I went again to the office of the agent but it was closed. They had moved away and I have never been able to find them since, nor have I been able to get back the sum of sixty-eight dollars which I had paid them on the orders for the first two tickets, or the additional ten dollars which I gave.

Another avenue of fraudulent practice is the notaries' office. The foreign notary has a peculiar leverage on his countryman, or one whose language he speaks, from the circumstance that in foreign countries the office of a notary is one of honor and importance. The holder of the office is a man of character and education and standing in the community. With this tradition in his mind the foreigner trustfully goes to the representative of this calling in the new country and confides his affairs to him. One notary who is also a real estate agent in Brooklyn drafted a bill of sale of a clothing store and antedated the document for the purpose of avoiding the payment of notes which had been protested. For this service he charged five dollars and the cost of filing the document. It is a common custom for these notaries to ask whether bills of sale are *bona fide* or are made to prevent creditors from collecting money due them. If the latter purpose is admitted a higher fee is charged for the document. The superintendent of labor complained against one notary for issuing fraudulent permits enabling children to work who are not legally qualified.

The list of offenses is long and many of them are ingenious in character and illustrate only too graphically that in their self-interest the notary public, the employment agent, and the immigrant banker are strong forces against the assimilation of the alien by the new country.

The banker does not want him to invest his money here as that would remove it from his own profitable custody, both from savings accounts and from passing through his hands to the foreign relatives. The employment agent is not interested in his buying a little farm; that might take him out of the ranks of the frequently unemployed who need his offices. The notary public is not enthusiastic that he should learn English, as that would equip him to attend to matters which the notary must now transact for him.

Some kind of clearing house or utility center is indispensable and the alien is naturally attracted to these professedly friendly countrymen rather than to impersonal corporations, however legitimate in character.

As conducted now, every function of the immigrant bank, the employment agency and the notary's office is open to abuse. There is no supervision; no one is disinterestedly concerned about the alien and in his ignorance he responds to overtures of professed friendliness, believing that it is all part of the wonder of the new country.

Here then is a suggestion of the alien's handicap: exploitation at docks and on trains and boats; traveling conditions which imperil safety and health; oppression at the hands of the *padroni;* isolation from family life and comforts; frauds on the part of the banker, notary, and steamship agent, and misrepresentation at the hands of interpreters and fraudulent lawyers when he violates the laws he does not know or understand.

The voices of a few "fervid spokesmen of the inarticulate and unassimilated" are being raised in petition that "the wires of communication" be put up without delay. It is true that the aliens are in a gravely different case from the native-born; that they form a great group of persons to be reckoned with; that the state has no record of them, and that its educational and assimilative powers do not reach them.

# II

# The Italian in America, 1891-1914

Emigrants waiting to embark, Genoa, 1910.

# 12

# The Philanthropists' View [1]

*Strangers Within the Gates*

*Charities* in this number[1] enters upon a new field, of which the first fruits, we are confident will be found by our readers to be both appetizing and rich with promise. The influx of immigrants of various races and nationalities brings the social worker into contact with peoples whose histories, characteristics, virtues and weaknesses it is important for him to know. It is our purpose to present some of the salient facts in regard to these various groups of strangers within our gates, not as they are viewed by unfriendly outsiders, whether of a little earlier arrival or of native stock; but as seen from the inside by those who know intimately the colonies that have been formed within our cities and states, and who, through sympathy and intimate knowledge, are in a position to lay bare the obstacles to complete assimilation. It is the purpose of these studies to prevent needless friction; to do what we can to insure that racial aptitudes which are worth preserving are not needlessly sacrificed either by ignorance on the part of the newcomers, or by misinterpretation on the part of their American neighbors.

It often happens that our conception of a foreign type is based upon a caricature. *Micky, sheeny, dago,* have a terrible power of impressing

1. *Charities*, Vol. 12, 1904. Pp. 443-455.
2. In getting out a special number of *Charities* which attempts to discuss so broad a subject as the social assimilation of two races, and that within the compass of a single issue, sacrifices have to be made somewhere. And, rather than omit material pertinent to the Italian in America, various departments have been dropped out of this magazine number of *Charities*, together with the customary paragraphs in philanthropy, reviewing the progress of social work here and abroad. They will be found in subsequent weekly issues. For the same reason articles of general scope have been published here, and contributions with special or local bearing — the Italians on plantations or in the northwest, for instance — will be printed later, as initial steps in sustaining that interest in the working out of assimilation aroused by this number.

themselves in places where the Irishman, the Jew and the Italian are entitled to stand with no shadow of a caricature behind them. Neither the opera singer across the footlights, nor the padrone-worked ditch digger, is, in any complete sense, the Italian in America; and the value of the Italian laborer is no more to be judged offhand from his looks, than is that of the singer, especially if the judge is one whose standard of physcial beauty happens to be rigid adherence to a Saxon type. We have therefore sought, in this Italian number of *Charities*, and have obtained, the generous and most valuable co-operation not only of representatives of the Italian government, but of Americans of Italian origin, men who, knowing both Italy and America, elect to become and remain American citizens, but who, knowing both Italians and Americans, are able to speak authoritatively of the former and instructively to the latter; and the co-operation also of American writers who have entered most fully into the peculiar hardships and dangers and successes of Italian immigrants who are struggling with the conditions of what is to them a new country.

### The Italian in America

It is clear that certain obligations rest upon American communities toward recent immigrants. What those are in reference to Italians is shown clearly in some of the papers which we publish. That there shall be a courteous reception to those who are invited to come — and in this respect Mr. Speranza is right in pointing out that permission to come is an invitation — a reception such as is advocated and typified by the Society for the Protection of Italian Immigrants; that child labor and garment making in tenement-houses shall be prevented; that the common laborer shall have the equal protection of the law; that there shall be strict sanitary inspection and a suitable provision for light and air in living and sleeping rooms — these are among the elementary obligations assumed by American communities, not primarily in the interests of the Italians, but from which, incidentally, direct benefit will come to them.

There is no one solution for the problem so keenly and fruitfully analyzed from the inside by our various contributors this month. Restriction, as is pointed out by Adolfo Rossi, the royal supervisor of emigration, in the significant and interesting interview which we publish, introduces an artificial selection very favorable, at least from a physical standpoint, for America. Arguments for further restriction were fully presented in the February magazine number of *Charities* and need not be repeated. Suffice it to say that we are not likely to have such a degree of restriction as will in any way affect the importance of the subjects which we are now discussing.

Neither will agricultural dispersion prove a safe sole reliance. Dr. Tosti, indeed, suggests that the Italian agricultural laborer may supplant the negro in the more diversified and intensive cultivation of land which is to be a characteristic feature of the new South, and the same suggestion was made by Cyrus L. Sulzberger in an article which *Charities* published two weeks ago. Mr. Sulzberger thinks that migration from southern Italy may result in bringing into our southern states a people who shall operate upon the negro "as migrations have always operated, either to lift him up to a higher communal walk, or to cause his dispersion over the entire country". In effect, however, this would mean the migration of negroes to the cities, a process already far advanced with results not calculated to awaken enthusiasm.

## Appreciation and Assimilation

If the dispersion of every Italian colony now to be found in American cities, and the closing down of the gates of Ellis Island against Italians as effectively as against the Chinese, were effected, it is doubtless true that the problems of the city would be simplified. If, however, that were accomplished at the sacrifice of American appreciation and American sympathy for the hardships, the struggles and the achievements of Italians in their own peninsula and on the Western continent, the relief would be too dearly bought. To use an Italian saying, "the world is one country". Breadth of sympathy and a feeling of the unity of the human race are worth infinitely more than economic ease and freedom from anxiety. It might, or might not, be better that the American people should be homogeneous. It is certain that in our American cities we are not that, and are not likely to become so otherwise than by assimilation.

We shall continue to think aloud about our country's guests in so far as their presence contributes to our social problems, but it need not follow that this thinking aloud must be of such a character as to be unpleasant to the guests. It is far from being to their interests that we shall begin to think in whispers; but they may rightly ask that we think justly, intelligently and fraternally. *Charities* takes great satisfaction in becoming the medium through which most valuable contributions to this end are made.

## The Italian Population in New York

Last July, on the initiation of Commendatore Giovanni Branchi, consul general, The Italian Chamber of Commerce appointed a committee on statistics which should make an investigation into the numbers and economic condition of the Italian population in the State and City of New York. The committee is composed of Signori G. Granata, D. A. Maffei, E. Mariani, and Prof. G. Rossati. Signor Branchi, who had been chosen chairman, transferred his office to the first vice-consul, Cav. Gustavo Tosti, under whose direction the work has been done.

The investigation of the committee, as outlined at its first meeting will include the following points:

(1) The Italian population.

(2) Occupations, professions, participation in political life.

(3) Real estate owned by Italians.

(4) Savings, including money sent back to Italy, and accumulation of capital.

In the March number of the *Bulletin of the Chamber of Commerce* is given the first section of the committee's report.

The estimate arrived at of the Italian population is derived from these elements:

|  | N.Y. State | N.Y. City |
|---|---|---|
| Population in 1900 | 272,572 | 225,026 |
| Excess of births over deaths | 18,322 | 14,121 |
| Excess of arrivals over departures, 1901-1903 | 195,281 | 143,628 |
| Total Italian population January 1, 1904 | 486,175 | 382,775 |

With a complete registration of births and of deaths and with a complete list of arrivals, not only from Europe, but from other places in the United States, as well as of departures to other points in the country as well as to Europe, no fault could be found with the method employed. The most serious source of error is to be found in the number of departures. There are no figures to show the number of Italians who leave New York, either City or State, by rail — nor is there any method of estimating how many such there are. This number, while not large, is undoubtedly sufficient to deserve consideration.

Nor is the number of arrivals, indicated merely by the declared destination of immigrants, quite satisfactory. This number includes, on the one hand, many persons whose immediate goal is New York, but who, within a few weeks or months, go on farther into the country, thus forming the class of departures just mentioned. It omits, on the other hand, Italians drifting back to the New York colony after a more or less prolonged stay in some other state. These are probably so few in number, though there are some, as to be a negligible quantity. The net addition made to the population of the city and state is, therefore, probably less than is indicated by the difference between the immigrants who give New York as their destination and the persons who go back from New York to Italy, because of our inability to trace the movement of the population from year to year within our own country.

The large excess of births over deaths among the Italians is testimony to a high degree of vitality, and the large percentage of men, and of both men and women below forty-five years of age, is an indication of the economic possibilities, and value, of the group. In this age-composition of the Italian population, showing a very high proportion of men and women at the reproductive ages, may be found one explanation for the remarkably high birth-rate, noted in the report, among the Italians in America — much higher than is found in Italy. Immigration of the youth of the country works in both directions to bring about this difference, since it reduces the birth-rate in the old country, at the same time that it raises it in the new. To a certain large extent, also, the high birth-rate in America is a response to the easier conditions of life found here, for, however hard the conditions of the average Italian immigrant may appear to the average spectator, they are undeniably less hard than his life under the feudal customs of agrarian Italy.

Not the least impressive point found in the report under discussion is the revelation made therein that the sum of the information contained in the United States census of 1900, in regard to the Italians of New York City and of New York State, is merely their number. More descriptive information may be found about the whole group of Italians in the United States, as well as about the whole group of the foreign born in New York, but about the Italians alone in any particular state or city, there is nothing more than the mere number. The courtesy with which Dr. Tosti alludes to this deficiency in our census, as well as the deficiency itself, deserves reflection.

## Immigration Considered Geographically

Where the Italians were in the United States in 1900, and whither have been bound the Italians coming to the country since then, are shown in the map on page 104.

The shading does not represent the actual number of Italians, but the percentage they made of the total population of the state. It is somewhat surprising to find that they are a more important element in the population of Nevada than in that of any other state. Though the Italians in Nevada numbered less than 2,000 they formed 4.5 per cent of the total population, while the 38,000 in Illinois were less than one per cent of the population of that state, and the 271,000 in the state of New York — over a third of the total number of Italians in the United States, amounted to only 3.7 per cent of the general population of the state. On the whole the Italian element appears to be distributed through the population of the country with greater degree of impartiality than is generally supposed. It is true that the distribution is in fact far less uniform than the map indicates, for the reason that the variations within each state can not be represented. In Illinois, for example, the Italians are not spread out in a veneer of uniform thinness, but three-fourths of them are massed in Chicago. An examination of the population of the states by counties reveals that the most important of these irregularities are in the older states with large cities. West of the Mississippi, in the agricultural and mining country, the actual distribution approaches in uniformity the conditions represented on the map. In Nevada, for example, there are some Italians in every county; in California there is only one county without any; in Louisiana, also, where they are an important element in the population, and in Colorado, Wyoming, and Montana, they are well scattered. It is noticeable that with the exception of Louisiana, they have not yet gone, to any extent, into the negro states.

If the Italians are considered in their relation to the land area instead of to the population, it is found that their density varies from such a statistical curiosity as two-tenths of one Italian in a hundred square miles, which is the proportion in Oklahoma, to twelve per square mile in Rhode Island.

The crosses and circles used to represent the addition to the Italian population since the census was taken stand for absolute numbers, not proportions, ranging from two destined for Oklahoma, and eighteen for South Carolina, to the 110,000 who have gone to Pennsylvania, and the 256,500 whose stated destination was New York. These figures are for the destination of the immigrants at the time of their arrival in America; no account can be taken of those, and they are not few, who after a few weeks in New York are attracted farther afield in the new world. It may be

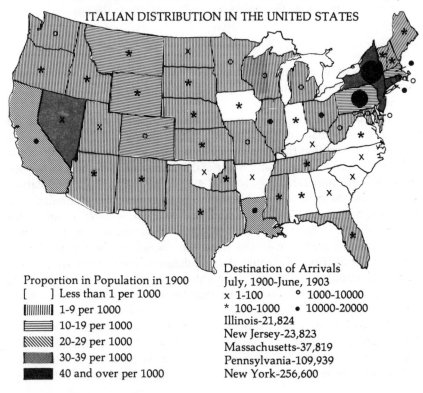

ITALIAN DISTRIBUTION IN THE UNITED STATES

Proportion in Population in 1900
[   ] Less than 1 per 1000
|||||||| 1-9 per 1000
≡≡≡ 10-19 per 1000
▨▨▨ 20-29 per 1000
▓▓▓ 30-39 per 1000
██ 40 and over per 1000

Destination of Arrivals
July, 1900-June, 1903
x  1-100        o  1000-10000
*  100-1000    •  10000-20000
Illinois-21,824
New Jersey-23,823
Massachusetts-37,819
Pennsylvania-109,939
New York-256,600

objected that, in dealing with an aggregate of hundreds of thousands groups of less than 100 or even 1,000 are negligible quantities and should not be represented. In this case, however, it seems worth while to take notice of the smallest figures, as evidence of centrifugal influences. It is surely significant that the Italians coming to America in the last three years have been bound for every state and territory in the Union.

### The View of the Italian Socialist

From an altogether different source comes evidence that Italian working-men not only appreciate the evils of the congested quarters of the larger cities, but that they apprehend that the overcrowding of certain industrial grades will be accompanied by further and more effective animosity on the part of American workers. *Il Proletario*, an Italian Socialist paper published in New York, has called attention to the reputed utterance of a delegate from the American Federation of Labor at a meeting of English unionists in Lancaster. It was especially toward southern Italians that he directed his attack in inveighing "against the torrent of the unhappy which yearly overflows this land, seeking for bread and labor".

In essaying to "point out the duty of the Italian government in the presence of these constant American threats", *Il Proletario* urges a line of action surprisingly in accord with the thought of Chicago settlement workers, with the recommendation of government experts in this country, and with the opinion advanced by the representative of Italy in New York — fresh example, this, of the fact that, however radical be the general panaceas they may advocate, an increasing number of working people are thinking — thinking hard and in some measure sanely — at the problems which stare society in the face. To translate from *Il Proletario:*

"The news from Italy shows no prospect of the rapid decrease of our emigration. Many years, if not decades, must pass before the yearly departure will cease of hundreds of thousands from our country, driven out by the sad material and economic conditions; and even when these are improved, if ever they are, the enormous fecundity of our race will force some of those born in Italy to seek elsewhere the means of subsistence.

"The seriousness of a possibly increased restriction of admittance to the United States becomes more evident when we recall that other places of refuge have already been closed or limited. We refer to the Argentine Republic and Brazil. The first, suffering from an economic and financial crisis, drives every year a larger number of its new inhabitants from its territory; the second is . . . a land of slaves and not of free and civilized men.

"The only country then which offers a sure and happy refuge for our people is North America, and it is from here that more and more are rising the cries of alarm against them.

"The southern Italian is disliked and despised because he stops in the great centers of industry, where he lowers the wages of labor, and offends by habits and customs too much in contrast with those of the majority of American citizens. Wherever our emigrant can find occupation in his own proper business of worker on the soil he is more acceptable and better liked.

"The duty then of the Italian state is to favor the formation of agricultural colonies in the United States."

## Our Health Obligations to the Immigrant

The discussion, by Dr. Brindisi of Boston and Dr. Stella of New York, of the health problems of the Italians in America, especially emphasizes two points. It is clear that the Italian immigrant brings with him health and strength. It is equally clear that he finds in large cities conditions which even his peasant constitution can not long withstand.

Statistics of deaths are the only general index there is to the health of the various elements of a population. But, in the case in hand, these records fail to reveal the undue measure of sickness among the immigrants themselves, partly because, as Dr. Brindisi points out, strong constitutions and temperate habits have helped Italians to recover in an unusually large proportion of cases, and partly because, especially if stricken with tuberculosis, Italians go back home to die. Dr. Stella's many years of experience among the Italians of New York gives weight to his testimony in regard to the prevalence of tuberculosis. It is necessary to conclude both that the amount of general sickness among the "first generation" is greater than is indicated by the death-rates, and that tuberculosis is far more prevalent than the very low death-rate would attribute. It is also necessary to conclude that it is our part to modify the conditions, as far as they are responsible and remediable, which make for physical deterioration among the peoples coming to us. What this means in a concrete, searching way is revealed by Miss Dinwiddie's study of the housing conditions of an Italian neighborhood in Philadelphia. This obligation is somewhat emphasized by the reflection that the Italian government, in its emigration disinfection station at Naples, does its part in seeing that its departing sons and daughters start for the new world aseptically clean.

## The Emigration Disinfecting Station at Naples

In an interview, published on another page, Cav. Adolfo Rossi, royal inspector of emigration from Italy, pointedly calls attention to the Italian emigration law about which hitherto so little has been generally known in this country. Those who have been somewhat skeptical about the enforcement of that law by the Italian Government will have to admit that the opening of the emigration disinfecting station at Naples is in the nature of evidence against them.

Among the provisions of this emigration law passed by the Italian Parliament in 1901, was one bearing directly on the hygienic conditions and safeguards of the emigrant and his baggage immediately before his embarkation.

The Department of Emigration naturally turned its attention first to the port of Naples, the chief port of departure. The plant is near the Maritime Station and within easy reach of all the steamship piers. On the ground floor are to be found disinfecting plant, special rooms for the vaccination of emigrants, and the office established by the Bank of Naples for the issuance of emigrants' drafts. The rest of the space is given up to waiting rooms. The emigrant, after delivering his baggage in the vestibule, passes out into the large portico on one side of the station to wait until his turn comes to receive it again. In the interval it has been opened, the contents inventoried and disinfected. The plant itself consists of two large steam sterilizers with a capacity for over two hundred pieces of baggage an hour. There is, moreover, a separate laboratory for formalin disinfection. At the extreme west end of the building are three vaccination rooms, with a common waiting hall but separate exits, thus insuring rapidity and preventing confusion.

A plentiful supply of water from the Serino is an added item for the "purification of the emigrant". Two large fountains are in the portico outside and smaller ones, with sinks and lavatories, are scattered throughout the building. Artificial light is supplied when needed, by an electrical plant in the basement feeding 100 incandescent lamps and six ten-ampere arc lights. The building, with all its accessories, is the product of Italian industries. The total cost was only about twenty-five thousand dollars.

"With the completion of this disinfecting and vaccination station", writes Signor Coen Gagli, the supervising engineer, "we have provided for one of the most urgent needs of the emigrant at the port of Naples." Then, with the splendid optimism and serious purposefulness that seem to characterize the awakening of modern Italy, he concludes his report. "But this is only the first part of the extensive program."

## Labor Abuses Among Italians

Reference is made in several articles in this number to abuses among Italian workmen. Evidence of what is meant was gathered by an agent of the New York Society for the Protection of Italian Immigrants, who investigated in detail into the labor conditions of his countrymen in West Virginia. There he found them in isolated camps, shut off from the outside world by high mountains; many, barbers and waiters, were unfit for the heavy work to which they had been sent under false pretenses by agents receiving so much per man sent — "dumped into West Virginia by the brokers in white slavery of the larger cities", the investigator called it. A boy of sixteen, "the incarnation of fatalism", answered "of course" when asked if he had ever been struck. Fifteen dollars carfare was invested by the contractor in every laborer taken out from New York, to be deducted from his wages. If the laborer attempted to leave when he found conditions not as represented, intimidation and force were resorted to hold him.

Armed guards were frequent. A man turned over to the boss after a fight was locked up in a shanty under a guard of negroes. In the night a shot was heard. The man was not seen again. One Italian made affidavit of being pursued by armed guards when he attempted escape, driven back at a run under the muzzle of a rifle, and made to lift alone so heavy a stone that he suffered a severe rupture. The contractor gave him one dollar when he went away for treatment. A gatling gun on a hill overlooked one camp. The contractors and their men carried revolvers and some rode with rifles in their hands.

*Criminality Among Italians*

An Italian who is qualified to speak on the subject of criminality among his people both by his experience as a lawyer practicing among them and by his membership in the New York Prison Association, writes as follows:

"I am convinced of two things:

"First, that while the proportion of crimes against the person may be somewhat greater in our Italian population than among natives, yet the proportion of all crimes to the population is less.

"Second, that a large percentage of Italians convicted of crime here do not have a fair trial.

"This second point is of great social importance as it constitutes a quasi justification for the alleged disposition of the Italians to take the law into their own hands.[3] The causes which militate against a fair trial are many. There is, first, the popular belief about the criminal tendencies of my countrymen. I have heard a judge charge from the bench that there is a presumption that Italians carry concealed weapons. A city magistrate was recently quoted as saying from the bench, 'It seems incredible that Italians would fight with their fists. Didn't they have knives or revolvers?' To which the accusing policeman replied, 'No'. The judge expressed the popular belief; the witness testified to the fact. A second cause is the ignorance of the accused regarding both the language and his rights under the law. There is further, among certain police officers, a pretty free use of the 'third degree'.

---

3. A brief article on the mafia, of special interest to social workers, and written by an Italian student of social conditions, Alberto Pecorini, will appear in a subsequent issue of *Charities*.

This doubtful method of obtaining evidence becomes a source of positive abuse with a people as imaginative and sensitive as the Italians.

"Finally, I do not hesitate to say that the character of some of the lawyers who defend my countrymen is an important factor in the miscarriage of justice. If a serious investigation were made of the methods used by certain lawyers in the Tombs, who practice fraud upon their clients and upon the court, we would have some startling revelations.

"The problem of excessive criminality, if it exists, must be solved, like every other social problem, not by palliatives, but by the slow method of social therapeutics — by education and good example.

"In conclusion let me say this: About seventy-five per cent of all crimes in the United States go unpunished, while of the crimes committed by Italians here I believe that, on account of their open character, seventy-five per cent are punished."

*Columbus Day*

Columbus Day — October 12 — has been celebrated by Italians in America for half a century. Bills have been before the last two sessions of the New York legislature, but whether or not Columbus Day will be added to the already long list of legal holidays in New York State, its observance by Italians is increasing in significance.

It was in the 40s or early 50s that a club of young men in the Leonard Street school started what was called the Columbo Guard. The membership was largely made up of Genoese, and for years their parades in uniforms suggestive of the *bersaglieri*, with feathered hats and blue suitings, paid a picturesque tribute to their historic fellow townsmen.

In the 70s, the United Italian Societies was organized as a representative body to celebrate the 20th of September, a date observed in commemoration of the unification of Italy. In 1897, the Sons of Columbus Legion was founded, and the following year observed October 12 with parade and picnics. Since then, both societies have participated in keeping both dates — celebrations which are not only patriotic in character, but bring before the colony the benevolent purposes for which these societies stand.

Madonna del Carmine, San Rocco, and the innumerable other saints' days give many opportunities for the festival spirit. But these are more or less local, or limited in their allegiance to the people of one church or from one part of Italy; and, on the other hand, the church does not officially participate in the observance of the 20th of September.

In Columbus Day, Italians in America have a festival which, it may be anticipated, in the future even more than in the past, will serve as an opportunity for all to unite in a common observance.

*Hull House and Its Neighbors* [4]
Jane Addams

The settlement which endeavors to reveal large foreign colonies to the rest of its city naturally pursues two methods:

The first is to secure speakers, teachers, club leaders from the more prosperous districts of the city, who shall form acquaintances and friendships as naturally as possible with the residents of the neighborhood.

The second is to provide for the various foreign colonists opportunities for self-expression, one of the most natural of these being through the drama. Plays have been given at Hull House in Bohemian, Yiddish, Italian and Greek, not only to the very great pleasure of the groups of colonists who heard them, but often to the surprise and always to the edification of their English-speaking auditors. These plays often serve a most valuable purpose, in so far as they help reveal the older people of the foreign colonies to the younger, and do something toward bridging the distance between fathers and sons.

The mass of the colonists, however, have no such means of expression. It was in the hope of giving them an opportunity that the Labor Museum at Hull House was started. It began with the methods of spinning and weaving, which we were able to collect from the neighborhood and to put into some historic sequence and order — the Assyrian, the Greek, the Italian, the Dutch, the Irish, the Colonial. Something of the same was done in weaving. The demonstration which takes place every Saturday evening attracts visitors from every part of the city, notably students from the normal schools and colleges. The children of the peasant women are much amazed at the attention their mothers receive and at the admiration which is given to the hand-made kerchiefs and petticoats. This, for the first time, breaks into their ideal of department store clothes. I recall a little Italian girl who came to the cooking class the same night and in the same building that the mother came to the Labor Museum demonstration. But she always took pains to deliver her mother at one door, while she entered another, not wishing to be too closely identified with the peasant who spoke no English and could not be induced to wear a hat. One evening she heard a number of teachers from the School of Education, of the University of Chicago, much admiring the quality of her mother's spinning, and she inquired whether her mother was really the best spindle-spinner in Chicago. On being assured that she probably was, because she had lived in a village on the edge of a precipice down which the women had dropped their spindles, and that therefore the village had developed a skill beyond its neighbors, she was much impressed, and regarded her mother with a new interest, being able, apparently for the first time, to give her a background and a setting beyond

4. *Charities*, pp. 450-451.

that of the sordid tenement in which she lived. At any rate, from that time forth, they entered at the same door.

During one of the Christmas seasons a number of Russian women who were working in a charitable sewing-room heard that there was to be a "party" at Hull House, and unexpectedly arrived, to the number of thirty. There happened to be no festivity on at the moment, although the disappointment was so obvious that every effort was made to produce one on demand. Music, photographs, even coffee, made but little impression upon the over-worked, hard-pressed women, but a visit to the Labor Museum produced an instantaneous effect. They at once began to try the spindles and the looms, to tell each other and their hostesses what was done in each particular family and in each special part of Russia, to exhibit specimens of the weaving and knitting of the clothing which they wore. In short, they began to be the entertainers rather than the entertained, to take the position which was theirs by right of much experience and long acquaintance with life. Their pleasure was most touching, and perhaps only their homely implements could have evoked it.

The old German potter takes great pleasure each week in demonstrating his skill, as do workers in silver and copper, and in wood mosaic. After all, the apprentice system, as a method of instruction, has much to commend it, and a well-trained workman can easily teach not only his own and his neighbors' children, but "swells" from other parts of the town, with a consciousness that his skill is but receiving its natural recognition. In a few years, we shall doubtless establish schools in America in which the children and grandchildren of these men may be trained in the crafts. In the meantime they lose the heritage which is theirs, the transmission of which would be of mutual benefit to both fathers and children, and do much toward restoring the respect which is often lost. Under existing conditions of factory work, it slips away without result or use to anyone. "I was a silver-smith in Bohemia, but I have carried pig-iron ever since I came to this country", or "I was a glass-blower in Vienna, but of course nobody wants such work in Chicago", are the significant remarks which one constantly hears. The shops at Hull House offer at least the space, tools, and material to the men who care to work in them, and are but a feeble beginning toward restoring some balance between the attainments of various sorts of people.

*Notes on the Italians in Boston*[5]

Robert A. Woods[6]

There is some question as to how the Italians will thrive physically in the New England climate. The death-rate among them increases with the second

5. *Charities*, pp. 451-452.                                    6. South End House.

generation. This is no doubt largely the effect of extremely close tenement quarters upon people who belong out of doors and in a sunny land. Their over-stimulating and innutritious diet is precisely the opposite sort of feeding from that demanded by our exhilarating and taxing atmospheric conditions. This fact suggests the first and perhaps the chief step in bringing about the adaptation of the Italian type to life in America. On the other hand, it is undesirable that the Italians should be in any considerable degree educated away from their love of the open air and their satisfaction in rural existence. Many Italian families have been sent from Boston into the country, with excellent results. The New England farmers are at first suspicious of them, but soon come to regard them as good neighbors.

The large majority of the Italians in Boston are industrious and thrifty. They carry on several kinds of small trade with commendable assiduity. Over two million dollars' worth of real estate in the Italian district is held in the names of Italian owners. The unskilled laborers sustain themselves by accepting a low wage standard; and still lay by money because they have an inconceivably low standard of living. In both of these respects — and particularly the latter — they do a real injury to the community, and give grounds for the enmity which their industrial competitors among the older immigrant elements feel toward them.

The artisan and the small trader among the Italians do not in general make very rapid economic progress. They show a certain lack of self-reliance and "push". Jewish artisans secure the low-grade building work, and the Greeks often get the best fruit and candy stands away from them. We have had Italian barbers for a long time. They increase in number but their shops do not seem to rise to a higher grade as to service and price.

The children of the early north Italian immigrants have now been through the public schools. Many of the stumbling-blocks which embarrassed their parents have been removed for them. They are beginning to take their proportionate place in the skilled trades, in commercial establishments and in the professions. One important industry which has had an educational effect upon the whole country and for which Boston has been the center, that of making plaster casts of the work of great sculptors — has been developed wholly by Italians. A few young people show signs of that genius for which no race has been more distinguished than the Italian.

There is a particular need and opportunity among the Italians for friendly and helpful influence. With no nationality does the right sort of encouragement bring more valuable results. A lack of force of will in their case goes often with unusual skill, intelligence and constructive imagination.

The new generation is many times hindered by the ignorant conservatism of the elders. One way of breaking the unfortunate tradition of illiteracy which exists particularly among the south Italians, and which leads them to put their children to work as soon as possible, will be to provide in the public schools greatly increased opportunities of manual and technical training along with book work. The tendency of parents to take their children away from the schools is in part a just judgment upon the narrow, abstract character of the school curriculum.

There is danger in Boston that with the gradual withdrawal from the Italian colony of the more progressive members who lose themselves in the general community, there will be left a distinct slum residuum. Not much degeneracy is yet evident among the Italians. But there is a steady continuance of a certain amount of violent crime. Among the large number of men without family connections there is gambling, beer-drinking, and licentiousness. The amount and variety of profanity which seems needed in order to promote the street games of some Italian boys is beyond belief.

These evils are to a considerable extent the result of city conditions. The laborers are without work for much of the year. They are huddled together so that self-respect and peace of mind are lost. It would be the work of a moral as well as an industrial reformer to transport the large surplus of Italian laborers to the agricultural regions of the south, and then to secure at least such restriction of immigration as would prevent new immigrants from creating a new city surplus.

When all is said, there is sound reason to believe that the Italians will prove a valuable factor in our composite population. They are beginning to appreciate and take to themselves our industrial standards and our political loyalties. We ought to begin to be deeply thankful for what they bring of sociability, gaiety, love of nature, all-around human feeling. The continental peasant has much to teach us. At his best he is a living example of that simple life which too many of us have so far lost that the words of two recent writers — one an Alsatian, the other a Swiss — seem like a breath of inspiration from some other sphere.

## A Working Colony as a Social Investment[7]

Bertha Hazard

Is it not possible that the Society for the Protection of Italian Immigrants, or some group of allied workers, should begin to offer in a somewhat extended manner, systematic opportunities for the founding of Italian colonies here in America, as an aid in the process of distribution?[8]

Questions such as this come naturally to mind in thinking of the make-up of the Italian quarter in the vicinity of Hull House. They press with special

7. *Charities*, pp. 452-453.
8. "The problem of immigration is essentially one of distribution." — Gino C. Speranza in *The Outlook*, April 16.

significance just now because of the pent-up agricultural enthusiasm of a young Italian belonging to one of the Hull House English classes. This Mr. N. is a graduate, I believe, of one of the best of the Italian universities. At two others he has taken special courses in mathematics and agriculture, and has, as he says, a "passion" for farm-life. He claims to have had practical experience in working on a small estate belonging to his family, he speaks English fairly well, and he seems to be adapted, personally, for the direction of men and things. Some weeks ago he took a fortnight's holiday from his present work in a factory, and, attracted by the advertisements of a Southern railroad which wishes to sell land, he went to the coast of Mississippi to see what promise there might be there for him and for some of his 'connazionali'. On the Gulf shore he found a small town, well situated, having good transportation facilities; there were canneries needing workmen, a lumber company wanting more hands, much vacant land which could be bought cheap, and various officials who would find it useful to have an Italian colony started in the neighborhood. The wages offered for day-laborers were less than can be earned during the summer in the neighborhood of Chicago, so that it would be useless to expect men to go so far to undertake work which might not prove permanent. But to found a colony, Mr. N. thinks that he could easily find here in Chicago a number of families who would be willing to go South with him in October, prepared to work hard for a mere living, until the first crops should have been gathered. On the one hand, therefore, we have desirable and inexpensive land; on the other, there are sober and industrious men who now add their share to the crowded and unsatisfactory living conditions of a large city. Between the two stands the man with directive power and enthusiasm and experience. The money alone is lacking. For want of this there seems to be no present hope that this new center of simple and healthy living can be formed.

In talking recently with another young man about the desirability of finding work for the summer in the country, I fell naturally into all the usual arguments by which the theorists strive to influence simple people to change their mode of living. The young man has been in America for some time: for at least one season he has worked in the country, and he knew out of his own experience whereof I was speaking. He heard me patiently to the end. Then he said, "Lady, you do not know. The city is not nice, but in the country *everybody* is bad."

In the gang where he had worked, the men had been treated like beasts, and, in this particular set, I suppose for the most part they must have acted like beasts; and this Hull House student would have no more of it. Of course I am unconvinced; naturally I do not feel that the city life *is* better, in general. Still, even under better conditions than this young man happened to find, life among gangs of laborers must at best be hard and more or less demoralizing, and at the end of the summer, for many of them, there seems to be nothing to do except to go back to the cities, to be idle, perforce, until spring comes again; and the chances are that in many cases the family and the city are each the worse off for the long idle winter.

Efforts have been made here and there during the past few years to establish Italian colonies in different parts of the United States. Some have failed sadly, some have succeeded, all have had difficulties. Still, a study of the experience of these colonies seems to justify the belief that nothing which has been done for the Italian has led to such permanently good results. If the sporadic efforts of various interested individuals and companies can show these occasional good results which are to be found in our country, should they not encourage a more generous plan and concerted action for the better solution of this "essential problem of distribution".

## The Sordid Waste of Genius [9]

Florence Kelley[10]

It is the frequently recurring duty of the writer to attend meetings of women's clubs in all parts of the country. Incidently this involves listening to the reading of the minutes of the previous meeting. Recently, in a small New England town, the minutes dealt with an afternoon devoted to music. The secretary, not a musical person, conscientiously reproduced, at forty minutes' length and as well as a defective memory permitted, the contents of a long paper on the music of Palestrina. Now in that little town it would have been quite impossible to get together an audience to listen for an evening to the music of Palestrina, even if there had been musicians capable of rendering his compositions. But because the composer had lived some generations ago, and at a distance of some thousands of miles, the club members had an agreeable consciousness of being engaged in the pursuit of culture when they first listened to a long account of his methods of composition, written at second hand (from an encyclopedia of music translated from the German), and then listened to a long reproduction, in the minutes, again at second hand, of that first paper.

As the writer sat through the ordeal, she could but reflect upon the living genius of the Italian children, here in America, which perishes every year for want of opportunity for development. How many beautiful voices are ruined forever, crying papers! What plastic power is crushed out in early childhood by the weary drudgery of artificial flower making in the tenement-houses of New York! It was a little Italian boy who flung himself down to sleep on the railway track, on his way home at two o'clock in the morning, after his

9. *Charities*, pp. 453-454.               10. Secretary National Consumers' League.

impossible toil in the glassworks, in southern New Jersey. He perished when the train came along.

It requires real love of music and real recognition of genius to discern both in the discordant cry of the dirty little chap on the sidewalk, who calls the last murder from his newspaper headlines. In one case, however, this was done by the music teacher of a settlement. The lad's parents were bought off for a stipulated sum, though they were more than ordinarily prosperous to begin with. For four years the child Angelo sang, with joy to himself and to all who heard him. Here was a real contribution to the nobler enjoyments of our all too sordid work-a-day life! Here was promise of a real gift of genius from Italy to America, discerned and developed in the new country! But a presidential election came, cold and sleet threatened the troop of children who huddled in newspaper alley until one and two o'clock in the morning awaiting the latest night extras and the first editions of the morning papers. Angelo was among them — the greedy peasant family had not withstood the temptation to get both the music teacher's gift and the newsboy's earnings. Weariness, cold and wet did their work; pneumonia followed the election night and Angelo never sang again.

### Mme. d'Arago, Charity Go-between [11]

The trustfulness and simple-mindedness of many of the Italian immigrants make them — especially before they know the English language or American customs — easy victims to all sorts of deception. By reason of the same qualities, they often figure as participants in fraudulent transactions. The impositions of the padroni, who, if they are Italian, have learned worse than Yankee business methods, are familiar. So are the naturalization frauds, in which the Italians themselves are generally but ignorant tools of political leaders. There are other ways, less well known, in which the Italian newcomers are "worked" to the advantage of more sophisticated fellow-citizens and to the detriment of their own reputation.

An example of this sort of thing is afforded by the history of a woman who has been known to the New York Charity Organization Society for twenty years. During the last ten or twelve years she has been living as a parasite on the Italians of the city, supporting herself by devices of unusual ingenuity, and coming, from time to time and by various chances, to the notice of the society.

In 1889, Mme. d'Arago, as she may be called, asked for help at a convent on the ground that she secured converts to the Roman Catholic faith. She took with her a man — apparently a German — for whom she tried to get assistance. This is the first recorded instance of the practice she later developed into a profession, of acting as an agent for her unfortunate

11. *Charities*, pp. 454-455.

acquaintances. A few years later she began work among the Italians, by attempting to proselyte in another direction, for she was writing to a Protestant clergyman: "I would wish God would help me to raise an Italian chapel and school in East New York in the Episcopal faith. I could canvass two hundred to three hundred Italians, together with their children, who now go to no religious worship." In a later communication she assured him: "I am able to unite forty families and more than two hundred Italians, to join a more intelligent religion".

For most of the time since 1893 she has lived among the Italians, getting a lodging and meals whenever she can, in return for services rendered to them. It has rarely been possible to find her "home", as the address she gives is generally a bank, a bakery, or a saloon, where she receives her mail and meets her clients. She says that at one time she was at service in Brooklyn. For a while she lived at a Salvation Army lodging house under the name of Bertha Klein, but generally she has kept to the Italian colony in which she was found in 1893.

Her most constant source of revenue has been derived from the profession she developed for herself. She made herself acquainted with the workings of many charitable agencies in the city, especially institutions for children, and advised her friends where to apply for aid whenever they wanted it. If her clients succeeded in getting what they asked for she would accept a fee from them; if not, she would write to the society to which they had applied, saying that they were "bad" and needed nothing. Her specialty was placing-out children. She got children into institutions for a consideration of ten or fifteen dollars apiece. She also secured the release of the child from the institution, when that was desired, for ten dollars. Unfortunately for her prosperity, her second application to an institution was apt to arouse suspicion and start an investigation. She also found homes for children in families. This was accomplished through advertisements in the Italian papers, one of which reads:

"A POOR WOMAN of the province of C____, left a widow with three children, six months, four and six years old, seeks a family which will care for them. They are healthy and very pretty. Address by letter, Mrs. d'Arago, at number 315 Margaret Street."

In 1903 she was still procuring "working papers" for children. When one mother for whom she had performed this service refused to give her as much money as she demanded, she told the little girl's employer that she had tuberculosis and thus brought about her dismissal. Another way in which she used her good offices is revealed in one of her letters asking for money. In enumerating her troubles and misfortunes she said: "And I got an Italian woman out of prison and for reward — she did not pay me".

Several letters addressed by her to the Bureau of Dependent Children seem to indicate that she used her wits against her enemies as vigorously as in behalf of her friends. These letters contain notes on families who have children in institutions, but who, she asserts, are perfectly able to provide for them at home. "Italians", she writes, "import children daily and get them in homes; parents who have children in homes keep groceries and beer saloons; husband works at shovel — and I will send you a list next week — hundreds I know." The promised list tells how mothers "dress in fine style" and the family has "fine whiskey, beer and wines", and live "luxuriantly" while "the city has to pay" for the maintenance of their children. These letters to the Bureau of Dependent Children may be one of her devices for getting children restored to their parents at the parents' request. The fact, however, that they were written while she was living in the Salvation Army lodging-house, as Bertha Klein, point rather to another explanation, that she took this way of revenging herself on her clients who had not come up to all her demands in the way of pay. In either case it is entirely possible that she had helped to place the very children under discussion.

From time to time, in the course of these twenty years, Mme. d'Arago has apparently become discouraged and thought of Europe with longing. Twice, it is known, she has obtained money avowedly for a return to Italy or to England, but she has used it for other purposes. In spite of her cleverness, her ingenuity and her fund of information in certain directions, she has never been prosperous. It is clear that life has been hard for her and that she has suffered much.

As for the Italians, her clients, it is difficult to estimate the harm that her good offices in their behalf have done them. By encouraging, and doubtless often suggesting, the theory that here in America the public stands ready and eager to assume the parent's duties, whenever he finds them inconvenient, this woman and others like her have had their part in creating and strengthening a characteristic for which the whole blame is generally placed on the Italian nature.

# 13

# How It Feels To Be A Problem: A Consideration of Certain Causes Which Prevent or Retard Assimilation[1]

GINO C. SPERANZA

The American nation seems to like to do some of its thinking aloud. Possibly this is true of other nations, but with this difference, that in the case of the American, the thinking aloud is not suppressed even when it deals with what may be termed the "country's guests". Older nations, perhaps because they lack the daring, self-sufficiency of the younger, prefer, in similar cases, to think in a whisper. All countries have problems to grapple with, economic, political or social; but with America even the labor problem is popularly discussed as if its solution depended on that of the immigration problem.

Now, considering the large percentage of foreign born in the population of the United States, it is a strange fact how few Americans ever consider how very unpleasant, to say the least, it must be to the foreigners living in their midst to be constantly looked upon either as a national problem or a national peril. And this trying situation is further strained by the tone in which the discussion is carried on, as if it applied to utter strangers miles and miles away, instead of to a large number of resident fellow citizens. Perhaps this attitude may be explained by the fact that to the vast majority of Americans "foreigner" is synonymous with the popular conception of the immigrant as a poor, ignorant and uncouth stranger, seeking for better luck in a new land. But poverty and ignorance and uncouthness, even if they exist as general characteristics of our immigrants, do not necessarily exclude intelligence and sensitiveness. Too often, let it be said, does the American of common schooling interpret differences from his own standards and habits of life, as necessarily signs of inferiority. Foreignness of features or of apparel is for him often the denial of brotherhood. Often, again, the fine

1. *Charities*, Vol. 12, 1904. Pp. 457-463.

brow and aquiline nose of the Latin will seem to the American to betoken a criminal type rather than the impress of a splendid racial struggle.

Then there is another large class of "plain Americans" who justify a trying discussion of the stranger within the gates by the self-satisfying plea that the foreigner should be so glad to be in the "land of the free" that he cannot mind hearing a few "unpleasant truths" about himself.

This is not an attempt to show that the time of immigration does not carry with it an ebb of squalor and ignorance and undesirable elements. It is rather an endeavor to look at the problem, as it were, *from the inside*. For if America's salvation from this foreign invasion lies in her capacity to assimilate such foreign elements, the first step in the process must be a thorough knowledge of the element that should be absorbed.

Many imagine that the record and strength of the American democracy suffice of themselves to make the foreigner love the new land and engender in him a desire to serve it; that, in other words, assimilation is the natural tendency. Assimilation, however, is a dual process of forces interacting one upon the other. Economically, this country can act like a magnet in drawing the foreigner to these shores, but you cannot rely on its magnetic force to make the foreign *an American*. To bring about assimilation the larger mass should not remain passive. It must attract, *actively attract*, the smaller foreign body.

It is with this in mind that I say that if my countrymen here keep apart, if they herd in great and menacing city colonies, if they do not learn your language, if they know little about your country, the fault is as much yours as theirs. And if you wish to reach us you will have to batter down some of the walls you have yourselves built up to keep us from you.

What I wish to examine, then, is how and what Americans are contributing to the process of the assimilation of my countrymen who have come here to live among them.

### The Attitude to the Newly Arrived

I have before me a pamphlet which a well-known American society prints for distribution among arriving immigrants. On the title page is the motto: *A Welcome to Immigrants and Some Good Advice*. The pamphlet starts out by telling the arriving stranger that this publication is presented to him "by an American patriotic society, whose duty is to teach American principles" — a statement which must somewhat bewilder foreigners. Then it proceeds to advise him. In America, it tells him, "you need not be rich to be happy and respected". "In other countries", it proceeds, "the people belong to the government. They are called subjects. They are under the power of some Emperor, King, Duke or other ruler", which permits the belief that the patriotic author of this pamphlet is conversant mostly with mediaeval

history. There are some surprising explanations of the constitution, showing
as wide a knowledge of American constitutional history as of that of modern
Europe — but space forbids their quotation. "If the common people of other
countries had faith in each other, there would be no Czars, Kaisers and
Kings ruling them under the pretext of divine right." This is certainly a gem
of historical exposition.

Then, in order to make the stranger feel comfortable, it tells him, "you
must be honest and honorable, clean in your person, and decent in your
talk". Which, of course, the benighted foreigner reads as a new decalogue.
With characteristic modesty the author reserves for the last praise of his
country: "Ours", he says, "is the strongest government in the world, because
it is the people's government". Then he loses all self-restraint in a patriotic
enthusiasm. "We have more good land in cultivation than in all Europe. We
have more coal, and oil, and iron and copper, than can be found in all the
countries of Europe. We can raise enough foodstuffs to feed all the rest of the
world. We have more railroads and navigable rivers than can be found in
the rest of the civilized world. We have more free schools than the rest of the
world. . . . So great is the extent (of our country), so varied its resources, that
its people are not dependent on the rest of the world for what they absolutely
need. Can there be any better proof that this is the best country in the
world? Yes, there is one better proof. Our laws are better and more justly
carried out."

Between such instruction and the welcome the immigrant gets from the
immigration officials, he ought to feel that this is certainly the "best country
in the world".

Perhaps the first impressions the foreigners receive are not a fair test of
what it really feels to be a problem — because the initial adaptation to new
and strange conditions is necessarily trying to anyone.

*The Italian Docile But Not Servile*

The real test comes after — years after, perhaps — and it is this aftermath
that I wish to examine. Perhaps I come from a hyper-sensitive race, and
what I say of my people cannot apply to the immigrants of other nationalities, but close and constant contact with Italians of all classes on the one
hand and twenty years of strenuous American living on the other, seem
justification for voicing the sentiments of my countrymen among a people,
many of whom look upon us as a menace. And the fact that though many
suffer, yet few cry out, may be a further justification for one from their
common average to speak for them.

Naturally, when one speaks of the Italian in America, the American
thinks at once of the ubiquitous unskilled laborer. He thinks of him as a
class or a mass composed of more or less picturesque elements, with no

particular individual characteristics. This is especially true of the men who employ such a class. Through the padrone system of engaging men, the employer never comes to know the employed. He gives an order to the padrone to get him "five hundred dagoes". The men are supplied, they do their work and are passed on to other jobs. However practical this system may appear, it is based on a vicious mistake. The chief characteristic of the Italian is his individuality, and a system that treats him as one of a homogeneous mass is essentially wrong and cannot yield the best results. When the Irishman supplied the labor market in America, it may have been a simple thing to deal with him in masses; to apply that system to the Italian is to lose sight of elemental differences.

## The Go-Between Padrone

In endeavoring to graft the system employed in the case of Irish labor on the Italian, employers discovered a new element which they did not care to study or did not know how. So they tried to patch up the difficulty by the introduction of the padrone. This Italo-American middleman is for the laborer, to all intents and purposes, the real employer. How can you expect assimilation of this vast class of laborers when you uphold and maintain a system which completely isolates the class from its American superior? It may be argued that the padrone system is a necessity in dealing with large bodies of Italian laborers; but this is an argument which stops short in its conclusions. It is like claiming that an interpreter is necessary in addressing a foreigner; he is, unless you learn the foreign language. And, moreover, if you depend too much on the interpreter you will oftentimes find he is not interpreting correctly. Against this it may be urged that it is the business of the foreigner to adjust himself to his American employer; but how can he when you interpose a padrone?

Now, as a rule, padrones are of a type hardly calculated to teach their men what is best in American life. They are generally shrewd fellows with a good smattering of bad English and well versed in American boss methods. But they know their men well; they count on their ignorance and implicit confidence, on their helplessness and loyalty to the *compaesano* — be he right or wrong. Naturally, the padrone will endeavor to keep the laborer from all contact with his American superior; he will make himself the final arbiter and supreme power. I know of several instances where, in order to prevent an appeal to the contractor, the padrone has taught the laborer to fear his superior as a cruel and unapproachable person. Hence this vast foreign mass touches at no point the American element or touches it in a way to make them desire to avoid it.

## The Isolation and Misapprehension that Results

Is it a wonder that the intensely sociable Italian herds with his fellows and will not mix? Foreign urban congestion is a real problem, but may it not be that the remedy has to come from others than the foreigners? You begin by drawing a sharp line against him; you distinguish him from others. The cultured among you persist in seeing in him only a wearying picturesqueness with a background of mediaeval romance and Roman greatness; the uncultured among you see in every *meridionale* a possible *mafioso*, in every *settentrionale* one more mouth to fill from that "bankrupt Italy".

The better disposed tell us we are hard workers and earn every cent we make; but even these speak as from master to man. Perhaps it is our friends that make us feel most keenly that we are a problem. They take us under their wing, they are zealous in their defense, they treat us like little children. They speak of the debt the world owes Italy, they benignantly remind their countrymen that these foreigners have seen better days. It is extremely trying — this well-meant kindness that disarms criticism.

Of course, criticism by the stranger within our gates seems ungracious; but whenever it is attempted it is suppressed by this common question: "If you don't like it, why don't you go back?" The answer is never given, but it exists. For the majority of us this is our home and we have worked very hard for everything we have earned or won. And if we find matter for criticism it is because nothing is perfect; and if we institute comparisons it is because, having lived in two lands, we have more of the wherewithal of comparisons than those who have lived in only one country.

Then there is the American press. How is it aiding our assimilation? It would not be difficult to name those few newspapers in the United States which give space either as news or editorially, to non-sensational events or problems with which Europe is grappling. As regards Italy, there is such a dearth of information of vital importance that little, if anything, is known by the average American, of the economic or political progress of that country. Columns on Mussolini, half-page headlines on the mafia, but never a word on the wonderful industrial development in northern Italy, never a notice of the financial policies that have brought Italian finances to a successful state!

What is the American press doing to help assimilate this "menacing" element in the republic?

"Why is it", was asked of a prominent American journalist, "that you print news about Italians which you would not of other nationalities?"

"Well, it is this way", was the answer, "if we published them about the Irish or the Germans we should be buried with letters of protest; the Italians do not seem to object."

It would be nearer the truth to say that they have learned the uselessness of objecting unless they can back up the objection by a "solid Italian vote".

One result of the unfriendliness of the popular American press is that it drives Italians to support a rather unwholesome Italian colonial press. Why should they read American papers that chronicle only the misdeeds of their compatriots? Better support a local press which, however poor and oftentimes dishonest, keeps up the courage of these expatriates by telling them what young Italy is bravely doing at home and abroad. But this colonial press widens the cleavage between the nations, puts new obstacles in the way of assimilation and keeps up racial differences.

*A Change in Attitude Needed*

To feel that we are considered a problem is not calculated to make us sympathize with your efforts in our behalf, and those very efforts are, as a direct result, very likely to be misdirected. My countrymen in America, ignorant though many of them are, and little in touch with Americans, nevertheless feel keenly that they are looked upon by the masses as a problem. It is, in part, because of that feeling that they fail to take an interest in American life or to easily mix with the natives. And though it may seem far-fetched, I believe that the feeling that they are unwelcome begets in them a distrust of those defenses to life, liberty and property which the new country is presumed to put at their disposal. They have no excess of confidence in your courts and it is not surprising, however lamentable, that the more hot-headed sometimes take the law into their own hands. You cannot expect the foreigner of the humbler class to judge beyond his experience — and his experience of American justice may be comprised in what he learns in some of the minor tribunals controlled by politicians, and in what he has heard of the unpunished lynchings of his countrymen in some parts of the new land. What appeal can the doctrine of state supremacy and federal non-interference make to him? Imagine what you would think of Italian justice if the American sailors in Venice, in resisting arrest by the constituted authorities, had been strung up to a telegraph pole by an infuriated Venetian mob, and the government at Rome had said, with the utmost courtesy: "We are very sorry and greatly deplore it, but we can't interfere with the autonomy of the province of Venetia!"

I am aware that the question is often asked: If these people are sensitive about being discussed as a problem and a menace, why do they come here? It is a question asked every day in the guise of an argument, a final and crushing argument. But is it really an argument? Is it not rather a question susceptible of a very clear and responsive answer. They come because this is a new country and there is a great deal of room here, and because you invite them. If you really did not want them you could keep them out, as you have done with the Chinese.

*The Italian Immigrant as Raw Material*

I am not attempting to minimize the bad aspects of large numbers of aliens pouring into a new land; it is because I recognize such bad aspects and the necessity of using means to prevent harm, that I urge the study of the question from a neglected side. If assimilation is the only way out, then I say, do not follow methods that negative all efforts toward such a desired end. This new material in your body politic you call *dangerous;* why not be more precise in your definition and call it *raw?* One of the most intelligent American women I know, when told of my intention to write on this subject, said to me in all seriousness: "You must take your subject broadly. Go back to the time when your ancestors watched the Goths come over the mountains into what seemed to your ancestors to be their land." Of course, if you approach the question in that spirit, if you see a similitude between a barbaric invasion by martial usurpers bent on destroying a great civilized power, and the peaceable and natural process of emigration of civilized peoples from a land of classic civilization to a new country in its infancy, then there is little hope for an understanding. If you approach this raw material as dangerous, you will force it back on itself and perpetuate racial distinctions; you cannot, in the nature of things, deal fairly, calmly and scientifically with what you fear. Certainly you cannot deal with it in a sympathetic spirit. But look upon this foreign contingent as raw and crude material, and then the opportunity for infinite possibilities is within your grasp. What is dangerous demands destruction; but you can mold the raw. And with the possibility of tangible results in such molding, is born hope and sympathy, optimism and enthusiasm.

Perhaps the hopefulness of this contention needs some proof of its reasonableness. In other words, what evidence is there that my countrymen, for example, should be considered rather raw material than a dangerous element? Let us study this point carefully, seeking arguments, if any there be, based not on the data of sentiment or from facts covering a short period or a small locality. Men and races cannot be judged by such standards. Let us rather examine historical, economical and political facts.

*Judged by a Historical Standard*

The racial traits and characteristics that have made Italy the "loved Mother of Civilization" are not ephemeral qualities any more than is the cephalic index of the Mediterranean. They are qualities that persist and count; they may be dormant or the opportunity may be lacking for their display or action, but they must be counted as an asset in inventorying an Italian. There is more than a reasonable presumption that the race that achieved the dual political and spiritual supremacy in the Rome of Caesar and in that of Peter, that saved Europe from the eastern rule and found for it a new empire in the West, has the seeds of great possibilities. Those that crossed the mountains and brought light to Gallia, and those after them who, in a gentler age, crossed beyond to the land of your forefathers as heralds of that humanism that ennobled all that received it, were the ancestors of these people that flock to you now and whom some of you dread. Until you can show that the advent of these people has had a harmful influence upon new neighbors in the past, your conception of them as a menace has at least no historic basis. The evidence is all the other way.

## Political Testimony

Let us examine the political testimony in the case. Here we need not go very far back; the memories of living men suffice. By a tremendous and heroic effort, Italy achieved the dream of political unity in 1870. Such accomplishment meant the destruction of the results of centuries of well-entrenched oppression and foreign bondage. But Italy was united as much by the political sagacity of Cavour as by the heroic qualities of Victor II and Garibaldi. It was the one country that justified its bloody struggle by the sanction of the political plebiscite. And ever since young Italy has patiently and bravely fought its way against tremendous odds toward its political ideals. Popular American belief to the contrary, as Dr. G. Tosti, one of the most scholarly of Italians in America, has shown, Italian financial policies have been so ably planned and handled that there has been a continuous rise in the value of Italian state bonds on foreign markets and a constant diminution in the rate of exchange.[2] Nor is it to be forgotten that, despite the heavy taxes imposed to meet the tremendous demands made upon her youth, united Italy has never admitted the possibility of bankruptcy and never paid her national debt in paper as, for instance, Russia has done.

Hence we see that the political and economic as well as the historic evidence tends to support an optimistic view of the possibilities of the Italian immigrant.

## The Standing of Italians in America

Not more relevant but more convincing, because more susceptible of direct and personal certification, is the evidence that the Italian immigrant himself furnishes in this country. It is true that, as a nationality, Italians have not forced recognition; though numerically strong there is no such "Italian vote" as to interest politicians. They have founded no important institutions; they have no strong and well-administered societies as have the Germans and the Irish. They have no representative press, and well-organized movements among them for their own good are rare. Those who believe in assimilation may be thankful for all these things; for it could be

2. "The Financial and Industrial Outlook of Italy", by Dr. G. Tosti in *American Journal of Sociology*, Vol. VIII, No. 1.

held that it is harder to assimilate bodies or colonies well organized as foreign elements, than individuals held together in imperfect cohesion.

Yet the Italian in America as an individual is making good progress. In New York City, the individual holdings of Italians in savings banks is over $15,000,000; they have some four thousand real estate holdings of the clear value of $20,000,000. About ten thousand stores in the city are owned by Italians at an estimated value of $7,000,000, and to this must be added about $7,500,000 invested in wholesale business. The estimated material value of the property of the Italian colony in New York is over $60,000,000, a value much below that of the Italian colonies of St. Louis, San Francisco, Boston and Chicago, but, a fair showing for the great "dumping ground" of America.

But the sympathetic observer will find the most remarkable progress on what may be called the spiritual side of the Italians among us. It is estimated that there are more than fifty thousand Italian children in the public schools of New York City and adjacent cities where Italians are settled. Many an Italian laborer sends his son to Italy to "finish his education" and when he cannot afford this luxury of doubtful value, he gets him one of the *maestri* of Little Italy to perfect him in his native language. In the higher education you will find Italians winning honors in several of our colleges, universities and professional schools. I know of one Italian who saves money barbering during the summer and on Sundays, to pay his way through Columbia University. I know of another who went through one of our best universities on money voluntarily advanced by a generous and farseeing professor. The money was repaid with interest and the boy is making a mark in the field of mathematics. I know of a third, the winner of a university scholarship, who paid his way by assisting in editing an Italian paper during spare hours; a fourth , who won the fellowship for the American School at Rome, and thus an American institution sent an Italian to perfect his special scholarship in Italy.

New York City now counts 115 Italian registered physicians, 63 pharmacists, 4 dentists, 21 lawyers, 15 public school teachers, 9 architects, 4 manufacturers of technical instruments and 7 mechanical engineers. There are two Italian steamship lines with bi-weekly sailings, 16 daily and weekly papers, and several private schools. Italians support several churches, one modest but very efficient hospital, one well-organized savings-bank and a chamber of commerce. They have presented three monuments to the municipality, one, the statue of Columbus, a valuable work of art. They are raising funds to build a school in Verdi's honor, under the auspices of the Children's Aid Society, and are planning to organize a trust company.

I have given the statistics for New York City because the Italian colony on Manhattan is less flourishing than those in other large American cities. So that what is hopeful for New York is even more promising in Philadelphia, St. Louis and Boston.

*Some Characteristics as Citizens*

As regards the dependent and delinquent classes among Italians, a good deal of misapprehension exists. There is no such thing as a dependent *class* of Italians in the United States. Mendicancy, which is pointed out by the foreign traveler as one of the sores of Italy, is practically unknown among Italians here.

Of the delinquent class, some consideration is necessary. While it is true that many Italians are arrested for "violation of city ordinances", these arrests are often the result of ignorance — being the infraction of *mala prohibita* rather than of *mala in se*. The viciousness or weakness which results in drunkenness seldom manifests itself in Italians. In several years of practice at the bar, I have seldom seen an arrest for intoxication among them.

On the other hand, I am aware that Italians are often guilty of crimes of blood. But because these are mostly crimes of passion, committed without secrecy, they make excellent copy for the newspaper writers. As we read of these, while less exciting crimes fail to be chronicled, the popular belief is formed that more crimes are committed by Italians than by any other foreigners. I have yet failed to see any reliable statistical proof of this assertion. I do not seek to justify crimes of passion when I say that it is something to remember that an Italian will stab or shoot, but seldom poison. His hot-headedness prevents his committing crimes necessitating subtle and careful planning. One result is that by such "open crimes" he always pays the penalty of his misdeeds because proof of his overt act is always possible, whereas the carefully planned crimes of others often go unpunished from lack of evidence.

We have rapidly surveyed the conditions of the Italian among us — his historic background and the political and economic achievements of his brother at home. To consider him without his hereditary possibilities is to measure him by an unfair standard. The most highly civilized and desirable immigrant cannot adjust himself quickly to the environment of a new land; probably the only fair test of the value of any immigration is what it contributes to the new land through the second generation. If this is so, all discussion on the menace of Italian immigration would seem premature.

There is one more question that an Italian, speaking for his countrymen here, may urge upon Americans who are interested in the problem of assimilation. It is this: That you should make my countrymen love your country by making them see what is truly good and noble in it. Too many of them, far too many, know of America only what they learn from the corrupt politician, the boss, the *banchiere* and the oftentimes rough police-man. I have been in certain labor camps in the South where my countrymen were forced to work under the surveillance of armed guards. I have spoken to some who had been bound to a mule and whipped back to work like slaves. I have met others who bore the marks of brutal abuses committed by cruel bosses with the consent of their superiors. What conception of American liberty can these foreigners have?

This, then, is the duty upon those who represent what is good and enduring in Americanism — to teach these foreigners the truth about America. Remember these foreigners are essentially men and women like yourselves whatever the superficial differences may be. This is the simple fact far too often forgotten — if not actually denied. And this must be the excuse if you discuss these people as a menace, pitching your discussion as if we were beyond hearing, and beneath feeling, and sometimes even as if beyond redemption.

Make us feel that America has good friends, intelligent, clear-sighted friends; friends that will not exploit us; friends that will not be interested merely because of what Italy did in the past for all civilization, but friends that will extend to us the sympathy which is due from one man to another. You will thereby make us not merely fellow voters, but will prepare us for the supreme test of real assimilation — the wish to consider the adopted country as a new and dear Fatherland.

Italian emigrants waiting to embark, Naples, ca. 1910.

# 14

# The Exodus of a Latin People[1]

WILLIAM E. DAVENPORT[2]

While it would be an exaggeration to say that any section of Italy has been depopulated by emigration, it is true that many towns in Calabria and Basilicata have lost one-tenth of their residents within the past two years, and one-fifth in a somewhat longer period.

The result of extensive emigration from any given section is usually advantageous to the institutions of the region in question and to the families of the emigrants remaining in Italy. The earnings of the father or older brother are largely sent back to the old land, and both the family and the village profit by this influx of money from abroad. At the same time the withdrawal of a great proportion of the able-bodied and enterprising men of a village or country place causes a certain unrest and dissatisfaction, and during the harvest seasons especially the need of these laborers is severely felt.

On every hand I heard the complaint that large land-owners suffer because it is difficult to find men enough to work their lands — and, of course, this means only that they must pay higher wages. The result has been in many sections that the pay of field laborers has risen from a lira (twenty cents) a day to twice that amount.

1. *Charities*, Vol. 12, 1904. Pp. 463-467.
2. Mr. Davenport is head-worker of the Brooklyn Italian Settlement. He has just returned from Italy where he was sent by his society to study the economic and social conditions of the peasants in the districts from which Italian immigration is chiefly derived. Although he has written letters from abroad to several New York periodicals, nothing like a résumé of his observations has been published before. Such a study by an American whose daily work brings him into intimate personal relations with the immigrant from the time of his arrival, is of unusual interest.

Occasionally a landed man will buy modern agricultural machinery to make good the lack of hands, but the inertness of these men in general passes all understanding. Many of them are selling off their lands piecemeal and others are living a life of idle discouragement while their holdings practically go to waste. This suicidal course seems to be common in Basilicata and parts of Calabria and even in the Abruzzi.

Meanwhile, the income received from America suffers no diminution and is regarded as second in importance only to the agricultural receipts from whole sections. The number of large families who withdraw permanently from the country is now on the increase, and this will mean in time smaller receipts from the United States. Perhaps then more of the communes will be obliged to purchase the land of wealthy proprietors and rent it at low rates to the villagers, as they are now doing in some cases.

The problem of the agricultural districts is a very knotty one, mainly because the communal taxes are often so high that the produce when brought to town scarcely pays the farmer the cost of production. In some towns the rate on wine amounts to one-quarter or even one-third of its retail selling price. The physical difficulties to be overcome, in sections where the farms lie eight and ten miles from the villages, are enormous. Often the laborer reaches the field only after four hours of hard walking. Large sections are so steep and rocky that the yield must of necessity be light.

Realizing all these things, the Italian peasant lends a ready ear to the tales of prosperity in America. He does not expect, like his predecessors from western Europe, to dig up gold in the streets of New York, but is really well acquainted with conditions here and knows the rate of wages he may expect. His going causes little excitement outside his own family circle, because to go to America is the ordinary, almost the popular, thing to do. He is almost as much in a rut when he leaves for the steamer at Naples as when he followed his antique plow in the uplands of Calabria.

### The "Emigration Provinces"

Sixty per cent of the Italian immigrants in the United States come from the Abruzzi, Basilicata and Calabria. A very large percentage of them — almost all of them, in fact — have been farm laborers, or men holding small tracts of land through inheritance. The conditions which they leave behind seem almost impossible to an American. Even where the man owns his little farm, the income is so small that he must work for a larger owner, while his wife and children care for his own place. His average wage is thirty cents a day, although during harvest time it may rise to two lira, or forty cents. The conditions under which he is employed involve practically all of his working hours. All of the houses are in the villages, and the fields are often miles away. So the workman must trudge for hours before he reaches his field. At work he is a digger, not at all a farmer in our sense of the word. Many of the owners believe that it is better to cut the earth with a spade or tear it with a mattock, than to turn it with a plow. The laborer spends his day digging over a small plot which an American plow would finish up in a few moments. On his own little place his wife swings a heavy mattock over her head and jerks out lumps of sod just as sturdily and for just as many hours as does he.

Italy has been called the garden land of Europe, but at least in these three provinces the term has no significance. They are mountainous, with sharply sloping fields full of rocks and incapable of fair returns. This, of course, is not true of all land in these provinces, for here are many of the best vineyards and olive groves in Italy. But from the physical conditions alone the farmer is doomed to work which is unremunerative, or at best, uncertain.

In Sicily, sending over twenty per cent of the emigration to this country, the soil, once rich, has been exhausted. This is largely due to the deforesting of the mountains and consequent diminution of the water supply. For six months in the year central Sicily looks like the barren lands of Arizona and New Mexico. I saw little rills trickling pitifully in the center of wide river beds, which had once held streams a quarter of a mile wide. In March and April there is a little rain, but none again until October or November. The principal crop here is wheat. An American farmer could feel only pity for the sickly, sparse, stunted crops and the gleaners cutting them with sickles as they did in the days of Ruth.

Sicily has probably the richest sulphur mines in the world, but here, too, primitive methods keep down proceeds and wages. The ore is carried up from the mines on the shoulders of boys who pass in long files up and down stairways cut in the rock. Some of the mines, I was told, have introduced machinery, but I did not visit any where other than hand tools were in use. In Sicily, also, are the richest groves of oranges and lemons.

These are the physical and economic conditions which the Italian leaves behind him to emigrate. His social condition is no less a marked contrast to ours. His house is nothing to him but a place to sleep. If it has a bed nothing else is needed; he has not felt the want of running water in it, or even near it, and sends his wife to the fountain in the morning and at sunset, for water. For everything except sleeping he uses the piazza, or public square.

The thought and pride which we expend on our own homes, the Italian contadino lavishes on his piazza and his village, his "paese", which is really all the world of which he has any knowledge. This is true not only of the contadino, but of many in the middle classes as well. On the piazza are the social club, the workingman's club, the café, the fountain, the pharmacy, the tobacco shop, the post office and the church. It is there that he receives his friends, talks politics and transacts business. The *circolo sociale*, the social club, has been transplanted to New York with slight variation from its original form. The piazza is the one place which is faithfully swept out every day.

Next to the civic pride is the pride in the local church. Very likely it was built in the open country and the village grew up around it. For centuries the church was first in the villagers' affections, but gradually it has been eclipsed by the love of the village itself, as a whole. When I met men whom I had known in New York, in Italy, they asked me first, "Have you seen my village?" Then, "Have you seen my church?" Not one asked if I had seen his house. It is this feeling which makes possible the handsome buildings and churches in villages where ninety per cent of the houses are barren.

I was strongly impressed with the evident growing away from the church, as an institution rather than as a religion, of many of the educated fraction of the population. Both religious ceremonial and priestly activity are constantly on men's tongues, and as constantly denied their former influence. This is partly due to the influence of the social clubs, where modern literary and scientific notes are discussed, and a general impatience with what are regarded as the pretensions of the church is freely expressed. Shocking as it is to Americans, nothing is more common than to hear educated Italians refer to the church as "the shop". Unquestionably, too, the position of antagonism maintained by the Vatican toward Italian unity wounds the Italian's pride and seriously affects his confidence in and esteem for the ecclesiastical organization.

This, indeed, is freely, though regretfully, admitted by leading churchmen. Whether or not it is a good thing that such a condition exists, is a matter on which there is naturally the greatest difference of opinion.

*Social Factors in Immigration*

The Italian is infinitely bettered industrially by emigrating, but socially he suffers a loss. In his own village he may have been of some small importance, but here he must long be content with a position at the bottom of the social ladder, as a laborer or factory worker. This social loss would be even greater were it not that families from the same province group themselves here in the same neighborhood. Thus, in the space of two blocks on Elizabeth Street dwell several hundred households from the Sicilian town of Sciacca; while in South Brooklyn, in close proximity, scores of Falernitan families have bought homes of their own and form a community by themselves. The continuity of this social life is conserved by constant accessions from the old land, by the frequent departure of grown sons (who came here in infancy) to serve in the Italian army, by the Mutual Aid Society, membership in which is based on one's nativity in a specific province or township, and finally by the local Italian news published in the great Italian-American newspapers, I had an illustration of this social loss in the case of a young man whom I knew in Brooklyn. He was of good family and standing at home, a graduate of a school, and ambitious. When he came to New York he worked in a factory at seven dollars a week for a time, and later was out of work. He became discouraged at the lack of work, and at the kind of work which fell in his way, and returned. Political influence, following the passing of very rigid examinations, secured him a place in a post office in a small village. The position demanded an expert telegrapher, and in addition he speaks French and is familiar with the classics. His salary is fifteen dollars a month. He pays ten dollars a month to live in the best hotel in the village, and his official position assures him social recognition. He has been convinced, however, that when he becomes a master of ready English his telegraphy will bring him seventy-five dollars a month in New York, and he told me that he should come back to stay. In the Italian post office his first advance in salary, probably five dollars a month, may not come for many years.

### The Industrial Side

I have in mind a household in Brooklyn which is an even better illustration of the industrial side of emigration. Just around the corner from our settlement four Italian men eat and live and sleep in one room which costs them five dollars a month. Two are brothers, the other two a father and son. They work as street cleaners, or diggers, and earn seven or eight dollars a week, perhaps more. The living for all four costs less than three dollars a week. Taking out all expenses, they have been able to send home fifty or sixty dollars a month, or thirty dollars to each of the two families. In the little villages where they came from this is a fabulous sum and quickly makes the rounds of the piazza. The mother or sister brags that Tony is paid seven lire a day. The brother at home earns two lire. Living as they do, the cost of living here is not high, and certainly is low in comparison with the wages. Is it any wonder that others follow quickly on?

The reports issued by the government undoubtedly stimulate emigration by a bare recital of facts. For instance, a report from the royal consul at New Orleans tells of the number of Italians in the city and state, their principal occupations, their wages, the average cost of living, the social and benevolent and church organizations. It is, in fact, a complete catalogue of answers to the questions which a prospective emigrant would naturally ask. When the head man of a village is asked for information of America, or of the best place to settle in America, he hands out the latest report. It has been my observation that these reports are carefully compiled and accurate, but the bare statement that for the same work, and probably shorter hours, a man receives from five to ten times as much wages, cannot fail to send ever increasing numbers.

These, briefly, are the points which I shall cover in my report to the Brooklyn Italian Settlement of over three months spent in Italy during the winter and early spring. From my observation both here and abroad, it seems to me that the needs of the Italian at our hand, after he has secured work — and he generally does secure work very soon — are educational. He must be taught English and he must be taught our customs and history. Public work attracts very large numbers of Italians, from its character and from the wages, so that they become citizens with alacrity. The right kind of instruction is essential to their becoming good citizens. Beyond this their pressing needs are chiefly for clubs and other substitutes for the piazza life and to fill in the time until their wives and families are brought to join them.

# 15

# The Effect of Emigration on Italy: An Interview with Adolfo Rossi[1]

GINO C. SPERANZA

When the papers announced that Adolfo Rossi would visit the United States, many an Italian here prepared joyfully to bid welcome to an old friend. Many an expatriate remembered him during his first visit to this country in the varied experiences which he afterward described in his two books: *The Land of the Dollar* and *An Italian in America*. An even larger number looked forward to his coming as to that of a friend — though they had never seen him. They knew him and loved him because he typified modern Italy, and because in his twenty years of quasi-public life he had brought honor to his country.

There are probably few living Italians more widely known among his people in Italy than Adolfo Rossi. As a journalist he gained prominence not merely by his up-to-date methods of gathering news, but by the fearlessness with which he expressed his views. As war correspondent in the disastrous Italian campaign in Abyssinia, he kept his countrymen fully informed of every bad move on the part of the commanding officers, no less than of every heroic deed of the subalterns. As a result of the former he was expelled from Africa; as a consequence of the latter he won the love of his people. Wherever he went as correspondent or investigator, he won laurels and friends — whether it was in the Graeco-Turkish war, in the investigation of the coffee plantations of Brazil, or in the Transvaal. A man of the people, modest and reserved, the casual observer would never imagine in seeing him

1. *Charities*, Vol. 12, 1904. Pp. 467-470. Adolfo Rossi is the Inspector for the Royal Emigration Department of Italy.

that he had followed royalty and been at home with the Papal Court. Above all it is his geniality with its subtle Venetian charm that makes him a general favorite at home.

It was in the beginning of 1902, shortly after the Italian emigration law went into effect, that Adolfo Rossi, now raised to the dignity of Cavalier Rossi, was appointed *inspettore* or supervisor of the emigration department. His wide knowledge of conditions in Italy and abroad, his keen power of observation and his tremendous activity qualified him in an unusual degree to fill the duties of his new office. These consist mainly in visiting the various points where Italian emigration is marked, studying conditions there, examining how the emigration law is enforced and ascertaining whether emigrants have fair play. And that is one reason why Adolfo Rossi is here.

"There seems to be a widespread belief here", he told me, "that the Italian government is encouraging emigration."

"Well", I said, "it is a fact that Italy is overcrowded and that, therefore, the government must favor the outflow of the overplus."

"I do not deny", said Rossi seriously — and when he is serious he is very serious — "that Italy has been overcrowded. Its population increases at the rate of about half a million a year, and this is approximately the number of those who emigrate during such a period. The right to emigrate is an inalienable right and my government cannot deny that right. Your own statutes", he added with a twinkle in his eye taking up a paper, "declare that 'expatriation is a natural and inherent right of all the people'. But the government can and does interfere with forced or artificial emigration, such as that stimulated by certain steamship lines. You see, these steamship companies have invested large capital in steamers for the emigration trade. Unless they get full shiploads for every trip they don't make a profit. Our emigration law of 1901, and its subsequent amendments, are aimed especially at such forced methods of emigration. If Americans would only examine that law they would see that my government is not aiding any process of dumping her sons here."

"Are the Italian steamship lines mainly responsible?" I asked.

"Let it be said to the honor of Italian capital that it has not lent itself to depopulate Italy by the method pursued by many of the foreign steamship companies", he answered.

"But people here", I prodded him on, "believe that while there may be a very drastic law on the statute books in Italy, yet this outpour from your country is too good a thing for Italy to expect that any law that would check it would be enforced."

"The curse of Italy seems to be that outsiders never judge her by her present; foreign opinion seems generally based on facts at least ten years old."

*Present Conditions in Italy*

Adolfo Rossi knows present conditions in Italy too well to sympathize with ignorance on the subject. "I'll tell you exactly what the facts are to-day", he went on, "and I will explain to you how far emigration is a blessing and where the blessing stops and begins to become a curse."

He began moving his fingers as if he were writing, which is always a sign that he is going to tell you a long story. "Of course, for a time", he began in that persistent drawl that is characteristic of Venetians, "emigration was a safety valve for the tremendous increase in the population of Italy. It also brought in money from those in America who had families in Italy. A good deal of money came in that way. Then undoubtedly it decreased crime — not because we sent you our criminals, but because many of the crimes committed, especially in the country, were due to over-population and poverty. Another good effect of emigration has been to increase wages all over Italy from one-third to one-half."

"Isn't that a whole list of blessings you owe to emigration?" I dared interrupt.

"Yes, but that's only one side of the picture, and the only side that seems to be known here. What you overlook is that the character of the emigration has changed in recent years. It is not hard conditions or starvation that now sends Italians to America; they come because they are eager for more money. A mason earning four lire a day in southern Italy, can live there comfortably, but he has heard that he can earn six a day in America. So he emigrates, and in such numbers that in certain parts of Sicily, Basilicata and Calabria, it amounts to a general exodus. This large emigration has been irregular or uneven in its distribution, that is, it has not been a few men from a number of villages, but all the able-bodied men of one village, for instance, have gone. In some places the village priest and the doctor, having lost their flock, have followed them to America. Certain municipalities have had to be consolidated and the parish church abandoned. You can see some decided disadvantages for Italy in this situation. First, it works harm to the landowners because despite the increase of wages they can't get laborers. Laborers have actually to be imported from Messina to Termini-Imerese during the olive-picking season. Many wheat farms have to-day become mere pasture lands from lack of hands to cultivate them. Sicily, called from ancient times 'the granary of Italy', to-day does not produce sufficient wheat for its own consumption and has to import some."

*The Men Who Leave Italy*

"But above all this excessive emigration is working a harm to the nation at large in that it takes from us the flower of our laboring class, which leaves Italy, not to seek a living, but greater comfort. To this, naturally, contributes the selection exercised by your immigration laws which let in only the good and reject the bad. My government allows the American commission of physicians of your own selection at Italian ports a pretty free hand. They do examine the emigrant not only for trachoma, but make a fairly thorough examination for hernia, for diseases due to senility, etc., thus adding a potent artificial selection.

"Then I notice that the newspapers write of the influx of a lot of poverty-stricken Italians. Just look at the facts: 84 per cent of Italians coming here are between 18 and 45 years of age. That means that 84 per cent of such immigrants belong to the working age. They are, in other words, producers. You get this product without the expense incurred in its raising. Every Italian of 18, for instance, costs his country, at the very lowest, $1,000 to bring him up. At 18, he begins to be a producer, but by leaving Italy the $1,000 invested by his country in him is lost. This 'human capital' of fresh, strong young men is the contribution of Europe to the new land. We spend a thousand dollars to bring up and develop a young man and then you reap the profits on the investment. We give you a good laborer, but I find you pay him less than other laborers. If it were not for his sobriety and thrift, he could not live on his hire. I think this is a manifest unfairness; first, because the Italian does not produce cheap work; and second, because you take advantage of his ignorance to underpay him. And then people think that he is underbidding other laborers."

"Don't these immigrants return to Italy in large numbers after they have laid aside a little sum?" I asked.

"That is another ten-year-old fact", he answered. "Many go back on a visit, but not to settle there. They go to bring their family or to find a wife; or they go back with a smattering of bad English to look over their 'estates' and be looked up to, and then come back. In some parts of Sicily, if a well-dressed stranger, even an Italian, goes on a visit, the villagers will say, 'He's from America'. But they do not remain, though they can live there comfortably. Four or five years of America seem to unfit the Italian immigrant for a return to live in Italy."

"But what is their idea of America — do the majority of them look upon it merely as a place to go to make money?" I asked.

"I believe that among many Italian peasants, America stands for more than the land of the dollar, even though they know little about it. I will tell you a story bearing on this point, and with it I shall insist on closing this interview, as I am leading a strenuous life. Some time ago, in a Sicilian village, a lot of peasants became dissatisfied with the mediaeval agricultural methods of the local 'feudal lord'. These peasants felt that they were neither chattels going with the land nor serfs. So one fine morning they gathered in front of the lord's house, bunched their shovels in a heap, and on top placed the following notice: 'Sir, do your farming yourself — we are going to

America'. And unless the immigration officials at New York have refused admission to these independent peasants, out of fear that they might become public charges, you will find them working on some of your railroads."

And, with a smile, Signor Rossi closed the interview.

Minnesota Mine Workers, ca. 1910.

16

# The Philanthropist-Padrone:
# What is Being Done to Raise the Standard
# Through Competition and Example[1]

CHARLES B. PHIPARD[2]

The majority of the 1,000,000 and over Italians who have come to this country since 1893, have had little or no capital, are uneducated, and, in consequence, manual labor is all they can do. In addition to this, the most of them, having been peasants at home, naturally drift to work in the open air with pick and shovel when they come to this country.

There is an abundance of this kind of work to be done and the Italian seems to be particularly fitted for it, but some medium is necessary by which he can be brought in contact with the employer and his work; this is done by the padroni or labor contractors. These men make it their business to supply laborers in any numbers. They are thus useful to employers, who as a universal rule would not themselves know how to get Italian laborers in any numbers, and who would find it impossible to proceed by picking up one man at a time.

The padrone has been very useful also, all in all, to the Italian laborer. The immigrant, in his ignorance of the language, could not find employment and could not look after himself in any way if he did. The padrone steps in and finds him employment, boards and lodges him while at work, collects his wages, writes his letters, acts as his banker, and engineers any and all dealings which the laborer may have with the concern for which he may be working. The padrone has therefore served a very useful purpose to both employer and laborer, and also to the public.

But the padroni as a class — for there are some honest and intelligent men among them — are not scrupulous in their dealings with the laborers with

1. *Charities*, Vol. 12, 1904. Pp. 470-472.
2. Manager of the Society for the Protection of Italian Immigrants.

whom they come in contact. Many of them engage in mean and petty swindling of one kind and another. Universally they overcharge the laborer for what they do for him. They never do anything to improve the condition of the laborer or to teach him to better his own condition for himself. They are ignorant men trying to make as much money as possible out of other ignorant men, who from their inability to speak the language and their foreignness, are peculiarly helpless. And there can be no great difficulty in judging the result.

To alter or remedy these conditions is no easy task, for it is necessary to possess some method of getting together the laborer and the work to be done, while improving the evil attributes of the padrone. Worse evils than those existing would ensue if the padrone were wiped suddenly out of existence.

It would seem that the best remedy for cases of actual swindling is through the criminal laws, and in these cases the laborer should have the assistance of public officials, charitable societies, etc. Even then, and with such assistance, his ignorance will be constantly a hindrance to his obtaining justice.

Overcharging arises from the dependence of the laborers on the padrone for provisions. In the majority of cases where a padrone places a gang of men at work, he conducts the commissary; and in such commissaries, where the work is located out of town, the padrone carries everything in stock which is necessary to the needs of the laborer, in the way of both provisions and clothing; and in a great many cases, or, perhaps, we should say the majority of cases, the prices charged to the laborer are exorbitant. Also, short weight or count is given, or the goods are of an inferior grade but sold at the prices of first-class goods.

This matter of overcharging could in part be regulated by passing laws to control the price of board, supplies and medical service to laborers when in contractors' camps. But overcharging cannot be prevented wholly except by the growth of a higher conception of their duty to the laborer on the part of employer and padrone. And it must be in this same way, too, that the general neglect and indifference to the laborer's welfare in other matters than overcharging on the part of the employer and padrone, can be rectified. The public is interested in preventing laborers from being treated like machines and allowed or forced to live like brutes. In a republic everything like this tends to debase the average character of the people, on which alone the welfare of the republic depends.

Accordingly, the Society for the Protection of Italian Immigrants has actively entered into the business of supplying employers with laborers and of conducting labor camps through trustworthy agents of its own. In these camps, the laborer will not be overcharged, and every effort will be made so that he can lead a healthful life, and not be brutalized in any way. Naturally, the entrance of the society into this field has been difficult of accomplishment on account of the opposition which it has met from the unscrupulous padrone and through the ignorance of the laborers, who do not as yet fully understand and appreciate that the society is doing this work solely for the betterment of existing conditions. Employers, also, have been hard to reach, as, for the past fifteen or twenty years, they have been in the habit of getting such uneducated labor as they have needed from the padroni, and they naturally look at the matter from a strictly business point of view. So long as the padroni can supply them with the desired number of men at the right time, they are not over particular, and in fact cannot be, as to the treatment accorded the men in the camps. The society has had the opportunity of demonstrating to both employers and laborers that labor camps can be conducted decently and on a legitimate business basis, and it has hopes that eventually its place in the regard of laborers will become firmly fixed. The main difficulty in weaning the ignorant laborer from his padrone is his habit of believing that the padrone is the only one who can supply his needs. This is repeatedly proved by the fact that no matter how badly one of these padroni may treat his followers they return to him for employment and advice in preference to all others. The padrone fully realizes this weakness and makes the most of it on every occasion. In consequence of this blind belief, it has been extremely difficult to win the confidence of the laborer, thereby making it additionally hard to demonstrate to the employer that the society can render him as good service in the matter of getting him men at short notice as do the padroni. The society feels confident, however, from experience, and from growing interest by the particular laborers with whom its representatives have come in close contact in labor camps, that the desired object will be accomplished — that the laborer and the padrone will both become sufficiently educated and enlightened so that the laborer will look out better for himself, and the padrone for him.

STRAWBERRIES
3 CARLOADS FOR "KATY FLYER"
APRIL 25 - 09. DICKINSON TEX. SCHLUTER
HOUSTON

# 17

# The Agricultural Possibilities of Italian Immigration[1]

GUSTAVO TOSTI[2]

The statistical investigation started by the Italian Chamber of Commerce may be said to constitute the first specific attempt toward ascertaining the number of Italians actually living in New York. The results obtained are all the more important inasmuch as the number of Italians residing here had, since the census of 1900, been largely a matter of guesswork.

The report of the Italian Chamber of Commerce shows the Italian population of New York State to be, on January 1, 1904, at least 486,175, while for the city of Greater New York we have on the same date a total of 382,775. It appears, thus, that the Italian population of the city represents 78.7 per cent of the entire Italian population of the state. We have here a most striking confirmation of the fact of urban congestion, generally suspected and only partially brought to light by previous research. The census of 1900 had already drawn attention to the peculiar concentration of our immigrants in the cities and especially in the city of New York. In fact, in 1900 the Italian population of the city amounted to 85.4 per cent of the total Italian population of the state — a percentage which shows, it is true, a slight decrease for 1904, but one too insignificant to modify the general tendency evidenced by the collected figures. The rush toward New York City continues unabated, and unchanged continue those conditions of congestion and overcrowding with their long train of evils which have fully been set forth in recent writings and discussions.

It can hardly be denied that this almost mechanical gravitation of the newcomers of all nationalities toward the cities in general, and toward New

1. *Charities*, Vol. 12, 1904. Pp. 472-476.
2. Acting Consul-General of Italy, New York City.

York in particular, constitutes the most serious aspect of the problem of immigration in this country.

We can easily understand that the evils resulting from the unwholesome promiscuousness of tenement life should lead certain observers to entertain a feeling of diffidence and fear toward the foreign invader. But we cannot understand how the dangers of the concentration of alien colonies in the large cities of this country can be used as an argument for a wholesale condemnation of immigration in general. The danger lies, as Commissioner-General Sargent has set forth in his last report, not in the increasing tide of immigration, not even in the individual deficiencies of immigrants, nor in their failure to come up to a certain ideal type or standard, but rather "in their congregation in alien colonies, usually in the great cities, where the competition for the means of subsistence is most strenuous, the contrast between wealth and poverty most conspicuous and most productive of discontent and resentment against such inequalities and the civilization which make such contrasts possible, and where temptations to vice are most numerous".[3] It is in the very nature of things that the members of such alien colonies, thus placed in the unhealthy surroundings of the tenement, should "pursue non-productive or but slightly productive occupations", or should lend themselves "to foster the avarice of 'sweatshop owners', thus depriving the employers of labor throughout the country of much-needed assistance that would bring good pay to the laborer, profit to the employer, and benefit to the country at large".[4] The problem, therefore, would seem to be not one of suppression, but one of organization of the foreign element. In other words, foreign immigration should be distributed where it could find needed and useful employment and supply equally useful labor.

*Rounding Out a Nation*

The systematic opponents of immigration, those who would build a Chinese wall around this country, seem utterly to forget that its tremendous size, compared with its actual population, will make immigration a necessity for years to come. It is only through the constant influx of a strong, healthy, vigorous immigration that this country may hope to develop adequately its almost inexhaustible wealth of physical resources and, as it were, to complete itself. The census of 1900 furnishes us with some interesting data on this very aspect of the problem. Leaving out of consideration the New England and north Atlantic states which are so densely populated owing to their predominant industrial character, and setting aside the north central states which are climatically unsuited to southern immigration, it appears that the

3. Annual Report of the Commissioner-General of Immigration, 1903, p. 121.
4. Ibid, p. 122.

very states where conditions would seem most favorable to our immigration, the south Atlantic and south central states, are just those in which the density of population is very low. With the exception of Maryland, where the relative population per square mile reaches a maximum of 120.5, the states in that section show a density varying from 48.4, in Tennessee, to 11.6, in Texas. The western states in an even more marked degree are sparsely settled. California, the most thickly populated of the western section, shows a maximum density of 9.5, while other states in the group give examples of almost desert places — Wyoming with 0.9, and Nevada with 0.4. If we compare the population of both the United States and Italy with their respective areas, we have the following results:

| United States, 1900 | | Italy, 1900 | |
|---|---|---|---|
| Population | 76,304,799 | Population | 31,856,675 |
| Area | 9,366,693 sq.km. | Area | 286,648 sq.km. |

We have, thus, an average density of 8 per square kilometer in the United States and of 111 in Italy. The half-deserted island of Sardinia has a population relatively four times superior to that of the United States, while Italy reproduces the average density of the thickly populated north Atlantic states. Of course, this is merely a mathematical relation, destined to convey only a general idea of the average density of population in both countries. In such a general formula, we leave out of consideration sectional variations in density as found; for instance, in the overcrowded eastern seaboard states, and in such regions of Italy as Lombardy, Sicily and Liguria, where, also, the relative population is much higher than the average above quoted.

A country having so low a density as the United States and showing, in its highest social classes, a tendency toward a sluggish birth-rate, cannot afford to stamp out immigration.

The very overcrowding of certain sections (Rhode Island 407, Massachusetts 348.9, New Jersey 250.3, Connecticut 187.5, New York 152.6), if compared with the low average density above pointed out, constitutes a social danger of the gravest significance, for the intensity of urban life cannot become an element of national strength unless it bears a definite relationship to the distribution of rural population.

## Farmers, Not Harvest Hands, the Solution

The necessity of immigration once realized, the main exigency of the situation appears to be the breaking up of these alien colonies in the cities and the distribution of their members in those parts of the American territory where their work is most needed. But how can this end be attained? Let it be said once for all that the solution of the problem lies in devising such means as will make the agricultural distribution of our immigration possible. Our immigrants must leave the congested cities and seek a purer atmosphere in agricultural work. But it must be understood that the question at issue is not how to transform our immigrants into farm workers, but rather, how to transform them into farmers and small land-owners. There is a misleading idea in certain quarters that the "agricultural distribution of Italian immigrants" should be obtained simply through the employment of a large number of Italians as farm workers and farm hands. This would be only a palliative measure. The character of agricultural work is, by its very nature, precarious. The Italian immigrants would thus find employment during a few months of the year, when, for instance, at harvest time, there is an enormous demand for labor in the western states and in California. But after a comparatively short period of occupation they would lapse into enforced idleness, which would undoubtedly drive them back to the industrial centers. The only way to get at the root of the question is to transform a large proportion of our immigrants into *land-owners* or *farmers*. But it is to be remembered that one of the important factors in determining the rush toward the cities has been the utter lack of facilities for the immigrant to acquire land and settle in the agricultural districts as a farmer.

Some forty years ago, when the much-talked of "homestead law" went into effect, conditions were totally different. Then, immense tracts of land were put at the disposal of would-be settlers under very easy conditions. And the land thus offered to the newcomers was chiefly situated in rolling regions, well provided with water, and highly productive. The immigrants of the northern races, especially the Germans and the Scandinavians, were not slow to take advantage of the facilities thus provided by the law; and thus they came to build up the prosperous middle western states out of the wilderness which was then known as the "Far West". But now the homestead law, although still in force, has no longer the same practical bearing. There are yet hundreds of millions of acres of public lands which can be acquired by prospective settlers, but these lands are mostly situated in the arid or semi-arid zone, and would require highly expensive irrigation works to place them under cultivation.

Conditions may change somewhat in consequence of the application of the so-called "reclamation law", which is destined to solve the irrigation problem in the tracts included in the arid zone, representing two-fifths of the total area of the United States (California, Colorado, Idaho, Kansas, Montana, Nebraska, Nevada, North Dakota, Oregon, South Dakota, Utah, Washington, Wyoming and the territories of Arizona, New Mexico and Oklahoma). Eventually the large proportion of public land included in this zone (about five hundred and fifteen millions of acres) will be utilized as an outlet for agricultural settlers. But as things are progressing with unavoidable slowness in the carrying out of the provisions of the reclamation law, we

may well leave public lands out of consideration for the present. The land
that can be furnished to the immigrants is now in private hands and must be
acquired from them by a society organized on the basis of a realty
corporation. Such a society should buy the land for the immigrant, sell it to
him on easy payments, furnish him with seeds and implements, and provide
for his maintenance until his first crop.

## The South as a Field for a Land Corporation

The organization of an agricultural colony is, of course, dependent for its
success upon various factors — the cost of land, the nature of the soil, the
salubrity of the climate, the atmospheric precipitation, the distance from the
railroads and from the markets. We shall not attempt here a survey, however
rapid, of the various sections of this country where there would be room for
agricultural colonies. Such work has been already exhaustively done by
Kate Holladay Claghorn.[5] The southern states, Atlantic and central, are the
very section of this country which seems most suited to receive Italian
immigration. It can hardly be denied that with the decline of old manners of
farming and the adoption of a diversified and intensive cultivation of land,
which is a characteristic feature of the economic growth of the south, a
demand has been created for European farmers with their knowledge of
intensive methods. For such an improved form of agricultural work the
general opinion seems to be that the colored laborer is not suitable. All the
circumstances thus seem to favor the introduction in the southern states of
European farmers, and the Italians are the best suited for this purpose,
owing to climatic reasons. The main point at present seems to be: How shall
the public mind in the south be gradually brought to look at the introduction
of foreign farmers without bias or prejudice. An educational campaign will
have to pave the way for the successful organization of a land corporation,
destined to operate in the south, along the lines mentioned.

5. The principal colonies are described by Miss Claghorn, in Volume XV of the *Report of the
Industrial Commission*, pp. 499 to 507. They are: Vineland, N.J.; Bryan, Tex.: Asti, Cal.: Dapue
and Lambert, Ala.: Sunnyside (which is again being developed after a practical abandonment)
and Tontitown, Ark.: Montebello and Verdella, Mo. Mention is made also of smaller groups
engaged in agriculture in almost every county of California; of the laborers on the plantations
of Louisiana and Mississippi, of groups of truck farmers and vine growers at Dickinson and
Gunnison, in Texas, and near Memphis, Denver, Pueblo, Salt Lake City, Cheyenne and many
other cities all over the country, and through the wine-producing belt of New York,
Pennsylvania and Ohio.

Our Lady of Pompei Church, New York City, ca. 1900.

# 18

# The Associated Life of the Italians in New York City[1]

ANTONIO MANGANO

It is generally supposed by those unfamiliar with actual conditions, that the Italian colony of the Borough of Manhattan is a well-organized and compact body of people, having a common life and being subject to the absolute control and leadership of some one person or group of persons. To the reader of popular articles describing Italian life and customs, in these days so frequently appearing in newspapers and magazines; to the enthusiastic and romantic slum visitor, who walks through Mulberry Street, and possibly peeps into the dark and dismal hallway of some dilapidated tenement and feels that he knows just how Italians live and act; to the theoretical sociologist, to whom all Italians look alike and in whose estimation all Italians are alike, think alike, and act alike — to such persons the mere mention of the Italian colony inevitably suggests unity of thought and action as well as of mode of life on the part of all who belong to that colony. And yet nothing is farther from the real truth.

Although many of the people of the Italian colony could not tell what the word *republic* means, and while none of them prior to coming to America have ever breathed the atmosphere created by republican institutions, it must be said that the love of freedom and the spirit of independence are elements inherent in the Italian character. Countless battlefields, made sacred during many centuries by the blood of those who rather than be subject to tyranny or foreign dominion offered their lives, as well as their substance, as a sacrifice, are unmistakable witnesses to the love of Italians for freedom and for liberty. When the Italian lands upon our shores and catches the spirit of the independence which prevails here, his own nature finds itself in a congenial atmosphere and begins to expand along those lines. Under the

1. *Charities*, Vol. 12, 1904. Pp. 476-482.

social and economic conditions in his own country, he could not assert himself; he was timid; he did not dare say his soul was his own for fear of being deprived of the means of subsistence. Here a very different state of affairs prevails. He somehow catches the idea that if he works faithfully and behaves himself, he need fear no man. This means an appeal to his manhood.

No one will deny that development along this line is good and wholesome. But, unfortunately, the good is accompanied by a shadow of evil. The spirit of independence seems to go to seed. The members of the Italian colony have a certain element in their general make-up which has rendered it virtually impossible for them to act unitedly and harmoniously. Each man feels that he is a law unto himself; each small group of men are a law unto themselves. They appreciate most keenly that it is their right and privilege to do as they see fit — providing they do not interfere with other people's rights — but they lose sight of this other great fact equally important, that personal rights and privileges should be modified by consideration for the welfare of the community — the only condition under which men can live together in any proper and mutually helpful relation.

But, now, if we are asked whether any plausible reason can be advanced as to why the Italians seem to lack natural capacity for a large co-operation, we would answer that they have for centuries lived in the midst of an environment which has tended to develop in them a spirit of division and sectional feeling. Prior to the formation of the present Italian kingdom, the country was divided into numerous dukedoms and principalities among which there was constant rivalry and bitter feeling, if not open warfare. As a natural consequence, the people not only have lacked sympathy for those outside of their particular principality or dukedom, but even have nursed a strong feeling of hostility toward them. Added to this, there is the spirit which prevails to-day in many parts of Italy — a clearly marked rivalry between two towns or two cities within the same province. Doubtless such contention has its good effect in inducing rival towns to put forth every effort for their improvement; but on the other hand, division and dissension are unconsciously fostered under the guise of a false patriotism.

The New York colony is composed of persons coming from nearly every nook and corner of the old peninsula. It is by no means strange, then, that they should bring with them local prejudices and narrow sympathies; it is not to be wondered that they feel that highest duty consists in being loyal to the handful who come from their immediate section and in manifesting opposition toward those who come from other localities. Thus it comes to pass that while a man may be known as an Italian, he is far better known as a Napoletano, Calabrese, Veneziano, Abbruzese, or Siciliano. This means that the Italian colony is divided into almost as many groups as there are sections of Italy represented.

There are, however, many signs which unmistakably point to a decided change for the better in the near future. There are certain forces at work which have for their ultimate object the development of a larger spirit of co-operation, which will enable the Italians as a whole to unite for the attainment of specific objects. The main purpose of this article, therefore, is to point out the chief Italian institutions which indicate the lines along which Italian organized effort is directed, and to describe briefly their operations.

## The Italian Chamber of Commerce

Among the agencies which have for their ideal united Italian action, there are none more potent than the Italian Chamber of Commerce. This organization, founded in 1887 with but a few members, to-day embraces in its membership of 201 a majority of the Italian businessmen in Greater New York. The objects for which it was established may best be stated by translating a few articles from its constitution and by-laws:

(1) a. To promote, develop and protect commercial relations between Italy and the United States.

b. To facilitate and protect orderly interests, both commercial and industrial, which the Italians residing in the United States of America may have with other countries, and especially with Italy.

(2) a. To act as interpreter to the Italian government, to public or private officials, foreign or domestic, in regard to all matters concerning the development of Italian commercial interests in the United States.

b. To study the existing commercial and industrial reports between Italy and the United States; indicate the causes which hinder the development and suggest remedies.

c. To transmit to the Italian government all such information which may be of value in matters commercial and industrial between the mother country and the United States.

d. To compile a general annual directory of all Italian merchants in New York City and in the principal centers of the American union.

e. In general, to lend its good offices in the settlement of any difficulties which might arise between Italians, or between Italians and other nationalities.

In addition, the Chamber occupies itself with a number of other things which are not specifically stated in the constitution. It aims at increasing Italian exports to this country and American exports to Italy; it acts as a medium in suggesting to dealers, both Americans and Italians, where they can secure the particular goods desired.

But to my mind, while I would not for a moment detract from the commercial functions of the Chamber, its greatest good is achieved along another line — one which is destined eventually to lead the Italians to drop sectional feeling and rejoice in the glory of a common nationality. That the Neapolitan, the Sicilian, the Roman, can all join this organization and have as the one object the advancement of Italian interests, is a step in the right direction and toward another end which is eminently wholesome and greatly to be desired.

## Columbus Hospital

The Columbus Hospital is situated on Twentieth Street between Second and Third Avenues. Organized in 1892 and incorporated in 1895, it has been from its beginning under the direct supervision of the missionary Sisters of the Sacred Heart. Were it possible for the hospital to secure increased accommodations and better facilities, it would be of far greater service to those in whose interests it is dedicated. The following paragraph is taken from the last annual report: "During the year, 1,098 patients were admitted, and of this number only sixty-three paid full board. When we consider that the hospital is devoid of endowment, annuity, or permanent fund for its maintenance, depending entirely upon the energies of the sisters and the voluntary contributions of those who have its well-being at heart, it becomes a problem which those unacquainted with the management would find difficulty in solving."

Columbus Hospital is generally known as an Italian institution, yet of the twenty-one physicians on its medical and surgical staff not one is an Italian, but the sisters who carry it on are all native Italians, and ninety-five per cent of the patients treated are of that race.

## The Society for the Protection of Italian Immigrants

The Society for the Protection of Italian Immigrants was founded three years ago, and since then has, without a shadow of a doubt, rendered more practical assistance to the thousands flocking to our shores than any other institution working in the interest of Italians.

Speaking of the conditions in which Italians find themselves on arrival, Eliot Norton, president of the Society, says in his annual report: "These immigrants are landed at Ellis Island, where they are examined by United States officials. From there some go into the interior of the country and some remain in New York. Almost all of them are very ignorant, very childlike, and wholly unfamiliar with the ways, customs and language of this country. Hence it is obvious that they need friendly assistance from the moment of debarkation at Ellis Island. Those who go into the interior of the country need to be helped in getting on the right train, without losing their way or money; while those coming to New York City need guidance to their destination and, while going there, protection from sharps, crooks and dishonest runners, and thereafter to have advice and employment."

The Society is constantly enlarging its activities. It has had the hearty co-operation of Commissioner Williams and of the police department. Its officials are stationed at Ellis Island and act as interpreters for the newcomers.

With such immigrants as have friends either on Ellis Island or on the New York side, awaiting them, the society does not concern itself. Its attention is fully occupied in attending to those who have no friends and who have not the remotest idea as to the place for which they are bound. These are taken directly to its office, at 17 Pearl Street, and later turned over to its guards or runners. For this service the immigrant is charged a nominal fee. During the first two years and a half, 7,293 friendless immigrants were conducted to their destinations, in or about New York City, at an average cost of thirty-two cents apiece, as against an average expenditure of from $3.00 to $4.00, which immigrants formerly were forced to pay by sharpers.

## The Italian Benevolent Institute

Closely associated with the work of the Society for the Protection of Italian Immigrants is the Italian Benevolent Institute. Within the past two years it has taken on new life. The work was encouraged by gifts from many quarters, the most noteworthy one being from His Majesty the King of Italy, which amounted to 20,000 lire. One of its encouraging features is the fact that it is maintained almost exclusively by Italians.

The institute has its headquarters in a double house, 165-7 West Houston Street, which is intended as a place of refuge for the destitute. It often happens that newcomers, bound for interior points, land in New York without a cent in their pockets, expecting to find at the post-office or some bank the sum necessary to carry them to their destination; it also often happens that the money expected does not arrive in time. To such persons as these the Benevolent Institute opens its doors. Then, too, there are immigrants who come with the intention of settling in New York. Such persons may have $8 or $10, but unless they find work at once they too are compelled to seek aid from some source. Further, New York has become, in a sense, a central market for Italian labor, and of those who go to distant points in search of work some fail to find it, and return to the city.

## Italian Benefit Societies

Attention has already been called to the fact that the Italian is lacking in the spirit of unity, and of association in a large sense. The last few years, however, have witnessed a few noteworthy victories in the interest of larger sympathy — mainly through the efforts of a few leading spirits who have been prominent in the affairs of the colony. If one can prophesy, in the light of tendencies already at work, the day is coming when the Italian colony will recognize its responsibilities, and, throwing aside petty jealousies, will launch out upon such a policy as will best enhance the interests of the Italians as a whole.

If we were asked, therefore, whether there is any bond which unites the

Italian colony as a whole, we must answer no. Even the Roman Church cannot be considered such a unifying factor in the attitude of indifference taken toward its claims.

It must be observed, however, that the Italian manifests a strong tendency toward organization with small groups for social ends and for the purpose of mutual aid. There are in Manhattan alone over one hundred and fifty Italian societies of one sort or another. "The moral disunity of the old peninsula is transplanted here."

The Italian does not lack the instinct of charity or mutual helpfulness; but at present he lacks the instinct in a broad sense. He would take the bread from his own mouth in order to help his fellow townsman; there is nothing he will not do for his *paesano;* but it must be expected from this that he will manifest such an attitude toward *all Italians.* Notwithstanding, were it not for this strong feeling, even though limited to small groups, we should have many more calls upon public charity on the part of the Italians than we now do.

*Amusements*

In matters of amusement and recreation, the Italian stands in great contrast with his American cousin who too often goes to extremes and excesses. When the Italian goes off for an afternoon's or evening's outing, he does not demand horse racing, cock fights, vulgar exhibitions or other forms of violent excitement. He finds boundless pleasure in comparatively simple things. Gathered about a table sipping coffee or wine, listening to some music, a stroll up and down the street, a game of cards in a saloon or in some friend's house — these are the chief amusements of the masses. Italian temperance along this line might well teach the American a wholesome lesson.

The Italian is fond of the theatre, and it is the better class of plays which appeal to him. The one distinctly Italian theatre, *Teatro Drammatico Nazionale,* which furnishes nightly performances in New York, is situated on the Bowery in the heart of the Italian population, and is fairly well supported. But there are numerous small places throughout the colony, mainly in connection with saloons, where light comedies and bits of tragedy are given. There is also the little marionette theatre in an upper room on Elizabeth Street, with its doughty knights and plaintive spokesman, and the clash of arms in its battles royal to the crooning of a violin.

It is music, however, which appeals most strongly to the Italian character. He is not carried away with our slam-bang-band music, nor do you hear him whistling and humming the so-called popular songs of the day. Negro melodies are pleasing to him because of their combined elements of sweetness and sadness. But it is the opera which lifts him to the third heaven. The favorite operas of Verdi, Puccini and Mascagni, always draw large Italian audiences at the Metropolitan, especially so if the leading artists are Italians, and often such is the case. With the love of music is joined a sentiment of patriotism. I have in mind a young barber — and he one of a class who earns less than ten dollars a week — who rarely, if ever, misses one of the great Italian operas. During the season — it is a common experience to hear shoe-blacks, and even day laborers, discussing the merits of this or that singer, and giving their reasons why this or that opera pleases them.

Italians from every nook and corner of the tenements largely make up the great crowds which listen to the park concerts at Mulberry Bend.

It is the custom of each of the small group societies to give an annual festival, and it is in connection with such festal occasions that the Italian manifests his love for show and pomp, uniforms, banners, music, elaborate discourses. Eating and drinking are the chief features, and order generally prevails.

On religious holidays the greatest and most extravagant celebrations take place. They, as a rule, occur in midsummer, when prodigal decoration, street illuminations — such as one sees so frequently in Italy, fireworks, processions, etc. — are indulged in. No inducement could tempt the Italian to miss these festivals. At such a one held three years ago in "Little Italy", in honor of one of the saints, it was claimed that no less than fifteen thousand men paraded up and down the streets each day, bearing banners on which were pinned offerings of money. In the three days, the contributions were said to have amounted to something over $20,000.

If the Italian is anything he is convivial. Nothing gives him more pleasure than to meet with his friends. In this strong desire within him for companionship may be found a cause of the herding of Italians together in certain "quarters" and of his reluctance to seek employment on farms where he would have far better opportunity for rearing his children.

*The Italian Savings Bank*

As one passes through the Italian quarter and observes the number of windows displaying the sign "Banca Italiana", he is naturally led to think that the Italians do nothing but deposit money. I am told on very good authority that in Greater New York the number of so-called "banks" — distinctively Italian — is beyond three hundred. It should be said, however, that ninety per cent of these banks are nothing more or less than forwarding agencies. They are constantly springing up to meet the needs of this or that group of persons, coming from a particular town or village. For example, here is a group of people from Cosenza. They want a place where they can have their letters directed. They need some one who can assist them in the matter of sending home money now and then. They look for information

regarding new fields of labor which are developing. It is in response to these
needs that the larger part of these so-called banks have been brought into
existence. They are generally attached to a saloon, grocery store, or cigar
store — sometimes to a cobbler shop. The "banker" is always a fellow
townsman of the particular group that does business with him, and this for
the simple reason that the *paesano* is trusted more, no matter how solid,
financially, another bank may be.

The one real substantial Italian bank, incorporated in 1896 under the laws
of the State of New York, is the Italian Savings Bank, situated on the corner
of Mulberry and Spring Streets. It has to-day on deposit $1,059,369.19. Its
report shows open accounts to the number of 7,000, and books up to date to
the number of 10,844. The moneys deposited in this bank, as might be
supposed, are generally in very small sums, but the figures show an average
sum on deposit of about $170. The depositors as a rule are Italians, but
persons of any nationality may open accounts if they wish.

This institution was started at a time when small Italian banks were
failing, and when there was special antagonism to such institutions, both on
the part of those who had lost money through the failure of the smaller
banks and on the part of those of the small banks which continued to do
business. But through determination and perseverance on the part of the
officers under the lead of Cav. J. N. Francolini, who was chosen president,
and who for two years gave his services free of charge, the institution was
placed upon a firm foundation, and is to-day a credit to the colony.

*The Churches*

Any discussion of the associated life of the Italians would be incomplete
unless some mention were made of religious organizations. There are in
Manhattan, 23 Roman Catholic churches which are entirely or in part
devoted to the Italians. As one enters these churches, he is struck by a
certain warmth and artistic display which are lacking in many of the other
churches. The Italian has had centuries of training in the matter of artistic
cathedral decorations and, taking into account the fact that so much of his
life has been centered about the church, it is but natural that his places of
worship should embody all that art and aesthetic natures can contribute.
The church does work for Italians among the lines of parochial schools, and
maintains a home in the lower part of the city for female immigrants.

In Manhattan, there are four regularly organized evangelical churches —
maintained by the Presbyterian, Methodist, Protestant Episcopal and Baptist
denominations. With the exception of the beautiful little Episcopal church
on Broome Street, the evangelical churches may be said to lack altogether
the very elements which the Italian, in view of his past training, deems most
essential to his environment for worship. And yet notwithstanding this,

these churches are well attended. There are several other missions established for Italians, but results of their work cannot easily be seen, simply because they lack the organization necessary to hold together the people whom they reach in a more or less effective manner.

## The Leonard Street School

Probably the institution which has done more than any other for the Italian colony in an educational way is the school on Leonard Street, devoted exclusively to Italians and maintained by the Children's Aid Society. This school, with its faithful body of teachers, has exerted a strong influence upon the Italian colony. The day sessions are conducted precisely along public school lines, mainly for children who do not enter the public schools for a variety of reasons. A night school is conducted in the same building, which aims primarily at giving instruction in the English language. There is an average attendance of men and boys at these classes of about three hundred. Besides this, there is a department of Italian instruction. A teacher who has this work in charge is supported by the Italian government. The building is also used for social purposes, and entertainments are held during the winter every Friday evening.

As an evidence of the esteem felt by Italians who have come under the influence of this school, a movement is now on foot among them to secure funds — $3,000 has already been raised — for the establishment of a similar school for the Italians in "Little Italy".

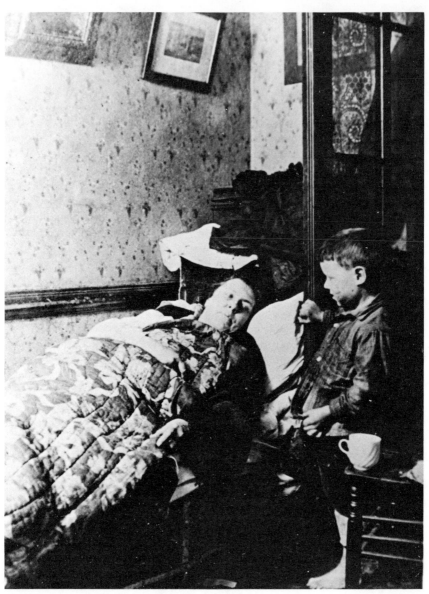

New York City tenement, ca. 1910.

# 19

# The Italian and Public Health[1]

ROCCO BRINDISI, M.D.[2]

The Italian immigrants, on account of moral and social faults rightly or wrongly attributed to them, have been generally characterized as undesirable; but everybody seems to be willing to recognize that they are gifted with at least two virtues: sobriety and endurance in performing the hardest kind of work. The first quality is an efficient factor of health, the other is a sure sign of psychical and physical vigor.

The major part of our immigration is made up of sturdy mountaineers of the southern Apennines inured to the most laborious agricultural work. The American immigration law, by excluding the weak and the old, has raised the physical standard of the immigrants. So it is that the Italian laborers in this country show a small percentage of disease and a still smaller one of mortality. This, however, is less true in regard to the second generation, whose vitality is impaired, principally by the unsanitary conditions in which they are forced to live.

In 1902, there were in Boston 641 deaths among the Italians. Of the deceased, 175 were born in Italy, and 466 were born in America of Italian parents. The total figures represent 6 per cent of the total number of deaths in the city of Boston and 11.43 per thousand of the population. This rate of mortality is lower than that of any other nationality except the Russians.

The largest percentage of sickness is furnished by the newcomers among the men, and by the women and the children.

The newcomers, especially when, as commonly happens, they land in the early spring, pay their tribute to acclimation by contracting rheumatic and

1. *Charities*, Vol. 12, 1904. Pp. 483-486.                    2. Boston.

respiratory diseases, such as rheumatism, bronchitis, pneumonia, pleuritis; but fortunately the proportion of deaths is moderate, owing to the strong constitution, the youth and the temperate habits of the patients.

The Italian women here are forced to change entirely their mode of living. From the active rural life in the open air they are plunged at once into a life of relative inactivity and seclusion, and consequently become more or less liable to general impairment of the organic functions. They are frequently affected with dysmenorrhea, dyspepsia, anemia, clorosis and kindred diseases; and their impaired physical condition has an injurious effect on the children, who contribute largely to the mortality.

Besides the maternal influence, improper nursing and insufficiency of fresh air and light are responsible for the great number of ailments and deaths among the Italian children. Rickets and tuberculosis are the most frequent general diseases. Bronchitis, broncho-pneumonia and pneumonia usually affect them in winter and intermediate seasons, while in the hot weather the dreadful host of the so-called summer complaints, from the irritative gastro-enteritis to the deadly cholera infantum, storms and ravages the Italo-American breed.

In substance it can be safely said that the morbidity, like the mortality, is larger among the children of the immigrants than among the immigrants themselves.

The following table shows plainly this disproportion of deaths in Boston during the calendar year 1902, as reported to the local board of health.

| Cause of Death | Born in Italy | Born in the United States |
|---|---|---|
| Typhoid fever | 6 | 12 |
| Tubercle of meninges | 2 | 15 |
| Tubercle of lungs | 18 | 25 |
| Meningitis simple | 6 | 30 |
| Meningitis cerebro-spinal | 7 | 20 |
| Bronchitis acute | 1 | 30 |
| Broncho-pneumonia | 7 | 44 |
| Pneumonia | 11 | 44 |
| Diarrhoea and enteritis | 1 | 34 |
| Nephritis acute | 9 | 12 |
| Congenital debility | 1 | 28 |

A word may be said here of the veneral diseases and alcoholism among the Italians.

It is a general opinion that the genital affections are very frequent among our immigrants, owing to the promiscuous and crowded conditions of their life. I am able to state, however, though I cannot prove my statement with statistics, that in the same class of people of other nationalities such diseases are not less frequent.

In one hundred Italian males examined and treated by me for different infirmities, during the month of December last, I find only seventeen cases of veneral diseases. It is to be noticed that I have taken into account only the males, as the most exposed to the contagion, and have purposely chosen the month of December, which is the time when our laborers are idle and provided with more or less money earned during the preceding seasons.

As everyone can see, this is not a large proportion by any means,[3] and there is reason to hope that the changed character of our immigration will still reduce the percentage. In 1895, states Dr. Bushee,[4] the excess of males in the Italian population of Boston amounted to 1,592. This inequality of sexes undoubtedly had an important bearing on their mortality; but since then the men have developed the tendency to call their families here and settle with them permanently or for a long period of time, with the consequence of considerable elevation of the moral standard and decrease in the number of loathsome diseases and alcoholics.

Of alcoholism, I need say very little, inasmuch as it is very rare among our people. Of the eighty-eight who died in Boston from alcoholism in the year 1902, none were Italian. During March of this year, 59 Italians were arrested by the police of Division 1, which is in the heart of the Italian quarter, and of these only 9 were for drunkenness. It is worthy of note that 5 were arrested on the eighteenth, that is, between St. Patrick's Day and St. Joseph's, which shows that they are not habitual drunkards, but go on an occasional spree on holidays. Lieutenant Rosatto, to whom I am indebted for the above information, states that during his long service of seventeen years in that station not one Italian woman was arrested for drunkenness.

The exceptionally numerous saloons in the North End are generally patronized by non-residents coming from other quarters of the city and suburbs. This excessive number of drinking places, besides lowering the moral tone of this section of the city, in which is located the Italian colony, increases the opportunity for the residents to indulge in alcoholic beverages. So it happens that some Italians become addicted to beer and hard liquors in preference to the light and rather harmless red wines, to which they were accustomed in the old country.

3. The death rate from veneral diseases among persons under forty-five years of age in the registration area of the United States in 1900 was higher for the Italians than for any other element of the white population; among persons of forty-five and over the Italians ranked fourth. —Ed.

4. F. A. Bushee, Ph.D., *Ethnic Factors of the Population of Boston.*

## A Threefold Problem

The problem that confronts the student of the hygienic and sanitary conditions of Italians living in the large cities of the United States is threefold, and involves the consideration of the dwelling-houses, the food and the race traditions. Let us examine briefly these three aspects of the important problem, and see where the faults are and how they can be possibly mended.

## Houses

The Italian immigrants have a tendency to live together in one section of the city, with the result that they transform it into a characteristic community, which is given the name of "Little Italy". The "Little Italy" of Boston is in the historic North End, which, although over a century ago the most aristocratic quarter of the city, is now composed of the oldest and most dilapidated buildings, and of the cheapest modern tenement-houses, ill ventilated, poorly lighted and scantily provided with modern sanitary improvements.

"In some of the principal streets of the North End", writes Dr. Bushee, "as well as in the smaller tenements of the back alleys, Italians live in a more crowded manner than any other people in the city. In 1891, when the tenement-house census of Boston was taken, two precincts of the North End occupied almost exclusively by Italians contained 259 families, or more than one-fourth of the total population, who were living on an average of two persons to a room; and 154 of the families were occupying single rooms. The average number of persons to a room for the two precincts was 1.41. Since that time the board of health has ordered vacated some of the less sanitary of these houses, and has improved the condition of others; in 1895, however, the average density of the population for the whole ward and probably also for the precincts was found to have increased somewhat, and in 1899 individual cases of crowding were discovered, which were worse than those reported in 1891. A partial census of another part of the North End, taken in 1898, shows comparatively little change in the average density of the population. In 1891 the average number of persons to a room was found to be 1.37 and in 1898, 1.39."

This gives an idea of how the Italians crowd together in the houses of the North End; but it is due them to say that the conditions described are now somewhat improved, as stated in the latest publication of the South End House, *Americans in Process:* "Many of the Italians are beginning to seek something better. They are now, in considerable numbers, moving into the more desirable tenements to the west of Hanover Street; and some families, especially of the second generation, are taking a more significant step in detaching themselves from the colony and settling amid pleasanter surroundings."

I know many Italian families in Winthrop, South Boston and Dorchester, living in their own houses, clean and comfortable. This is the most convincing proof that the much-slandered Italians, as well as any other people, are capable of bettering themselves.

Dr. S. H. Durgin, the chairman of the Boston Board of Health, writes me: "In a general way I would say that, while the Italians are prone to overcrowding, they are in other respects found to be in a fair sanitary condition, and decidedly improving from year to year in our city."

The progressive improvement of the sanitary conditions of the North End is largely due to vigilance of the Board of Health which, especially in the last decade, has caused the demolition and partial reconstruction of many bad tenement-houses. Undoubtedly the total destruction of all and every building would be the most efficacious means of inducing the inhabitants to scatter themselves in the rest of the city and suburbs; but such radical treatment being impossible, for obvious reasons, it is to be expected that the work will be gradually performed by the combined efforts of the health authorities and the more progressive Italians. There is already a North End Improvement Association, which is looking toward the betterment of the sanitary conditions of this quarter, and perhaps the appointment of Italian health inspectors, chosen among competent and honest young men, would contribute to the final success.

## Foods

Many an American, taking as standard of dietetics his own mode of living, assumes that the Italians feed themselves poorly, because they do not eat a sufficient quantity of meat. This is a mistake. The Italians in Boston — and I think the same may be said of all the large cities of the United States — eat much more meat than they used to consume in the old country, and still suffer immensely more from stomach troubles here than they did in Italy. There is no physiological law which determines how much meat a man must eat, in order that his organism may be kept in good running order. A difference exists between individuals, and a still wider one between peoples and races on account of differences in climates, habits and constitutions. People of the same nationality may differ in their dietetics according to the different latitudes. The northern Italians, for instance, eat more meat and less vegetables than the southerners. Many times I have cured dyspepsia, constipation, or more serious digestive ailments, by simply reducing the quantity of meat and increasing the proportion of vegetables in the menu.

The fact that it is the Italians who have introduced in the American kitchens the dandelions, the celeries, the fennels and many other greens, and that they have increased the use of fruits in this country, shows their natural taste — which is a natural need — for these edibles, a greater abundance of which would be a real blessing to all. "The Italians have in fact", to quote again from *Americans in Process*, "created a wholesome appetite for fruit among the mass of the people...Even the newest immigrant, with his push-cart, makes his wares attractive, and unwittingly acts as the dietetic missionary of the back streets throughout the city."

It is true that there are Italians who, rather from a mistaken spirit of economy than from lack of means, feed themselves poorly; but their number is very small. The old shame of rummaging the garbage barrels in search of decayed food is gradually disappearing, owing to the general sentiment of reprobation among the Italians, which I am confident will in the near future sweep away definitely this degrading habit.

I have already said that the Italians here learn to drink beer and hard liquors, which were utterly unknown to them in Italy. Fortunately, the abuse of these intoxicants is limited, and the number of drunkards among our immigrants is daily decreasing, owing to the moral effect of family life. Another important cause of temperance is, in my opinion, the light red wine which the Italians manufacture for their own use.

*Race Traditions*

The Italians, like all the peoples with ancient habits and traditions, cling to many prejudices and superstitions, which often hamper those who work with them.

Among these prejudices, I will quote the horror they generally have for hospitals. Many of them still hold the opinion that hospitals are strictly devoted to the treatment of destitute patients left to the mercy of heartless physicians. In the majority of cases, to advise an Italian patient to enter a hospital arouses the hostility of the patient and his family.

Superstition, aided by ignorance, frequently makes them cheerfully submit to the extortions of the many professional swindlers and dupers. Charms, amulets, ex-votos, oftentimes defeat hygiene and baffle the efforts of the health authorities and the physician. It is to be noticed, however, that no prejudices are to be found among the educated Italians. The Italian mind, when unbiased and untrammeled by ignorance and superstition, is wide open to the reception of truth. And it is, in my opinion, education alone, that most powerful factor in the progress of humanity, which will accomplish the work of regeneration among the Italian immigrants. It is education, through the public institutions and the missionary work of the physicians, that will bring the principles of hygiene and their practical benefits into the Italian homes, while waiting for the more substantial fruits of the schools.

There is not the slightest doubt in my mind that the rising generation of our Italians will be, in regard to sanitary conditions, on the same level with the American people.

# 20

# Tuberculosis and the Italians in the United States[1]

Antonio Stella, M.D.[2]

In spite of the traditional renown of Italy as the paradise of Europe and one of the most healthful countries on earth, notwithstanding the fact that she really yields less victims annually to consumption than any other nation on the continent under similar demographic conditions, it is an undoubted fact, and a truth sadly brought daily to the attention of physicians, social workers, and others in a position to know, that tuberculosis is very prevalent among the Italians emigrated to these shores.

To have an idea of the alarming frequency of consumption among Italians, especially in the large cities of the Union, one must not look for exact information to the records of the local boards of health and the registry of vital statistics; they are, for the very reason of the mobility of the Italian emigration, very fallacious, and show a low figure; but one must follow the Italian population as it moves in the tenement districts; study them closely in their daily struggle for air and space; see them in the daytime crowded in sweat-shops and factories; at night heaped together in dark windowless rooms; then visit the hospitals' dispensaries; and finally watch the out-going steamships, and count the wan emaciated forms, with glistening eyes and racking cough that return to their native land with a hope of recuperating health, but oftentimes only to find a quicker death.

This desire and tendency on the part of all Italians, whether rich or poor, to go back to their homes as soon as informed that they are affected with phthisis, is the chief cause of the discrepancy between the *actual high* number of consumptives existing among the Italians in the United States and the

1. *Charities*, Vol. 12, 1904. Pp. 486-489.  2. New York City.

*official low* figures of the various health boards.

In fact, in a recent table of the New York Health Department as to the mortality from consumption among the different nationalities between the ages of fifteen and forty-five years, we find that the Italians occupy only the tenth place in the list, losing but 149.9 per 10,000 population, as against 548.4 and 428.0 lost, respectively, by the negroes and the Irish, who lead the way. On the contrary, Italians come second in the table, where the mortality is considered below the fifteenth year of life (children generally being allowed to die here); and the same high percentage would certainly be found for the adult generation, were the statistics arranged not according to the death-rate, but according to the infection-rate, which is simply appalling.

From some tenements in Elizabeth and Mulberry Street, there have been as many as twelve and fifteen cases of consumption reported to the Board of Health since 1894.[3] But how many were *never* reported? How many went back to Italy? How many moved away to other districts?

My personal experience with some of the houses in that particular neighborhood is that the average has been not less than thirty or forty cases of infection for each tenement yearly, the element of house-infection being so great. I remember some rear houses in Elizabeth Street, and one in Mott Street, now torn down, through the operations of the new tenement law, that yielded as many as twenty-five cases in the course of a year to my personal knowledge alone.

And how could it be otherwise?

### The Causes in Back of the Appalling Infection Rate

When we consider the infectious character of tuberculosis on the one side, and the overcrowded and filthy conditions of some tenements on the other, where a population of men, women and children is herded together at the rate of eight and ten in every three rooms (in some "flats" on Elizabeth Street this number can often be doubled), a population, besides, made up chiefly of agriculturists, fresh yet from the sunny hills and green valleys of Tuscany and Sicily, abruptly thrown into unnatural abodes and dark sweat-shops — a population, at that, over-worked, underfed, poorly clad, curbed with all the worries and anxieties of the morrow, and only free, thank God! — from the worst ally of consumption — alcoholism — where could the Koch bacillus find victims more prepared, where a soil more fertile than among such surroundings?

We know now-a-days that the penetration of a pathogenic germ into our system is not sufficient to cause a disease. It must find our body in a state of

3. See diagram, "Italian Quarter", *Handbook on the Prevention of Tuberculosis*, published by the New York Charity Organization Society, p. 90.

temporary paralysis of all its natural defenses, to be able to give rise to certain morbid processes, the evolution of which constitutes a disease.

No one will deny that the integrity of our respiratory organs depends chiefly on the quantity and quality of air we breathe. Every individual in normal condition should have at least 35 cubic meters of air as it is reckoned for hospitals, and the air we breathe in should not contain more than one per cent of all the expired air (Rubner). In many tenements, on account of the overcrowding, the quantity of air left for each person is reduced to three or four cubic meters, and the expired air in the sleeping-rooms represents one-half or one-sixth of all the air available. We can well say, then, that the atmosphere of those places is largely made up of the emanations from the bodies of the various persons living together.

What deleterious effect on the lungs and on the system in general the sojourn and sleep in these rooms must have, is beyond all calculation. The haematosis and oxygenation are first affected, and then appears that train of obscure and insidious symptoms (persistent anaemia, progressive fatigue, emaciation, etc.), which represent the ante-tubercular stage, and actually prepare the ground for the bacillary invasion.

Those that feel this change most keenly, and fall victims to tuberculosis with marked rapidity, are not the second generation of immigrants, as generally believed, but the very first arrivals, especially those coming from the rural districts of Italy, unaccustomed yet to the poisoned atmosphere of city life.

## The Indoor Cramp of an Outdoor Race

Among those — and they are the large majority — who seek work in factories and shops, instead of pursuing their natural occupations in the open air, the stigmata of progressive physiological deterioration and general low vitality are most apparent. Six months of life in the tenements are sufficient to turn the sturdy youth from Calabria, the brawny fisherman of Sicily, the robust women from Abruzzi and Basilicata, into the pale, flabby, undersized creatures we see, dragging along the streets of New York and Chicago, such a painful contrast to the native population! Six months more of this gradual deterioration, and the soil for the bacillus tuberculosis is amply prepared.

For the Italians, though, besides the abrupt passage from rural to urban life, and the unsanitary housing accommodatiions, which stand among the foremost influences responsible for the spread of tuberculosis among them, another potent factor must be mentioned, and this refers to certain trades and occupations, that are especially favored by our countrymen, and which may well be called phthisiogenic, on account of the important role they play in the development of tuberculosis.

Suffice it here to mention the rag-sorters, sweepers, bootblacks, hotel cleaners, continually exposed to the inhalation of dust contaminated with dried tubercular sputum; the plasterers, marble and stone cutters, cigar makers, printers, pressmen, upholsterers, cabinet makers, barbers, tailors, brass and glass workers, who all stand near the head of the list in the mortality from consumption, and among whom we find thousands of our Italian immigrants.

In many of those occupations, besides the direct irritation to the bronchial mucous membrane from the inhalation of dust, the work itself requires a sitting position (cigar makers, tailors), in which the chest is bent forward, and thus prevents the expansion of the lungs, and directly interferes with the proper aeration of the pulmonary apices.

*The Women Workers*

Still worse is the condition where the sweat-shop system flourishes at home, either as extra work, done late in the night, by young men and women already exhausted by ten hours of work in a crowded factory, or as a regular practice, by poor housewives, desirous of adding to their husbands' earnings.

Words can hardly describe the pathetic misery of these Italian women, compelled to sew two or three dozen of pants for forty cents, using up their last spark of energy to make life better, when in fact they only accomplish their self-destruction. For their health is usually already drained by a too-productive maternity and periods of prolonged lactation; they live on a deficient, if not actually insufficient, diet; they sleep in dark, damp holes, without sunshine and light, and have already had enough to exhaust them, with the raising of a large family and the strain of hard housework.

This practice explains in a measure the somewhat higher death-rate from phthisis of Italian women than men, especially among Sicilians, and the fact that we often find among them consumption in the quick form, that is, miliary tuberculosis of the sub-acute or the very acute type, which, rather than a clinical rarity, is of quite common occurrence in this class of patients.

And this high susceptibility is not due to any inherent lack of vitality in the race. The Italians otherwise show the most wonderful elements of resistance and recuperation, as may be seen in the favorable manner they react to surgical operations, extreme temperatures, and all sorts of trials. Nor is it dependent upon any individual hereditary predisposition, for while the younger generation, emigrated to America, die rapidly, their parents at home live to a surprising old age. Their rapid fall is due solely to an ensemble of deleterious causes, acting simultaneously, steadily and forcibly on their constitution, and in a manner so complete, that the fertilization of the ubiquitous Koch bacillus must result of necessity.

The pulmonary form, however, while by far the most prevalent, is not the only manifestation of tuberculosis among the Italians in the United States. Tuberculosis of the peritoneum and intestines, of the bones and glands, is seen very frequently among adults, in contrast with the common experience elsewhere that it is chiefly prevalent in early life; in the same way you will hear from physicians of large hospital practice, that many obscure conditions in the pelvis and adnexa, in the brain, kidney and other internal organs, occurring among Italians, prove at the pathological investigation to be tubercular, when everything else would have pointed to a different cause.

In view of these facts and the present state of our emigration, we must then consider the prevalence of tuberculosis among Italians as a function of their special economic and social conditions in their new environment, and if any remedies can be expected in the future to stop the spread of the scourge among them, they must be found in the betterment of those conditions and a thorough change of their present aspirations.

The statistics show that the higher we move up in the social scale, the lower the mortality from consumption; or as Gebhard puts it, "the death-rate from tuberculosis among the various classes, in large cities, is in inverse ratio to their individual income". This inequality of fortune in our modern society plays really the most important role in the spread of tuberculosis, and as long as present conditions prevail, we shall always find tuberculosis to be "the disease of the masses" par excellence, and the inseparable ally of poverty.

Now every one knows that the Italians in this country represent almost exclusively the working class, and in some quarters the very poor class. To raise them to a higher social level, economically speaking, besides being a matter of slow evolution, implies a problem of such magnitude and such distant realization at the present, that we can only hint at it in passing by, and leave the social workers and economists the full discussion of it.

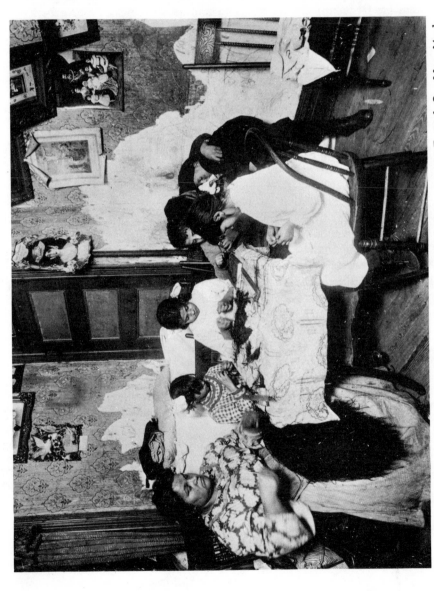

Mrs. Mary Mauro and family working on feathers in their home at 309 E. 11th St., New York

# 21

# Some Aspects of Italian Housing and Social Conditions in Philadelphia[1]

EMILY WAYLAND DINWIDDIE [2]

Philadelphia's "Little Italy" is one of the most picturesque sections of the city. For about thirty-five blocks the Italians are closely packed together. One can walk the streets for considerable distances without hearing a word of English. The black-eyed children rolling and tumbling together, the gaily colored dresses of the women and the crowds of street vendors all give the neighborhood a wholly foreign appearance. The rag shops and macaroni factories are an important feature of the district.

An overwhelming majority of Italians was found in one block in which every house was visited. Classed according to the nativity of the father, or of the mother where the father was dead, of the 366 families here 358 were Italian; 4 were Russian; 2 American; 1 German; and 1 Swiss. The Russian and German families were all Jewish.

The principal occupation of the heads of families, given in the order of the number of persons engaged in each, were those of laborers, shopkeepers, rag-pickers or rag-dealers, tailors or engaged in tailoring trades, peddlers and vendors, unskilled employees in factories and stores, barbers, street cleaners, cobblers and shoemakers, and musicians.

1. *Charities*, Vol. 12, 1904. Pp. 490-493.
2. As an inspector of the New York Tenement House Department, Miss Dinwiddie was granted a year's leave of absence, by former Commissioner Robert DeForest to make an investigation of housing conditions in Philadelphia for the Octavia Hill Association. The investigation was begun last fall and has been carried forward with thoroughness. The need for remedial action has been shown to be pressing, and an energetic housing campaign is about to be inaugurated. One of the neighborhoods which came under Miss Dinwiddie's detailed study is inhabited largely by Italians, and her description of conditions found there, written for *Charities*, is the first publication of the results of her investigation.

Of the special work carried on within the apartments rag-picking took the lead. Next came tailoring and cobbling and last scissors sharpening and umbrella mending.

Though not the subject of special study, some general information in regard to amusements was gathered. Gambling in various forms was frequently seen. Social drinking in the homes was not uncommon. A large proportion of the houses had casks or barrels of wine in the cellars. Drinking in the saloons seemed less frequent. Of the 180 buildings of every kind in the block investigated, two were saloons. This did not seem a large proportion of the total of eighty-one stores and places of business. The Italian marionette theatre is crowded every night with men and boys, who hang in breathless attention upon the continued stories acted there from evening to evening. In spite of the reeking tobacco smoke, the jammed and uncomfortable condition of the audience and the absence of women in the assembly, a more orderly or better disposed gathering could scarcely be found. The church festivals are also attended by great crowds and form a striking part of the neighborhood life.

Aside from the character of the population the district itself is full of interest. Like most of the older parts of the city it is intersected by small alleys in such a way that the interiors of the blocks are covered over with numbers of rear houses. Of the 167 occupied dwellings visited in the block previously spoken of, seventy-three were rear buildings. Where back yards are covered over in this way the space left for light and air is sometimes dangerously small. One row of seven alley houses, back to back with another row so that all ventilation from the rear was cut off, received such light and ventilation as it had from a court, four feet three inches wide, with buildings on the opposite side extending almost the entire length of the court. The occupants of these houses were obliged to keep lamps burning all day.

## Overcrowding and its Results

That overcrowding by land areas is much greater here than in other parts of the city is proved by the census statistics, which show that the Second, Third and Fourth wards, within which nearly all the Italian district lies, contain more than one-sixteenth of the total population of the city in less than one one-hundred and fiftieth of the area.

Overcrowding per room, however, is a much more serious evil than overcrowding by numbers of persons to the acre. In one tenement-house 30 Italian families, 123 persons, were living in 34 rooms. Of 366 families visited considerably more than one-fourth had only one room each. It is difficult to imagine what this means without having seen life under such conditions. In some cases as many as seven persons cook, eat and sleep in one room.

Except in freezing weather the members of the family who are able to do so stay out of doors until midnight because the rooms are unendurable. Cleanliness is impossible and decency is utterly disregarded.

Much of the overcrowding is due to the common practice of taking lodgers, and the fact that the adult occupants of the rooms are often not related to each other in any way makes the promiscuous herding together even worse in its influence upon morals than in its effect on health. There was difficulty in ascertaining the separate rental of the living quarters of each family visited, as some rented a shop and several living rooms together and could not give a clear account of the proportion paid for each. Definite statistics were obtained in regard to 335 families. Of these 34 owned their living quarters, 2 occupied their apartments rent free in return for janitor's services, 16 families stated that they paid no regular rent, being relatives of the owner or sub-landlord of the house. Of the remainder 26 were sub-landlords, leasing entire houses, occupying one apartment and subletting others; 75 rented and occupied whole houses used solely as dwellings; and 182 had each a separate apartment in a house tenanted by two or more families.

The average monthly rent of a house used solely as a dwelling for one family was $7.99. The average rent for a single apartment in a house occupied by two or more families was $5.51. It will be seen that the rent per apartment is less in the houses containing several families than in the one family buildings. The rent per room, however, is greater in the houses occupied by several families. In these the average is $3.33 per room, as opposed to $2.28 in the one family dwellings. The reason for this is in the fact that the great majority of single family houses are rear buildings with small rooms and without water in the house or conveniences of any kind, while the building having two or more families are usually on the street, have larger rooms and are better fitted up. This accounts for the greater per room rent in the latter. The smaller rent per apartment is because of the smaller number of rooms occupied by the families in these houses.

The figures given above take no account of the amount of rent repaid by lodgers within the apartments, doing no independent housekeeping. The number of these is very large, as has been previously stated.

*Cellars and Their Inhabitants*

Lack of space not infrequently leads to the use of cellars for living purposes. One cellar kitchen seen lacked only a few inches of being entirely below ground and had no ventilation except by two doors. The door which communicated directly with the outer air, the tenants informed me, was kept closed and fastened up during the entire winter. The filthiest room I visited in the district was a cellar bedroom which the family above let to lodgers for ten cents a night.

Many of the cellars which were not inhabited were in an unhealthful condition. One had a stream of considerable size flowing through the middle from a broken water pipe in the yard. It had worn a fairly deep channel in the earth floor and the tenants said that it had been pouring through for over a month. This cellar, however, was less offensive than others, where the leakage consisted of foul water and sewage instead of fresh water.

As if the human occupants of the house did not furnish sufficient life, some of the families kept fowls or animals of one kind or another. During a visit to one house the door from the inside cellar steps was pushed open and a goat stalked in to join the family circle, having apparently grown weary of the dark cellar. The worst case was that of a slaughter house and dwelling in one building. About 30 sheep were kept on the second floor, which was reached by an inclined plane. Downstairs a room was used for slaughtering and about one hundred sheep were killed every Saturday besides numbers every day. The butcher and his wife lived in the house and had a kitchen on the ground floor. This was in a closely built up block with houses adjoining on every side.

Lack of cleanliness in the rooms was not surprisingly bad in view of the overcrowding and the inadequate water supply. It was frequently the case that the living rooms and especially the bedrooms were much cleaner than the halls, cellars and yards.

The insufficient water supply would excuse much. I have found eleven families, having as sole water supply one court hydrant for the whole number. Ten other families used another hydrant in common. Considerably less than one-third of the Italian families visited had exclusive use of one or more water fixtures each. In the block specially investigated, counting in all fixtures from which water could be drawn — yard hydrants, sinks, baths, stationary tubs and basins — there were in all 237 fixtures for 366 families and 81 stores and places of business.

The number of baths was of course small, yet 17 out of 167 houses had one each. For the whole block the average was one bath for each 22 families, 102 persons to a tub. Five of the tubs were said not to be used for bathing purposes and three more were reported to be so used only in summer. This appeared to be due to their location and condition rather than to lack of appreciation on the part of the tenants. One tub, for example, was in the middle of a large bedroom, without enclosure of any kind. In another case a family of eight had one room and a bath. They used the bath compartment as a sleeping room, the tub serving as a sink. The three tubs used only in summer were in extension rooms which were extremely cold, so that the pipes froze in winter.

*Tenements and Rear Houses*

No attempt to describe conditions found in the district would be complete without some special notice of the evils of the tenements and rear houses. It is often said that Philadelphia has no tenement-house problem, yet of 167 dwellings in one block, forty-one, or nearly one-fourth, were each occupied by three or more families doing cooking on the premises and so came under the legal definition of a tenement. These tenement-houses are nearly all buildings apparently intended for private residences but used without alteration or with only slight changes for three or more families. The families in most cases have no fire protection. They are overcrowded. They have miserably inadequate sanitary accommodations of every kind. There is very little oversight. A special janitor or housekeeper is almost unknown.

In the rear houses evils of a slightly different kind are found. The buildings are small, usually containing only three tiny rooms. As many houses as possible are crowded together on the lots so that a large proportion have no yard space at the rear or side. The houses which have yards usually have to throw them open to the entire court because they contain the hydrants or other accommodations for all the buildings. Frequently they have only surface drainage and where they are defectively paved and graded, slops and filth remain stagnant under the windows of the buildings. One row of rear houses has already been spoken of as containing seven buildings back to back with another row and getting all their light and air from a space in front, four feet three inches wide. This same row had one hydrant for all the houses, but last fall the hydrant got out of order and the water supply was cut off, remaining cut off for several months, during which time all the tenants went to a neighboring house to borrow water. The occupants of most of the houses were very neat and kept their rooms clean, but the alley was filthy. It received the drainage from a stable at one side and a tenement at the end, so that the gutter, which occupied a large part of the passageway, was constantly foul.

Thus far I have spoken of the bad conditions found, but it must not be thought that the picture is altogether dark. Some comfortable houses, equipped with modern conveniences and occupied by one family each, were seen. A large proportion of the worst houses were occupied by recent immigrants who had not had time to work their way up to living in more expensive dwellings and did not know where to seek redress for the discomforts they suffered from in their present quarters, if they knew or desired anything better.

Clam seller in Mulberry Bend, New York, ca. 1900/10.

# 22

# A Transplanted Birthright: The Development of the Second Generation of Italians in an American Environment[1]

LILIAN BRANDT

"Dear and most gracious Signora A____", wrote Giulio, aged twelve, to his teacher in an industrial school when she asked for letters containing certain information. "My father has been two years in America, and he follows the trade of carpenter, and...he would like to make of me an honest, industrious boy, with, at the same time, a trade better than his, and he sends me to school so that when I am grown I may be an educated man and useful to others.

Later I wish to make machines for factories, and thus to have better wages than others.

Having nothing more to say I kiss my hand to you and assure you that I am

Your

Giulio."

This letter is typical. Its grace and courtesy, and the ambition it reveals, are characteristic of the Italian children in America. The first two qualities are an inheritance that has come down to them through the centuries; the third is developed, or at least given a chance for expression, by American conditions.

Italian children, whether born in Italy or here, find America much to their taste. They are prompt to adapt themselves to the freedom of the new country and use all the facilities at their disposal for rising to a higher economic level than their parents. Modification of their names is one of the familiar external evidences of a disposition to become truly American, as it is also an example of the American tendency to make all things conform to

1. *Charities*, Vol. 12, 1904. Pp. 494-499.

our own ways. The transformation of Vincenzo Campobello to Jim Campbell, the general dropping of vowels and consequent condensation, are inevitable, and are but a repetition of the changes that occurred when Goth and Roman began to live together or when the Normans settled in England. But because the American element which furnishes standards for the Italians is usually of Irish origin, and because the Italian is actuated by a deeper motive than mere convenience, the names of Patrick O'Neill and Mike Mahoney are frequently borne by olive-skinned Sicilian boys; and the soft-eyed Lucia, not yet a year from Naples, may be heard to say, "Faith an' I won't then!" with the true Celtic inflection, thus bearing unconscious testimony to the assimilating properties of the older and better established elements of the population. The boy or girl is seldom willing to go back to Italy. Mr. Davenport, in his letters to the Brooklyn *Eagle*, has described the misfits arising from the return of New York City public school products to an Italian village. In their enthusiasm for America, the children too often develop a tendency to despise the ways of their fathers and lose their love of Italy and their pride in being Italians. Too often, also, their sudden plunge into unaccustomed freedom has, as is ever the case, its evil results. The removal of the old restraints, whether of tradition or of law, before the self-governing power has been developed, is apt to produce an intoxication which makes the transition period trying to all concerned. In the case of the Italians, it is especially trying to the parents, in American tenement neighborhoods, who are completely at a loss as to how to deal with their children when they are mischievous or unruly.

They are almost equally disturbed at assertions of independence which are, to American minds, quite legitimate. They wish to keep the children, and particularly the girls, close at home, and think them "wild" if they show any desire to get out of the crowded rooms and onto the street. Mothers do not want their daughters to go to evening schools. "Why should she learn to write?" asked one of them, "she'd only write to her 'fellas'." The impossibility, under the conditions of New York life, of bringing up children according to traditional ideas of what is proper, is responsible for a large part of the eagerness with which Italian parents seek to patronize institutions for children.

The institution to them is not only a *collegio*, where good instruction is thoughtfully provided by an interested public, but it is also too often a place where the child will be kept off the streets, broken of his "wild" ways, and properly cared for until he arrives at an age of self-support.

### Economic Aspirations

The most striking manifestation of the American spirit is, perhaps, found in the economic aspirations of the children. They are rarely content to remain at their fathers' level. The ambition which in Italy would have been kept dormant by social traditions, is roused in America by the all-pervasive and generally effective idea of "getting ahead". It is the exception if the son of the immigrant who "works at shovel" or "goes with the hod" grows up to use the same tool. If the son of a bootblack chooses that profession, it is generally found that, while his father carried a kit, his idea is to advance at least to the dignity of a chair, which represents a certain amount of capital invested and a comparatively stable business. Another common instance of advancement by this evolutionary process is from fruit-peddling with a push-cart or even a basket, to the proprietorship of a corner stand. Children going out from the higher grades of the public schools generally hope for clerical positions; failing that, they choose factory work.

The four Italian schools of the Children's Aid Society in New York represent probably the poorest part of the Italian population of the city — the part with the least natural opportunity. The older children in these schools were asked, a few weeks ago, to write letters to their teachers, telling them what they would like to "be" when they grew up. As a result of this the writer has authentic records of the economic ideals of 143 Italian children between the ages of nine and fourteen. Some of them have been in America only a few months; others were born here: all are from families in which the struggle for daily existence is not uniformly successful. The fathers of these children are tailors, hod-carriers, laborers, street-cleaners, boot-blacks, shoemakers, stone-cutters, peddlers, bricklayers, carpenters, rag-pickers, macaroni and candy makers, and bar-cleaners, with single representatives of such better-paid occupations as butcher, grocer, policeman and postman.

## The Boys and Their Ambitions

Of the 143 children, sixty-six are boys and seventy-seven are girls. Four of the boys were undecided about the career they would choose and one pathetically confided, "My papa used to work in a laundry...He does not work for a long time because he is sick. When I can work I will do any work I can get because I have to help mamma because papa is sick."

Among the other sixty-one, ten of the younger boys elect to follow their fathers' calling. In two cases the father's occupation is not indicated in any way. The other forty-nine are all looking forward to something which seems to them higher. Four, whose fathers are a hod-carrier, a tailor, a bricklayer, and a macaroni maker, would be doctors, one adding confidently: "And I will learn very hard, for I like to be a good doctor, and I will make a lot of money, and I will come to be a rich man, and I will give my mother some money to buy a machine". Two, son of a street-cleaner and son of a tailor, propose to be lawyers. One wants to be a "music man and play mandolin and all the new songs, and play guitar"; another will be an artist; another, the heir of a day-laborer, says, "I am going to write books and people will say I am a smart man". One, whose father "goes all over with a street piano", hopes to "write in an office, write down numbers and count them up and write names". To "write in a bank" is the goal of another. A shoemaker's son aspires to be a "printer man, to printer the papers to sell — the *Journal*, the *Sun*, the *World*, the *Telegram*, the *Globe*, the *Mail and Express*, and lots of other papers, and our Italian *Bolletino della Sera*, that's the best work that I could do".

A fourteen-year-old, whose home is one of the most insanitary tenements of the city, and whose father is a peddler, writes, "If fortune favors me I shall continue my studies". The occupations of tailor, carpenter, bookkeeper, engineer, butcher, messenger, druggist, elevator-runner, truck-driver and store-keeper all have votaries. Seven of the boys indicate definitely that their choice is determined by the desire to "make a lot of money". A few, however, are actuated rather by pure love of glory or adventure; these are looking forward to being a policeman, a fireman (who will "blow out the fire") or even a soldier. Several show that they esteem respect and appreciation beyond gain, for they mean "to be called smart". An interesting declaration is this: "My father is a grocery, and I am going to be a farmer". Perhaps the most dramatic choice is that of twelve-year-old Luigi. His father is a coat presser, but Luigi spurns the colorless, hateful drudgery of the tailor shop, and will have a life of interest and excitement for he "would like to be a horso racing".

## The Girls and Their Ideals

The seventy-seven girls show less variety and less individuality. The Italian girl, even more than the average girl, expects to be occupied, and at an earlier age than the average girl, with the care of her own household. Whatever her expectations, however, every girl indicates some one occupation as her choice. Forty-seven wish to be dressmakers and thirteen give their teachers the sincerest testimony of admiration by choosing that profession. Several of the would-be teachers explain that they will teach the children to sew, and one justifies her choice by the comment, "And then I will do as I please". Two would like to work in a candy shop, two in a tobacco shop, two would be hairdressers, two milliners, two "grocer girls". "My father shines", wrote one of these, "but I want to be a grocer girl". Another "would like to be a sister of the church", and the rest are attracted by the occupations of nurse, box-maker, "news-carrier", typewriter, cash girl, and "joiner" — whatever that last designation may imply.

## Art and Handicrafts

On the whole, the work chosen by the girls is less indicative of ambition than of another prominent characteristic of the Italian children — their aptitude for handicraft. In book learning the general estimate of their teachers is that they are bright and quick when interested, but restless and lacking in continued application. Similarly, they are not always the greatest credit to their settlement friends, judged by the standard of regularity of attendance; for, as one head-worker expresses it, "a gang of Italian boys may start for the settlement in time for their club, with every expectation of being there, but be diverted on the way, and not show up".

In manual training, however, drawing, and whatever requires skilled fingers and artistic sense, they are easily leaders. It is not for nothing that they have lived for centuries in the land of beauty. Italy gives her children an instinctive knowledge of the beautiful in color and contour, which they unconsciously apply to practical affairs and which we others spend hours, and years, of effort to acquire. The attractive arrangement of fruit stands, the picturesque gaiety of the Italian quarters in our cities, the groups of pilgrims from those far-away quarters who may be seen in the art galleries of Boston and New York on any "free" Sunday afternoon: these are familiar evidences of a racial characteristic which should be recognized as a distinct contribution to American life.

The girls in the evening schools of the Children's Aid Society — for some parents can be persuaded to countenance their daughters' attendance — are especially interested in tissue paper work, embroidery, and crocheting, and they work hard and show much ingenuity in making pretty things for their homes.

A teacher of drawing in the public schools of a New Jersey town[2] which has a large Italian population, has found the Italian children far more talented, on the average, than the others. The first day that her classes were given brushes and paints, she noticed that the Italian children held the brushes correctly and handled them as if they had been using them for years, and that they scrupulously confined the paint they applied to the drawn outline, while the little Germans and Americans splashed cheerfully beyond the lines and seemed to find a paint brush as unfamiliar to their hands as Charlemagne's pen was to his. The teacher was surprised to find, also, when she gave a lesson on the principles of composition in pictures — a lesson generally very difficult of comprehension — that the Italian pupils seemed to have an instinctive appreciation of what the others were obliged to accept on faith, and that they applied the rules with unerring judgment. These general observations seem more significant than individual instances of talent, since, as a small German girl objected when this teacher was commending the work of Antonio and Giuseppe and Tommaso, "But teacher, Max Schneider can draw too". Individual instances are, however,

2. Hoboken.

of interest, and might be cited indefinitely — the boy who filled a book with views of the school building and many architectural details; the one who, when the attitude of a little girl posed by the teacher for the class to draw did not seem to him, from his desk, wholly pleasing, deliberately walked up to the model and changed her position to suit him better; and the one who spent his evenings at the settlement in painting daffodils while his comrades revelled in exciting games.

## The Abuse of Talent by Italians

The art sense of the Italians is one of the most valuable contributions they bring to their new country, because it is one of the qualities which we most conspicuously lack. At present, however, this contribution is largely wasted or misused.

It is misused when the parents, by reason of that most commendable trait, so often associated with the land of their adoption — the ambition to make money and "get on" — exploit their children while they are yet children. Italian boys and girls in institutions are demanded again by their parents as soon as they reach the legal working age, and are put to work at whatever offers. Tiny children are so deft with their fingers that they are kept working every day after school hours and at night at artificial flowers or feather-curling, or some similar occupation engaged in by their mothers at home.

The parents are responsible for a part of the waste, as well as for the exploitation, of their children's artistic ability. As for themselves and their own gifts, the struggle for a living makes choice impossible. But even when an opportunity offers for the proper education of a gifted child, the parents too rarely resist the temptation of an immediate advantage.

Another factor which contributes to the waste of these special gifts is the race prejudice which every new element in our population has had to encounter, from the day when the Indians saw, with dissatisfaction, the invasion of the first white men. There is in New York City a factory where ornamental brass and iron work of unusual beauty is done. The superintendent welcomes Italians, but his German foreman will have none of them. One young man, who did remarkably artistic work, was complained of again and again by the foreman, but no definite charges were made. He insisted on the boy's dismissal. Finally the superintendent said, "Well, what is your objection to Rocco? Did you ever see him do anything wrong?" "O! no", replied the foreman, "he's too smart for that; but nobody could be as smart as that Rocco is and be all right."

Public school teachers do much, by calling to the attention of the older children the superior points of their Italian classmates, to break down these barriers of prejudice and disdain. The drawing teacher quoted above was recently given somewhat disconcerting evidence that her efforts in this direction had borne fruit. The town, it should be said by way of preface, is one in which the contemptuous appellation of *Dago* is supplanted by the equally contemptuous *Ginney*. The teacher one day placed before the children a toy animal for them to draw and asked if any one knew its name. A little Irish girl, with all the courtesy at her command, vouchsafed: "I know that out in the park they call it an Italian pig".

## Repression by Americans

The chief responsibility for the waste of this aptitude for artistic handicraft possessed by the Italians rests not on the parent's avarice nor on race prejudice, but on the American educational system and our failure to appreciate the value of what we are throwing away. The whole tendency of the public school system is to divert the children from manual work of any sort to clerical pursuits, and there is comparatively little instruction in a marketable kind of handiwork in the classes and clubs carried on by private enterprise to supplement the public school education. Manual training, as generally taught, is valuable rather as training the fingers and senses, furnishing entertainment, and suggesting possibilities of improving the home, than as supplying any education which would help toward earning a living. The explanation of this is to be found in the fact that there is practically no demand for hand work. Our age has little regard for beauty if it costs more, as it generally does, than ugliness. We must first, if we are to accept and use to our own advantage the gifts which the Italians come bringing, educate ourselves into an appreciation of those gifts. When that is done there will be a market for the things they can do better than we, and the provision for trade education will quickly follow.

The dismay with which we ordinarily contemplate any modification of "the American type" suggests that we are losing that sense of humor which we flatter ourselves is a conspicuous American characteristic. For surely an unprejudiced scrutiny of the American type does not establish the conviction that there is nothing further to be desired. There are points at which we are susceptible of improvement; there are qualities, of which we have now only a faint trace, for whose possession we should be justified in making some sacrifice. The Italians have a delight in simple pleasures, an appreciation for other things than mere financial success, a sense of beauty, a natural kindliness and social grace, which would be not wholly unendurable additions to our predominant traits. It rests with us whether we shall recognize these qualities, foster them, and assimilate them, or, by persistently ignoring and despising them, stamp them as undesirable, un-American, and mold the Italian immigrant in our own image.

Italian Shop on Mott Street, N.Y.C., ca. 1910.

# 23

# The Story of a Clock[1]

MARION F. GURNEY[2]

"But how did you manage to pay last month's rent?" queried the visitor, lifting her eyes from the finely embroidered linen sheet presented for her inspection. It was the sole remnant of the elaborate trousseau worked by Aida's skillful fingers before the fever of the gold-quest, burning in her father's heart, had driven him from his native Abruzzi to this strange new world. God knows what innocent, girlish dreams and hopes had been wrought into its delicate tracery of leaf and flower; but the day of fulfillment seemed far enough away, for the betrothed had been left behind in the sunny valley of the Apennines and the fabled American gold had thus far eluded its seekers. Bit by bit, under the stern pressure of necessity, the pile of snowy linen had dwindled until now the chest was quite empty, for to-day this last relic must be sold. All this the assembled family had related while showing their guest pictures of the distant home.

"So different from New York, *signorina;* no tall houses, but great mountains capped with snow, and the air like wine, so pure and strong, all scented with the fragrance of the pine trees. You would not think that there we were looked up to by everyone, and that Federico was secretary of the commune, while here we are called always *Ginney.* What does it mean, this *Ginney?*"

Then it was that the visitor had attempted to stem the rising tide of homesickness by hastily turning the conversation into the practical channel of rent. Her first question brought no response, and she repeated it a trifle impatiently. "And what about last month's rent?"

The head of the family, thus addressed, looked distinctly embarrassed

1. *Charities*, Vol. 12, 1904. Pp. 499-501.
2. New York Association for Improving the Condition of the Poor.

and fumbled with his watch fob. The watch itself had long since gone to join Aida's trousseau, but he still retained the fob, believing that it marked him as a person of consequence.

"Well, *signorina*, I paid it with a clock."

"With a clock! Do you mean that the landlord accepted a clock in place of the amount of your rent?"

"No, not exactly that. You see I have a friend, a Hebrew man, very good and kind. Your ladyship cannot imagine how gracious. Last month when we had no money to pay the rent and my wife was crying night and day, then came this good Jew and said to me, 'Dear friend, I know that you have much trouble and that you have no money to pay your rent. Is it not so?' 'Yes', said I, 'it is so'. 'Then this is what we will do', said he. 'You see this beautiful clock? It is well worth eighty dollars. See here, I will let you have it for sixty'. 'But no', I said, 'I know not if I shall have a home and what should I do with a clock?' Then the Hebrew man laughed loud. 'You are innocent', he said. 'You know nothing at all. Can you not take this beautiful clock to a *Monte di pieta*? Will not the pawnbroker gladly give you a month's rent for it? Yes, and more too, and do you suppose that I am unwilling to accommodate a friend? No, indeed; I am glad to do you a good turn, and you need only pay me ten dollars a week until the sixty are paid'. And so, because I knew no other way, I took the clock."

The visitor leaned back wearily in her chair, making an effort to follow the mental process by which the ex-secretary of the commune of S_____ had convinced himself that this was a good business proposition.

"How much did you get for it?"

"Fifteen dollars."

"Don't you see", she demanded with some asperity, "that in paying sixty dollars for an accommodation of fifteen you are paying interest at the rate of three hundred per cent, to say nothing of the pawnbroker and the legal penalties to which you have made yourself liable?"

But with the insouciance of his race the ex-secretary refused to disquiet himself.

"The *signorina* does not understand. This man is my friend. If I have not the money he will surely wait for me. Was it not he who proposed that I should pawn the clock? Oh, he is a very good man."

A week slipped by before the *signorina* passed that way again. She was not surprised to find the mother in tears.

"And the villain, the *birbante*", sobbed the excited woman.

"What is the trouble? Has your husband been arrested?" inquired the visitor.

"No, no, not yet, thank Heaven, but we have been so terrified. That clock man has just been here and we did not have two dollars. Your ladyship knows that no one is working. And when we asked him to wait until next week he said he would send my husband to prison, and then he stormed and screamed until all the neighbors came running in, and now we are forever disgraced."

"But how did you settle it finally."

"Oh, Joseph sold some chairs to the second-hand man."

Thenceforward the clock loomed before the family's mental vision as an insatiable monster which must be propitiated. Stick by stick the furniture disappeared. When at length Joseph found work in a factory at three dollars a week, but one dollar could be devoted to household expenses. Insufficiently nourished, the fragile Aida grew more pale and wan until the day when she returned from her factory only to fall in a dead faint at her mother's feet. So the struggle has gone on and on and is still continuing, for it will be at least three months more before the family can own a clock for which they have no use, and which they will probably forfeit ultimately to the pawnbroker.

In the Italian colony, especially among the better classes who struggle frantically to keep up appearances, one sees much of such speculative methods of raising money. It will often explain the existence of apparent need in a family whose income should be sufficient.

But few immigrants, even among the intelligent, have taken the precaution to learn English before they arrive here. The Italian laborer can readily find work, but the skilled artisan and the professional man must, for the most part, be prepared for long months of enforced idleness, until such time as he has acquired at least a rudimentary knowledge of the language of the country. Very few have the necessary capital to carry them through this period. That they should borrow money from some source is almost unavoidable. A well-conducted Italian loan association would be of incalculable benefit in protecting the simple country people from uncrupulous money lenders, and in preventing such grotesque financial transactions as the one cited above.

The intelligent Italian might avoid debt altogether, however, if the curse of Babel had not closed the door of opportunity for him. Among the families personally known to the writer an expert accountant is making hats in Houston Street, a tragedian and an ex-professor are both washing dishes in a restaurant, a bank clerk is keeping a laborers' boarding house, a decorator and designer is wearing out his strength handling beer barrels in a saloon, while his brother, formerly a teacher of manual training, acts as bartender. These and many more are doing work for which they are unfitted, with much mental distress to themselves and probably without satisfaction to their employers. Many of them have attended the city's night schools, but they feel that the present course is not adapted to their needs. A trade school and business college with a course in English especially suited to Italians and conducted by teachers familiar with both idioms, would go far towards enabling our Italian immigrants to give of their best to their adopted country.

Italian emigrants in the town of Chiasso on the Swiss border, ca. 1910.

# 24

# The Italian Under Economic Stress[1]

KATE HOLLADAY CLAGHORN[2]

The average American has a preconceived idea that the Italian of the poorer classes is a natural beggar and a constitutional pauper. This idea he gets from purveyors of the picturesque in literature and art, who find the professional beggar of Rome, or the careless, idle *lazzarone* of Naples, far more catching to the eye and more available for "copy" than the sturdy, hard working peasant, who quietly tills his field, unobserved and undisturbed, except by the tax-gatherer and the landlord.

Yet it is almost entirely from this laborious, self-sustaining peasant class that our great Italian immigration is drawn. The picturesque beggars for the most part stay at home, and the applicants for relief among Italians in American cities are, mainly, of the working class, who have met with distress owing to sickness or lack of work, and are as desirous as anyone could ask, to get on a basis of self-support again.

It is a curious fact, in view of the uneasiness aroused by the preponderance in the Italian immigration of illiterate, unskilled laborers with little money capital, that this appears to be, according to charity records, just the class most able to care for itself in this country and keep from charity. A study of all the Italian cases recorded by the Charity Organization Society of New York for five city blocks, showed that where there was a male head of the family, nearly a half were skilled workers — about the same proportion of in the case of the unskilled laborers, while in immigration, the proportion of skilled to unskilled for 1903, for instance, was only one to five. Not only the

1. *Charities*, Vol. 12, 1904. Pp. 501-504.
2. Assistant Registrar New York Tenement House Department.

"skilled", but the "professional" worker seemed to be at a disadvantage. There were less than one-half of one per cent of the professional class in the immigration of 1903, but five per cent of the charity cases received were of this class.

It is easy to see why this is so. There is a definite demand here for unskilled labor of the kind the Italians furnish, but not so much demand for their skilled labor, while the educated Italian is only too likely to find his education a misfit for American needs.

As the causes of Italian distress are so largely economic, it naturally results, as we have already seen, that the unskilled gets along better than the skilled, and the uneducated better than the educated.

A typical case of the distress the educated but poor Italian is likely to meet, was that of a teacher who, with his two young sons, of twelve and fifteen years, came to this country, after losing his life-long savings by the failure of a bank in Italy. On this side he was unable to find employment suited to his talents, and was obliged to apply for relief within four months of his arrival. When his application was made he was endeavoring to keep soul and body together by rolling cigars in a little tenement room. Unfamiliar with this trade, he was obliged to confine himself to the cheapest grades and succeeded in earning only about forty cents a day.

In only too many cases, educated Italians can succeed here only by beginning at the bottom of the ladder, and, greatly to the credit of their manhood, many of them do this, quite cheerfully and uncomplainingly.

*Temperance of Italians*

Of course, the Italian has his faults, which appear in his experience as a dependent — he would not be human otherwise — and perhaps not even interesting. Like "Tommy Atkins" he "aren't no thin red 'eroe", but he "aren't no blackguard too", and — we should always be careful to remember the last line — "most remarkable like you". That is, in certain situations of stress, he gives way to his natural inclinations, or turns to his own uses the opportunities that offer, much like the rest of us.

Let us first absolve him from the stigma of drunkenness. The full extent of the influence of this vice on the growth of pauperism is hard to determine, as both directly and indirectly it contributes to the breaking down of the physical health, and to the nourishing of moral disorder and crime. From the investigation made by the Committee of Fifty of nearly thirty thousand cases in the records of organized charity, it was shown[3] that while in twenty per cent of the German cases, twenty-four per cent of the American cases, twenty-five per cent of the English cases, and thirty-eight per cent of the

3. *Economic Aspects of the Liquor Problem:* Koren.

Irish cases, the principal cause of distress was intemperance; in only three and a half per cent of the Italian cases was intemperance the cause.

## Wife Desertion

One of the faults of the Italian, above alluded to, is that he sometimes deserts his wife, leaving her and the children to be cared for by the general public. In most cases, there is no deep design about this. The hot Italian blood boils up in the close association of domestic life under difficulties, and husband and wife violently separate, mutually unwilling to bear the yoke any longer.

The Italian particularism — provincialism if you will — is shown by the fact that in many cases of separation, what is held to be a good and sufficient reason is found in the fact that the husband is from the north, the wife from the south of Italy; or the one from Naples, the other from Sicily.

Sometimes the man of the family cannot endure his wife's relatives, who flock about and make trouble. Sometimes, he even objects to his own married children, and will allow his wife no communication with them.

There are also many cases of distress due to the deliberate desertion of a wife in Italy, and the taking of another in this country. It should be said with regard to these cases that this is not the habit of the average immigrant.

## Commitment of Children

One consequence of the desertion of wives is the commitment of children to some charitable institution. The Italian, indeed, has acquired a rather bad reputation on this score, being thought far too ready to throw off the burden of responsibility for his children.

However, in the study made by the present writer of Italian cases in five city blocks, where commitment of children was asked, it was found that three-fourths of the instances where commitment of children was asked were in families already broken up, either by the desertion of the husband, or by the death of husband or wife.

Take for instance, the case of a laboring man of fifty-five, whose wife had died, leaving him with three small children. There is also a son of twenty, who works on coats at from six to seven dollars a week. He is a "good son", and helps the father all he can, but his earnings cannot sustain the family, nor can the old man go out to work and care for the children besides. The family is well spoken of by neighbors and janitor. There is evidently no escape from committing these children, as the old man is not strong enough to earn sufficient to pay someone to take care of them, nor have they relatives to assume the care.

In general, Italian parents are unwilling to give up their children permanently, by adoption or otherwise. It is hardly fair to say, however, that this is wholly due to a desire to make use of the children as wage-earners. In many cases, this desire to have the children again is plainly due to parental affection. In one instance noted, a young woman who was left a widow, was obliged to commit her young child. Marrying again in about a year, almost her first act, with the full approval and consent of the step-father, was to get the baby back again. In another case, a father who committed his children eleven months before, because he was out of employment, asked their discharge, as he was earning ten dollars a week and could care for them.

It is rather strange to find so many Italian parents allege as a reason for committing their children that these are so "wild" they cannot discipline them properly. Some of these "wild" children in the cases studied had reached the hardened and ungovernable ages of eight and nine. One young sinner of six was "so bad" his mother said, that "the other day she fairly bit his ear". And there was still another hardened reprobate of four and a half!

The fact is that the Italian mother is as much a child as her children, and plays with them, quarrels with them, and loves them, just as another child would. If Villari may be taken as a trustworthy witness, this lack of government of children is not confined to the lower classes. In contrast to repressed, nursery-bred English children, he shows Italian children "here, there and everywhere", and "not only seen but heard"; they are "allowed to sprawl over the guests, and if they can talk, they frequently interrupt their elders or contradict them". He says further: "The average Italian mother, especially among the bourgeoisie, has absolutely no notion as to how children ought to be brought up. She indulges them in every way, and lets them eat whatever they ask for, and then scolds them for insufficient reason."[4]

On reading this a dim sense of likeness is felt to something we know pretty well in native American circles, and we wonder if, after all, the Italian is not already pretty well assimilated to American ways.

In some instances, the trouble is more serious than is indicated above. One case is typical and saddening. An Italian boy of about fourteen, seen in the street one cold night in January without shirt or shoes and stockings, told a pitiful tale of distress and cruelty on the part of parents, who sent him out in this condition to pick up wood, or anything else he could find. The case being referred for investigation, the visitor, on going to the home, found a comfortable place with no indication of want. The father was a hod carrier, earning $14.50 a week, and was both able and willing to do everything needful for the boy. The latter, however, was running with a

---

4. *Italian Life in Town and Country*, p. 118.

"gang", and would be away a week or more at a time, before his return pawning or selling all the clothing off of his back. The father and mother found in this boy the trouble of their lives, but seemed to be unable to do anything to improve the situation.

There seems to be considerable commitment of children because our Italian population has, unfortunately, acquired the idea that commitment is a custom of the country, which they may as well take advantage of. The following instance is typical: A widow with four children, two of whom were earning something, wanted the two younger ones committed on the ground that she could not earn enough to support them.

The visitor, however, gained the impression that the woman could continue in very much the same circumstances (i.e., living on her daughter's earnings and her own), but had been moved by the example of several families of her acquaintance. Both the mother and the mother's sister held a long argument with the visitor to the effect that they could not see why other people's children could be committed when they had both parents, while Mrs. C_____ was a poor widow. A sister-in-law lived nearby in a well-furnished place, at a good rent, indicating comparative prosperity, but would not help, for she, too, thought the children should be committed. After a period of visitation and advice, during which the mother received some temporary relief, she decided that she could get along, keeping all the children with her, and, by this time, she preferred to do so.

As there is no such general system of disposing of children in Italy, the practice and the idea have both grown up here, as a result largely of unwise methods of care for the poor.

With the doors of our asylums, which are aided by the city in proportion to the number of their inmates, flung hospitably open to every child for whom even a remote claim for support can be made, what wonder is it that the innocent immigrant, marveling at the kindness of the great government, regards the "collegio" as only another and superior variety of public school, needing no truant officer to drive the children thither as it draws them with the attraction of free food and shelter?

The more careful regulation of commitments has already checked this evil, and its continuance with wider extension of the placing-out system, and a course of education on the part of visitors in poor Italian families, would entirely do away with the idea, and leave the Italian parents in possession of normal feelings of responsibility.

*Other Influences at Work*

Another influence pushing the Italian immigrant toward pauperism is the well-meaning impulse of the charitable who, coming in contact in one way or another with a very poor family, assume that they are in need of charitable aid, and "refer the case" to some society. In some instances the persons visited have indignantly denied that they needed aid; in others, they have accepted the aid and the situation, and have thus taken the first step on the road to beggary.

There is especial danger along this line in the work of some of our Protestant missions. By birth and by training the Italian is a Catholic; by nature and instinct, if uprooted from that faith, a skeptic. It is no wonder, then, that the material aid offered in one way or another by the missions, should in many cases prove to the needy Italian the main attraction to attendance there.

On other pages of this paper is given an account of co-operative activities among Italians, which include, of course, the care of the poor.

It is very desirable for the best good of the Italian poor that the more prosperous Italian members of the community should take their welfare as a matter of personal concern. True charity does not consist in giving a few days' food, a little coal, a bundle of old clothes; it consists in finding the true cause of need in each individual case of distress, and meeting that by the appropriate means, whatever they may be. To do this requires patient, continuous attention to each family taken in charge, a sympathetic appreciation of their situation, and the means that should be employed to better this, not for the moment, but permanently.

And who should be able to understand and sympathize with the Italian, so well as a brother Italian? Who could so well know his hopes and aspirations, his likings and repugnances?

The century-long aloofness of Italian from Italian is giving way in the home country before the growing feeling for Italian unity. This sentiment may well be reflected on this side in an Italian solidarity of interest in his kind that makes him none the less a good American. Notwithstanding all the excellent work now being done by Italians for Italians, there is reason to think that their feeling of responsibility for their fellow countrymen might be developed still further.

An excellent model in this regard is the Jew, who, as strong an individualist as the Italian, so thoroughly looks after his kind that no Jew in distress can ever feel that he is an utter outcast while there is another Jew in the same community.

It would be one of the best gifts of the new country if there should arise here a similar feeling of Italian for Italian.

# 25

# Are the Italians a Dangerous Class?[1]

I. W. HOWERTH

Although the existence of dangerous classes in the United States is perhaps undisputed, opinions differ in regard to what elements of our population should be classed as dangerous. Much depends upon who is using the term. The unemployed and the idle rich hurl the epithet at each other. The A.P.A.'s and the Roman Catholics would hardly agree upon its application. In every case, however, the idea meant to be conveyed by "Dangerous Class" is doubtless the same, namely, a class hostile to our institutions or to the best interests of our civilization, and which is, or is sure to become, a disturbing element.

Of our immigrants the most refractory are undoubtedly the Italians. This fact with certain other characteristics makes them in the eyes of many the worst of all our immigrants. Their rapid increase within the last few years has called forth the most dismal forebodings from the American press, and the opinion has become current that individually and collectively they are a very dangerous people. And thus it is that the adjectives lazy, filthy, cruel, ferocious, bloodthirsty, and the like, are supposed to be particularly applicable to this class of immigrants. No epithet is too insulting to apply to the "Dago".[2]

There is of course a certain justification for this opinion. Blood-curdling stories about the secret society known as the Mafia are circulated. The conspiracy a few years ago in New Orleans resulting in the assassination of the Chief of Police and the bloody retaliation of the Americans, has not

1. *The Charities Review*, Vol. 4, 1894. Pp. 17-40.
2. This term was originally used in the South to designate a descendant of the Spaniards who settled there. It is probably a corruption of "Diego", a proper name very frequent among them.

been forgotten. Italian laborers occasionally engage in a strike, in which case their excitable disposition is likely to give them more notoriety than their number would seem to warrant. Frequent stabbing affrays among them have led many to think of the Italian and the stiletto as inseparable, a thought considerably strengthened by the recent assassination of the French President.

Now it cannot be denied that the Mafia exists, that Italians do sometimes resort to violence, nor that some of them have very inadequate conceptions of law and order. But bad things may be said about some of the representatives of every nationality, and perhaps after all the Italians are not so bad as their reputation. We certainly ought not to judge them by their worst element; and this we are likely to do. When we read, as in the Associated Press dispatches from the scene of the recent mining troubles, of the "enraged and violent Italians", "big ferocious looking Italians", and find them generally designated as Anarchists, we are likely to conclude, unless we are very ignorant of the Italian character, that strict veracity has been sacrificed to the exigencies of newspaper reporting. One thing is certain, the American press gives more space to the vices of Italians than to their virtues. It may be a question with some whether they have any virtues. To such it will appear strange to find anything said in their favor, and especially, that any one thinks it worthwhile to ask, "Are they a dangerous class?"

It is perhaps appropriate to say here that, being an American, I have no interest in the Italian element of our population other than humanitarian. It is not my purpose therefore to present an *ex parte* argument to prove Italian immigration desirable, or that these immigrants are in no sense a dangerous element. I wish only to present a few statistics and the facts of my own observation, and then leave the reader to draw his own conclusions.

When we are told that during the decade 1880-90 Italian immigration increased 312 per cent, we are likely to conclude, especially if we look upon immigration from southern Europe as undesirable, that the number is becoming too large for rapid assimilation. A statement of per cent, however, may be misleading. All depends upon the basis of calculation. In the decade 1850-60 Austrian immigration increased 2549.15 per cent, and Chinese 4591.95 per cent, and yet the country was not over-run by these nationalities. With regard to the Italians, the fact is that in 1890 there were only 182,580 in the United States, less than half the number of Germans in the city of Chicago. The following table will show the increase by decades since 1850:

### Italians in United States

| 1850 | 3,645 | 1880 | 44,230 |
|------|-------|------|--------|
| 1860 | 10,518 | 1890 | 182,580 |
| 1870 | 17,157 | | |

Since 1880, as the table shows, the increase has been comparatively rapid. This is better shown by the following, from the *U.S. Statistical Abstract* for 1893, giving the yearly immigration from Italy, including Sicily and Sardinia, from 1880 to the present time:

| | | | |
|---|---|---|---|
| 1880 | 12,345 | 1887 | 47,622 |
| 1881 | 15,401 | 1888 | 51,558 |
| 1882 | 32,159 | 1889 | 25,307 |
| 1883 | 31,792 | 1890 | 52,003 |
| 1884 | 16,510 | 1891 | 76,055 |
| 1885 | 13,642 | 1892 | 62,137 |
| 1886 | 21,315 | 1893 | 72,916 |

Why this rapid increase? Undoubtedly the enterprise of bureaus of emigration, which are engaged in the philanthropic purpose of enriching themselves by violating our laws against the importation of contract labor, and the rivalry of steamship companies, which has greatly reduced the price of passage, have had something to do with it. And then, too, successful immigrants return to Italy and fire the imagination of the people by displays of their newly gained riches, and by stories of the ease with which they were acquired. But the increase is not entirely due to the discovery that the United States is a good place to come to. Italy is a splendid place for the poor man to leave. A few years ago Dr. Strong (*Our Country*, p. 48) wrote: "The Italians are worse fed than any other people in Europe save the Portuguese. The tax-collector takes 31 per cent of the people's earnings. Many thousands of small proprietors have been evicted from the crown lands because unable to pay the taxes. The burden of taxation has become intolerable." This describes pretty well the condition to-day. The enormous sum necessary to maintain the large armies, and the consequent economic crisis which weighs so heavily upon all Europe, and especially upon Italy, induces the over-taxed peasantry to leave their native land. I have myself talked to immigrants who have rented their farms in Italy without other compensation than the payment of taxes.

Taxation being one of the chief causes of immigration it should be expected that a great part of Italian immigration is from the rural districts. This is true. Perhaps nine-tenths are *contadini* or land laborers. Others are brick-masons, plasterers, white-washers, tailors, barbers, etc. There are also a few clerks and a few members of the liberal professions. Here is a summary of the classification of occupations of the arrivals during the year ending June 30th, 1892:

| | |
|---|---:|
| Professional | 232 |
| Skilled | 4,948 |
| Miscellaneous | 32,957 |
| Not stated | 3 |
| None | 21,020 |
| Total | 59,160 |

Those described as miscellaneous, or as having no occupation, include the large class above referred to. It is a mistake to suppose that Italian immigrants are as a rule the "off-scourings" of their native land.

There is another prevalent misapprehension which should be corrected here. Inhabitants of southern Italy including Sicily, as compared with those of the north, have acquired a bad reputation. Sicily is the home of the Mafia. Now, it is commonly asserted that almost all our Italian population is from southern and insular Italy. How far this is from the truth will appear from the following table, showing the total emigration from the different parts of Italy for the year 1892:

| | | Permanent | Temporary | Total |
|---|---|---:|---:|---:|
| | Piedmont | 13,154 | 20,709 | 33,863 |
| | Liguria | 3,987 | 264 | 4,251 |
| | Lombardy | 13,051 | 8,851 | 21,902 |
| Northern Italy | Venetia | 19,664 | 63,113 | 82,777 |
| | Emilia | 3,309 | 2,591 | 5,900 |
| | | 53,165 | 95,528 | 148,693 |
| | Tuscany | 5,806 | 5,895 | 11,701 |
| | Marches | 719 | 117 | 836 |
| Central Italy | Umbria | 15 | 1 | 16 |
| | Latium | 120 | 4 | 124 |
| | | 6,660 | 6,017 | 12,677 |
| | Abruzzo and Molise | 6,838 | 2,207 | 9,045 |
| | Campania | 20,531 | 1,728 | 22,259 |
| | Apulia | 1,209 | 466 | 1,675 |
| Southern Italy | Basilicata | 7,024 | 303 | 7,327 |
| | Calabria | 9,733 | 280 | 10,013 |
| | | 45,335 | 4,984 | 50,319 |

(continued)

(continued from p. 202)

|  |  | Permanent | Temporary | Total |
|---|---|---|---|---|
|  | Sicily | 11,435 | 477 | 11,912 |
| Insular Italy | Sardinia | 47 | 19 | 66 |
|  |  | 11,482 | 496 | 11,978 |
|  | Grand Total | 116,642 | 107,025 | 223,667 |

| | |
|---|---|
| Total immigration from Northern and Central Italy | 161,370 |
| Total immigration from Southern and Insular Italy | 62,297 |
| Total permanent immigration from Northern and Central Italy | 59,825 |
| Total permanent immigration from Southern and Insular Italy | 56,817 |
| Total temporary immigration from Northern and Central Italy | 101,545 |
| Total temporary immigration from Southern and Insular Italy | 5,480 |

The division of emigrants into permanent and temporary is made by the Italian government. Permanent emigrants are those who go away for an indefinite time without intending to return to their native land; temporary, those who go abroad in search of work, intending to return. Now the figures in the third column show that out of the entire number of emigrants 161,370, or 72.15 per cent were from the northern and central provinces, while 62,297, or 27.84 per cent were from the south and the islands of Sicily and Sardinia. Only 62,137 of these emigrants landed in the United States. If we could assume that these were distributed in the same ratio as the total immigration we should have only about 17,000 from Southern and Insular Italy as compared with 45,000 from the center and north. This might not be a fair comparison, however, since so large a portion of emigration from the north was temporary.[3] But in both forms of emigration the north outranks the south. Popular opinion supposes Naples to furnish us a large and objectionable class. The total Neapolitan immigration however was only 3,236. This idea, then, that all our Italian immigrants are from southern Italy must be dismissed as a delusion.

Having now an idea of the number and character of our Italian population, let us inquire how it is distributed. All are agreed that among the Italians there is a strong tendency to concentrate. And many suppose that the entire drift of Italian immigration has lodged in a few of our large cities. On the contrary, Italians are found in every state and territory of the Union. New York contains the largest number, Pennsylvania the next, and California with 15,495 is third. The following from the census of 1890 will give an idea of their distribution by states:

3. Notice that the claims that the bulk of our Italian immigration is from southern Italy, and that Italians do not come here to stay, are not consistent.

Distribution of Italian Population in 1890

| North Atlantic States | 118,621 |
|---|---|
| South Atlantic States | 4,894 |
| North Central States | 21,837 |
| South Central States | 12,314 |
| Western States | 24,914 |
| | 182,580 |

Turning our attention now to the distribution by cities, we find that in 1890 about fifteen cities had an Italian population of more than 1,200. New York City with 39,951 heads the list. But this is more than four times the number in any other city. In the 124 cities having a population of 25,000 or more there were 107,337, or 58.79 per cent of the total Italian population. In our 50 largest cities there were 98,148 or 50.37 per cent. This is slightly less than the percentage in the same cities in 1880, which was 51.13. At that time the Italians constituted 1.16 per cent of their total foreign population. In 1890 the latter percentage had risen to 2.85. These figures show that the tendency to congregate in cities, perhaps the most deplorable feature of Italian immigration, is not on the increase. From this time on for reasons that will appear later, one can safely predict that it will rapidly diminish.

So much for Italian immigration in general. Let us now turn our attention to the Italians themselves. And as they are everywhere pretty much alike, we may confine our observations to the Italians of Chicago.

The Italian element of Chicago is of recent and rapid growth. In 1870 the census report shows only 552 persons born in Italy. In 1880 the number had risen to 1,357, and ten years later to 9,921. Of course these figures based on nativities do not represent the real number present. Children of Italian parents owing to their mode of life are Italians in every essential but birth. At present the Italian population is variously estimated from 25,000 to 50,000. A conservative estimate, I think, is 30,000. Here is material for the alarmist if he chooses to deal in percentages, for the percentage of increase since 1870 is 18,400. These 30,000 Italians are distributed in nuclei of various dimensions all over the city. At the presidential election in 1892 four wards registered more than 50 votes. These wards were the following:

| Twenty-third | 58 |
|---|---|
| First | 137 |
| Seventeenth | 208 |
| Nineteenth | 278 |

The nineteenth ward, which contains the largest Italian population, lies on the West Side, and is bounded by Van Buren Street on the north, the Chicago River on the east, W. Twelfth Street on the south, and on the west by Throop and Sibley Streets. It contains an area of .822 square miles, and has 22.7 miles of streets. Its population, according to the school census of 1892, was 54,172. The subsequent increase may be safely estimated at 6,000, making the population of the ward at present about 60,000. This population is a most interesting conglomerate. The total vote cast in the presidential election of 1892 was 9,155. This analyzed, is as follows:

| | | | |
|---|---|---|---|
| Irish | 1,035 | Scotch | 99 |
| German | 721 | Swedes | 39 |
| Russian | 477 | Poles | 38 |
| Canadians | 438 | French | 35 |
| Bohemians | 468 | Hollanders | 35 |
| English | 285 | Norwegians | 18 |
| Italian | 278 | Danes | 14 |
| Austrian | 187 | All others | 61 |

The ward is credited, also, with 56 Mongolians and a few Greeks and Armenians. The section in which the Italians dwell lies east of Halsted Street, between that street and the river. It contains about one-third of the area of the ward, and perhaps about two-thirds of the population. There are, then, in this part of Chicago about 120,000 people to the square mile, a dense population for Chicago, but, of course, not to be compared with the most thickly settled parts of New York, where they have over 380,000 to the square mile.

I choose this Italian settlement, not simply because it is typical, but also, because it is the largest in Chicago, and contains chiefly Italians of the lowest class. By general consent it has received the name "Little Italy". The line of densest concentration lies along Ewing Street, running east and west. Here, on a summer evening, one may get an idea of the density of the population, for they are all out; men, women and children, crowding the doorsteps, the sidewalks, and even the streets. On observing the small, tumble-down houses, one asks, "Where in the world did they all come from?" The fastidious eye quickly observes the filth in the streets, the dirty aspect of both houses and people, and the general appearance of squalor on all sides. People with sensitive olfactory nerves are likely to find little pleasure in the spectacle. The sidewalks contain an orderly array of well-filled garbage boxes. In walking from Halsted Street to the river, a distance of four blocks, I counted seventy-one boxes, capacious, and most of them well filled, all on the sidewalk. They are placed there by the city. Our Irish authorities seem to think anything is good enough for these "furriners". In spite of their thoughtful provision, much of the garbage remains to defile the streets and to send visitors away with the idea that nothing good can come out of "Little Italy". But after all, there are some elements of poetry in the scene. I doubt whether Goldsmith had anything better upon which to base his beautiful description of "Sweet Auburn! Loveliest village of the plain".

One may see groups of men in full enjoyment of health and strength engaged in playful banter or intent upon the achievement of some feat of skill, — for the drinks, to be sure, but that would probably be overlooked by the poet. Mothers with unconcealed enjoyment are watching the frolics of children who in spite of their surroundings are having a happy time. Strong men, good looking girls, happy children, parental affection, friendship, love and courtship, are all in the picture along with the disagreeable features. There is plenty of color and, I was about to say music, but that would be too great a stretch of poetic license.

Before making a closer acquaintance with these people let us review briefly their chief characteristics. Their physical appearance is too well known to need elaborate description. In stature they are usually below the average. Wiry is the term commonly used to describe the Italian physique, but those of the lower class are usually of stout build, dark hair, and swarthy complexion. But on Ewing Street you may see now and then fair complexion and auburn hair. Somehow these unusual features never figure in stories of Italian violence. Perhaps they do not lend themselves to the purposes of the reporter. It is always a dark or swarthy "villain". We should never be horrified by an account concerning "a big, ferocious looking, red-headed Italian".

As to the women the older ones usually present a miserable appearance, but the girls with their dark eyes, white teeth and olive complexion are often decidedly pretty. All like a good deal of color in their dress, and are extravagantly fond of cheap jewelry. The little girls dress exactly like their elders, and consequently look like small pocket editions of their mothers.

With all their ignorance the Italians are very bright. They are shrewd, highly imaginative, voluble, and volatile, expansive and explosive. Over a trivial incident they grow excited, all talk at once, and bluster and gesticulate as if it were a matter of great moment. Morally much may be said in their favor. They are sober, industrious and economical. To strangers they are uniformly polite. Their experience with Americans has taught them to be suspicious, but their confidence once gained they are affable and hospitable. All Italians are proud and high-spirited, and, when ill-treated, are defiant and revengeful. Amongst the women there is very little of the coarser commercial forms of vice. Emphatically, Italians are not lazy and thriftless. I do not forget that they are dirty as well as economical, but I do not allow the dirt to hide their better qualities. On this subject I shall have more to say later on. All I am concerned with at present is to sketch the outline of a picture which we may now proceed to fill in. Let us begin with an account of their family life.

If we walk down Ewing Street at a time when the inhabitants are within, and stop to knock at one of the greasy doors, we shall be greeted with an unanimous "Come in!" All Italians have learned to speak that much English. On entering we are likely to find half a dozen men at a table playing cards, a woman busy at some household industry, and three or four children who take advantage of any unoccupied territory. If it happens to be wash-day, we are likely to find the clothes hung out on lines stretched from wall to wall, making it necessary for us to dodge about as we move toward the chairs offered us. After sitting down and looking about us we find we are in the main room, parlor, sitting-room, dining-room, wash-room and bed-room all in one. Usually there is an extra bed-room, sometimes two. Besides the table and chairs, there are two or three old trunks, a bed, a stove, a decrepit sofa and two or three pieces of carpet. On the walls we may see a few old prints, saints perhaps, or highly colored chromos used to advertise some brand of groceries. A railroad map or a flashy advertisement may also serve for ornamentation. While we have been making this mental inventory, the *padre* has disappeared, and he now returns with a pail of beer, a glass of which each of us is expected to drink. Our refusal is interpreted as an indication of a more highly developed gastronomical taste than this simple beverage is designed to satisfy. Will we have some wine? No? Whisky? No? Well, then, smoke a cigar. Our continued refusal convinces him that we have no desire to be sociable, and he becomes suspicious. If we desire the acquaintance of that family it is probable that we shall have to call again. I have had to refuse hospitalities three or four times before I could make a family understand that I meant to be friendly without taking the preliminary steps which they thought essential.

Who are all these people who constitute an Italian family? Besides the parents and children, and perhaps a daughter-in-law or son-in-law, there are almost sure to be a few boarders, kinsmen or friends whose wives are either not yet selected or have not been brought over from Italy. As a consequence, the rooms being small and few, human beings in the Italian quarter are packed somewhat closely together.

My observations do not lead me to the conclusion that the number in an Italian family is above the average. The same is not true of the average number of people to a dwelling. In Chicago in 1890 the average number to a dwelling was 8.26, and the average family 5.01. In a tenement house containing 48 families and 350 people, or about 7 to the family, I found the real average to be only about 4. In 83 families taken at random, the average number of children was 2.84. From these figures, it is safe, I think, to say that the rapidity of increase among our Italian population has not a threatening aspect.

A somewhat closer study of the Italian family will repay us. "The family", says Mr. H. B. Adams, "oldest of institutions, perpetually reproduces the ethical history of man, and reconstructs the constitution of society." And continuing, he points out the fact that school and college, town and city, state and nation are after all but modified types of family institutions, and the true method of advancing sociology is to study this element of social life. Let us then inquire as to the relations of the personal elements of a typical Italian family, and the economic, social and educational factors that are visible.

In the first place, the Italian marries for love. No prudential consideration, not even a visible means of support, is a prequisite to matrimonial alliance. His married life is, therefore, likely to begin with one small room and a banana, but there is pretty sure to be conjugal love and constancy. The infrequency of divorce among Italians is not due entirely to their religion. In the home the wife is treated with consideration and respect. She is expected to be a helpmate, and there are no nice scruples about the kind of work she shall do. Usually she manufactures macaroni, sausage and other edibles, and spends her spare moments in doing patch-work. But often she is an outdoor laborer, picking rags, selling fruit, or accompanying her husband on his hand-organ excursions. All who are in the slightest degree acquainted with Italian life bear testimony to the virtue of Italian women. It is only a suggestion, of course, but of the 2,439 women reported to have been received in the New York Florence Crittenden Mission for the ten years ending April 19th, 1893, only three were Italian. To the honor of Italian women let it be said they fill neither our police stations nor our brothels. This is due not simply to the jealous guardianship of Italian husbands, but to the discipline of the home. Young girls are trained to habits of obedience, and are not allowed the unprotected freedom of American girls, which is to say the least a questionable good. As a sample of the wild statements made concerning Italians, take an article which recently appeared in the *Chicago American* in which it is stated that in Italy 21 per cent are born out of wedlock. The actual percentage as given in our consular reports for May, 1892, is 7.5.

Before passing from this subject I wish to dispel another illusion, and that is in regard to the age at which Italians marry. You will be told that the girls are married before they are 16, and that marriage at 13 and 14 is a common occurrence. The latest Italian census shows that more men marry between the ages of 24 and 26, and more women between 20 and 22 than at any other age. In the Italian quarter of Chicago about one hundred families taken at random showed only one woman married at 14 and but one man at 18. Girls until they are 18, and boys until they are 21, turn their earnings into the family till, and parents therefore discourage their marriage until they have reached their maturity.

This leads me to speak of the economic phase of the Italian family. Every member is expected to earn something. The father is a laborer, rag-picker, fruit-vender, peddler. Whatever he is he works hard at his business. Boys sell papers and black boots. Girls manufacture various articles of use and beauty. It is very difficult to estimate the family income and expenses. No account is kept and I have so far found it impossible to have them do so. I thought that in one case I had succeeded, but found that various items had been omitted. There were a good many "little things", they said, which they didn't suppose I cared about. According to the best I could find out here is the way a family of my acquaintance, consisting of nine persons, four adults and five children, managed to make both ends meet in the month of January, 1894.

The family had three small rooms on the second floor of a tenement house. The father was ill with bronchitis, his brother earned the money, and an old gentleman, the wife's father, was out of work. The two oldest children were in school. I doubt whether the account given me is absolutely correct. I remember now that one day when I was present they had tomatoes for dinner and they do not appear in the bill. It is probable too that there was a small expenditure for beer. Italians have a particularly strong prejudice against Chicago water.

Income

| | |
|---|---:|
| Earnings of one adult (peddler) | $ 19.12 |
| Aid from County $1.50 per week | 6.00 |
| Total | $ 25.12 |

Expenses

| | | |
|---|---:|---:|
| Rent | | 8.00 |
| Fuel | | 3.00 |
| Doctor | | 1.00 |
| Medicine | | .50 |
| Groceries, etc. | | |
| Cabbage | $ .60 | |
| Macaroni | 1.60 | |
| Soup bones | .45 | |
| Milk | .60 | |
| Bread | 3.40 | |
| Meat | 1.00 | |
| Rice | .20 | |
| Sugar | .60 | |
| Coffee | .60 | |
| Potatoes | 1.00 | |
| Eggs | .40 | |
| Lard | .25 | |
| Kerosene | .32 | |
| Fish | .60 | |
| Beans | .40 | |
| Cheese | .60 – | 12.62 |
| | | $25.12 |

As showing the variety of food I give also the grocery bill for one month of another family of two persons, a man and his wife:

| | | | |
|---|---|---|---|
| Bread | $ .52 | Olives | $ .10 |
| Macaroni | 1.03 | Tobacco | .09 |
| Beans | .25 | Sugar | .10 |
| Fish | .32 | Eggs | .09 |
| Sausage | .03 | Soap | .10 |
| Kerosene | .20 | Sweet oil | .10 |
| Candle | .05 | Grapes | .05 |
| Nuts | .10 | Lamp chimney | .06 |
| Cake | .01 | Cheese | .05 |
| Pepper | .10 | | |
| | | Total | $3.35 |

Here again I cannot be sure how much is not included in the bill. The absence of fruit, except grapes, is suspicious. Some will be surprised to find soap among the other items.

The inference likely to be drawn from these two illustrations is a true one. The standard of living in the average Italian family is very low. Many of them, especially those who know anything about the American standard, realize it and long for something better. But it is the exceptional Italian who has ever seen from the inside an American home. One of the most surprising phenomena to be observed in the Italian quarter is the dense ignorance of everything American, except money getting. Coming from Italy with their tastes and habits fixed, they reproduce in the midst of our civilization the life to which they have been accustomed. By comparison we find that their food here is pretty much the same as in Italy. According to our Consular Report for May, 1892, the kind and amount of food consumed per week by a workman in Italy were as follows:

| | Central Italy | Northern Italy | Southern Italy |
|---|---|---|---|
| Meat | 1.65 lbs. | 5 oz. | 11 oz. |
| Bread | 10.38 lbs. | 4.41 lbs. | 13.88 lbs. |
| Macaroni | 1.98 lbs. | 4.41 lbs. | 6.61 lbs. |
| Meal | 3.09 lbs. | 8.82 lbs. | —— |
| Cheese | 9 oz. | 5 oz. | —— |
| Rice | 1.87 lbs. | 1.1 lbs. | 5 oz. |
| Salt beef or fish | 9 oz. | 5 oz. | 2.21 lbs. |
| Vegetables | 4.41 lbs. | 4.41 lbs. | 8.82 lbs. |
| Wine | 4 to 5 qts. | 1 qt. | |

At first thought it may be surprising that the higher wages in this country do not lead the Italian workman to a higher plane of living. But higher wages are largely offset by increased expenses and by the uncertainty of employment. In Chicago the Italian laborer does not expect work for more than half the year. His yearly earnings are therefore likely to fall within $150. In many cases it is as low as $110. During the last winter getting employment was out of the question, consequently income in most families was measured by charity.

When I said income was dependent upon charity I did not mean municipal and other outside charity, for as long as they have anything to share Italians keep their relatives and friends. Sociability is one of their strong characteristics. Formal visiting among them is not frequent, but they are so well acquainted that they are accustomed to walk into each other's home whenever they please, even without the formality of knocking. Such close relationships, although fatal to privacy, necessarily give rise to friendship with its consequent claims. Hence in time of need an Italian family, as a rule, looks first to friends. Last winter it was not uncommon to find two or three families living together in order to save rent, and often the burden of support rested on one family alone. While these social relations help to knit an Italian community into a compact body, they serve also to make the family a strong unit, and this is not of itself a pathological condition.

As might be expected the educational influence of the family is not what it should be. While parents desire to have their children learn, they are too ignorant to realize their own duty or to appreciate education beyond its money value. It is often said that they have no care for the education of their children. I must assert that I have not found it so. In the poorest hovels I have seen the father painfully trying to collect his meager and scattered knowledge in order to teach his child; and I have learned that the best way to get on favorable terms with an Italian family is to offer to teach the children. As I have said, children are usually trained to habits of obedience and politeness. That they are trained to pilfer and steal, as we are sometimes told, is a mistake. If they get this training at all it is upon the street.

For fear I may draw too favorable a picture I will say again that I am purposely showing the good traits in Italian life, for in order that the picture may be true these traits must be emphasized. If I were inclined to take exceptional cases I could present the Italians in a very unfavorable light. I have seen families in which the degradation was indescribable. I have seen parents who encouraged their children in vice, and Italian children who needed no encouragement. But these, I say, are exceptional cases and if dwelt upon would be misleading. It may be said that, granting all that is claimed for the Italian family, the Italians as a class are a dangerous element in our civilization. It may be so. Let us try to get at the truth.

It must be admitted that ignorance must be classed as a factor which goes to make up a dangerous class. And Italians are ignorant. But how ignorant? Since 1859 Italy has had a compulsory education law. Until 1877, however,

it was a dead letter. According to the *Annuario Statistico Italiano* for 1892
illiteracy in Italy since 1861 was as follows:

| Census | All Ages | 18-20 Years of Ages |
|--------|----------|---------------------|
| 1861 | 78.06 | 71.45 |
| 1871 | 72.96 | 62.53 |
| 1881 | 67.26 | 54.30 |
| 1891 | 55 to 60 (estimated) | 42.00 |

This showing is bad enough, but it is much better than their condition is
usually represented. I have before me an article in which it is said that 85 per
cent of the Italians are illiterate. Here in Chicago I am inclined to think that
the percentage is about 60.

But ignorance is not the worst charge made against the Italians. They are
popularly supposed to be responsible for a large share of our drunkenness,
pauperism and crime. The facts about this matter will be to some a surprise.
In 1888 the deaths from alcoholism in Italy in 1,000,000 of population were
14, Russia 20, Ireland 29, England 50, Belgium 51, Sweden 65. In southern
Italy they are only 1 in 1,000,000.[4] Here in Chicago one does not often see a
drunken Italian. Beer is the favorite drink. It is usually bought by the pail
and drunk at home. In prosperous times the average Italian will spend $3 a
month for this drink. As to criminality and pauperism the census of 1890
shows 82,329 prisoners in the United States. Of these only 38 had one or
both parents Italian. Of the 73,045 paupers in our almshouses only 12 had
one or both parents Italian. To show the condition here in Chicago I have
constructed a table showing the standing of the principal nationalities in our
penal and charitable institutions. I was unable to get the statistics from the
various institutions for the same time, but the percentages are perhaps not
greatly affected. It is impossible to get the number of arrests of each
nationality. Owing to this fact the information in regard to criminality is
not as full as one could wish. Criminals sent to the Bridewell are under 21
years of age. Although the Italians, as shown by table below, are exceeded
by the Poles and Hollanders in the percentage of families relieved by the
county, it must be admitted that they make a very bad showing. Two things
however should be said in explanation: first, the actual Italian population is
perhaps three times as great as the figures of the census upon which the
computation is based; and second, the hard times of last winter, owing to
the fact that so many Italians live just above the line of self-support, drove a
great many to apply for aid. Of the 1,072 Italian families reported as
receiving help, 727 or more than two-thirds applied during the months of
December, January, February and March. The figures here given are in each
case taken from the official reports:

4. Consular Reports 1892.

| Nationality | Population in 1890 | No. of families receiving aid from county from Jan. 1, 1893 to April 30, 1894 | Per cent of native population | No. sent to county poor house for year ending Feb. 1, 1893 | No. per 1,000 of native population | No. adjudged insane February 1 to Dec. 1, 1893 | No. of families aided by Relief and Aid Society for year ending Oct. 31, 1893 | No. sent to Bridewell in 1892 | Children in Chicago orphan asylum 1892 | No. in Washington home for inebriates in 1893 |
|---|---|---|---|---|---|---|---|---|---|---|
| Germans | 384,968 | 10,521 | 2.7 | 396 | 1.02 | 152 | 857 | 614 | 71 | 96 |
| Americans | 292,463 | 6,625 | 2.2 | 851 | 2.90 | 174 | 680 | 6,067 | 182 | 823 |
| Irish | 215,534 | 8,548 | 3.9 | 754 | 3.49 | 85 | 787 | 1,209 | 45 | 310 |
| Bohemians | 54,209 | 5,116 | 9.4 | 58 | 1.09 | 21 | 197 | 59 | ..... | 5 |
| Poles | 52,756 | 10,394 | 19.7 | 47 | .89 | 21 | 220 | 96 | ..... | 11 |
| Scandinavians | 45,877 | 3,365 | 7.3 | 218 | 4.75 | 75 | 478 | 207 | 23 | 47 |
| English | 33,785 | 1,026 | 3.0 | 91 | 2.69 | 18 | 310 | 251 | 8 | 100 |
| French | 12,963 | 556 | 4.2 | 32 | 2.46 | 4 | 80 | 33 | ..... | 6 |
| Scotch | 11,927 | 298 | 2.4 | 50 | 4.19 | 5 | 125 | 144 | 12 | 38 |
| Hollanders | 4,912 | 639 | 13.0 | 11 | 2.24 | 0 | ..... | 12 | ..... | 6 |
| Italians | 9,921 | 1,072 | 10.8 | 19 | 1.91 | 3 | 190 | 43 | 4 | 7 |

Passing over the figures referring to indoor relief, let us notice the ratios of criminality as shown by the Bridewell report. If it is true, as some assert, that Italian children are trained to steal, they are quite successful in escaping detection. The Scotch, for instance, with only 2,000 more population have in that institution more than three times as many criminals; the English, with less than two or one-half times the population, almost six times as many, while the Americans, with about thirty times the population, are responsible for 141 times as many. These figures are immensely significant.

I have already said that Italians are not lazy. Perhaps for this very reason they are a menace to our welfare, for they are more likely to appear as a factor in the labor problem. Their standard of living being low, they are willing to work for low wages. If engaged in business, as fruit selling, they can undersell their American competitors. In spite of this, however, little danger may be apprehended. For Italians finding themselves unable to compete for the higher forms of labor, engage in labor which others, owing to their ideas of self-respect, are likely to shun. They may become rag-pickers, street laborers, scavengers. This will be so as long as the Italians crowd into the cities. Many unthinking persons suppose that Italians choose these ignoble tasks. On the contrary, they are forced into them. The more intelligent among them are deeply chagrined that they, sons of Italy, which gave to the world a Dante, a Michael Angelo and a Columbus, should be forced to gain their living in such a manner. A few years ago *L'Italia*, one of the two Italian newspapers of Chicago, appealed to the pride of its readers to induce them to let rag-picking and such disgraceful labor alone. A mass meeting was called and a committee of fourteen was appointed to see what could be done. At their own request an ordinance prohibiting such labor was drafted and passed. But the rag-pickers, unwilling to starve, banded together, and by threatening political vengeance, made the ordinance a dead letter. Not a desire for *such* work, but a desire for *work* impelled them to resist its enforcement. Few realize how difficult it is for an Italian to find work, and how they are imposed upon by unscrupulous rascals.

In spite of their disadvantages they manage to find some kind of work, and in ordinary years save money. They run no sweat shops, and under no circumstances do they reinforce our army of tramps. Whatever may be said, then, of the Italians with reference to the labor question, their energy, manifested in the first place by their presence among us, their industry and economy, are encouraging to those of us who hope to see them become a prosperous and desirable element in our country.

"But they are all Catholics", some will say, "and that shows plainly enough that they are a dangerous class." Granting for a moment that Catholicism is a menace to our institutions, it does not follow that on this account Italians are a bad lot, for in the first place they are not all Catholics, many of them belonging to the Evangelical church,[5] and in the second place, most of them who are Catholics are only nominally so. Even in Italy the priests have lost much of their power. In this country we have nothing to fear from the Italians on account of religious fanaticism. There is more danger from religious indifference.

While I am unwilling to grant that we have anything to fear from Italians as Catholics, I readily concede that they may prove dangerous as voters. Like other ignorant classes, they easily become the tool of demagogues and thus enlarge the baleful influence of the latter. They are not quick like the Irish to see the benefits of citizenship, and do not, therefore, hasten to become naturalized. But the zeal of party workers goes far to supply this deficiency, and their indifference to politics in general, makes the Italians supporters of the highest bidder. Here, I think, is where this element of our population presents itself in the most unfavorable light. Unless they can become interested citizens of our country they are sure to become a dangerous class. And because there is a possibility of their possessing political power without a feeling of responsibility, we owe them a duty. But before describing this duty, let us see what we are already doing for them and what they are doing for themselves.

What we in Chicago are doing for our Italian element is soon told, for it is next to nothing. The Hull House, situated on the edge of the Italian district, gathers in a few of the girls and teaches them how to sew. Beyond this there is no systematic effort to ameliorate their condition. To be sure, the city has licensed in their neighborhood 115 saloons to quench their thirst, and to supply their social demands, but some would question this method of amelioration. There is not a park, bath-house or church in the whole district. The only free bath-house in the city is in this ward, but not in the Italian district. It was opened in January, 1894. In the first three days after opening 1,244 availed themselves of the bath and many were turned away. The Italian quarter seems to be pretty much delivered over to the people who inhabit it and they are not doing much for themselves.

The most potent elevating factors at work among the Italians are the two Italian journals, L'Italia and L'America, both very respectable weeklies. The former has a circulation of 20,000, the latter 5,000. Of course they reach a much greater number. It is not unusual to see a cluster of Italians gathered to hear what il editore del giornale has to say. There are also in Chicago several Italian societies organized for mutual benefit. The wealthier class have a social club, but there is nothing of this kind in "Little Italy".

---

5. In Chicago we have an Italian church of the Presbyterian faith. It is often said that in Italy 99 per cent are Catholics. This was true in 1871. Since that time, however, the census schedules have omitted the question in regard to religion. Hence there are no reliable figures. See Annuario Statistico Italiano, 1892, p. 87, note.

What I have mentioned are about all the visible efforts put forth to better the condition of Italians in Chicago. More may be in progress in other cities. Here the Italians are not doing a tithe of what they should be doing for themselves with our customs and institutions, and to learn our language. To protect themselves against the schemes of the contractor, the banker, the lottery, the hotel-keeper, and the saloon-keeper, they should form a society to assist Italian immigrants by information and advice; to protect them by moral influence, and if necessary by the laws, against ill-treatment, imposition and swindle, and to provide work for them and to give them necessary assistance in every possible way. The Germans have such societies all over the country. The one in Chicago, during the last year, found work for 2,577 persons, and aided 585 families, 1,653 children and 266 single persons. The Italians need such a society more than the Germans.

While there are many things the Italians can and ought to do for themselves, there is much that must and should come from without. Rightly or wrongly we have permitted them to come to this country. Let immigration be further restricted if you will, we still have them with us and it is our duty to help them to a higher plane of living. To do so we must give them, first, our sympathy. Most of our newspapers heap upon them the most bitter sarcasm, and a large part of population regards them as proper objects of contempt and ridicule. No wonder that Italians sometimes conclude they are in a hostile country and either avoid everything American or return to their native land. "Who would have anything to do with a filthy Italian?" So ask many who seem to misinterpret the passage of scripture which reads, "He that is filthy let him be filthy still". The Italian quarter is filthy because it is neglected by the City. Under our present sanitary system somebody is bound to be neglected, and as the Italians are easily imposed upon they suffer most neglect. Our sanitary officer speaking of our contract system says, "Competition for the work (cleaning the streets and alleys) is sharp, the result is low bids. To thoroughly perform the work is impossible; the contractor devotes his entire attention to working out a plan whereby he can shirk and make both ends meet, the citizen complains of the slovenly way in which the work is performed, and the lack of regularity of service, the officer is accused of partiality in cleaning certain portions of a ward to the detriment of other portions, and finally he grows discouraged, and hopes for an improvement, an open fall and winter, or a cancellation of the contract."[6] We should clean up the Italian quarter. The old wooden garbage boxes should be removed from the sidewalk and destroyed. Metal boxes should be used and kept in the yard or set in the fences. Unfortunately in some cases there is neither yard, fence nor alley. In such cases the duty of the city is plain. There should be free bath-houses, and Tee-to-tum clubs should

6. Report of the Health Department, 1892, p. 26.

divide the patronage of the saloons. Not to be utopian, however, I insist only on the things first mentioned, namely, sympathy and good sanitary service.

Next in order we should enforce compulsory education. This is earnestly demanded by the more intelligent Italians. When children are old enough to earn money Italian parents are strongly tempted to keep them out of school for that purpose. We owe it not simply to the Italians but to ourselves that every child be kept in school until it has acquired the rudiments of an education. Children left to grow up in ignorance, to become familiar with all the vice of the street, to have no idea of their political duties and responsibilities, these constitute the really dangerous class. Education, sympathy, personal influence, all these should be brought to bear upon elevating the standard of life among the Italians.

Just here is where the church could do a great deal. If the church members of Chicago who are anxious to have missionary work carried on would each select an Italian family and visit it occasionally, not to preach to it but to hold before it an example of a higher standard of life, the results would be immeasurable. Italian families as a rule are never visited by Americans. Now and then a zealous missionary calls and leaves a tract, but Italians need sympathy and a good example far more than tracts. It is a fact, I think, that our benevolent and religious societies pay little attention to Italians. This neglect leads one of their number[7] to write, "Had they (the Italians) displayed the vices or criminal inclinations which prevail to a deplorable extent among the low classes of other nationalities they would soon have been brought to public notice and taken care of by our benevolent and religious societies, but they cannot be reproached with intoxication, prostitution, quarreling, stealing, etc., and thus escaping the unenviable notoriety of the criminal they fall into a privacy that deprives them of American benevolence; and there is no instance of any visitor having ever been appointed to explore this fruitful field of operation." This ought not to be true, and would not be true if the Italians were not grossly misrepresented and misunderstood.

As long as Italians concentrate in "quarters", and do not exert themselves to form bonds of union with the outside world they will counteract most of the work that will be done for them by the church and by individuals. The tendency to concentrate, as has been said, is the worst feature of Italian immigration. This is recognized by friends and by the more intelligent of their own number. As soon as an Italian lands in America he hastens to the Italian quarter and there he is likely to stay. He finds men and women who speak his own language. He lodges with an Italian, eats at an Italian restaurant; stores kept by his countrymen supply all his wants. Bankers, employment agents, lawyers, interpreters, physicians, musicians, artisans,

7. A. E. Cerqua, quoted in "Dangerous Classes of New York", p. 197.

laborers, grocers, bakers, butchers, barbers, merchants, all are there, a town within a town. Hence the "Italian quarter" has great cohesive force. Now it seems plain that even if we cannot dissolve the nucleus that is already formed we should keep it from growing larger. There is but one way in which this can be done, and that is by colonization. The remedy for centralization is decentralization.

I have already said that about nine-tenths of the Italians who come to this country are small farmers and fruit raisers. Is it any wonder that when these men find themselves in the heart of a great city, with no work at hand to which they have been accustomed, they take up such work as rag-picking? As has been wittily said, "they have grown so accustomed in their own country to picking fruit that they think they must pick something, hence apply themselves to rags and garbage boxes. Bad as that business is, however, it is not so bad as picking pockets." If now, Italians are successful farmers and fruit growers the place for them is not in the city but in the country. But the question arises: "How can they be induced to go there?"

All that is necessary to induce Italians to go to the country is to let them know that they can do better there than in the city. And that is true. In the South especially, land adapted to fruit growing may be had for nothing. The climate there would suit the Italian better than that of our northern cities. The South would welcome them. Railroad companies would furnish cheap transportation. Therefore it would not be a difficult matter to direct the incoming tide of immigration to this part of our country. All that would be necessary would be a society such as that already mentioned as operated by the Germans. When an Italian lands he should be asked about his former occupation and what he now wishes to do. If he has been a farmer he ought to be directed to a place where he can continue that occupation.

There are, of course, objections to colonization. It would cost some trouble and perhaps a little philanthropy. It would be, however, only the ounce of prevention that would save a pound of cure; for to make a useful rural population of our Italian immigrants would be one step toward solving our municipal problems. It is urged, also, that Italians do not come to this country to stay, and therefore they would not settle on a farm. To this it may be replied that, although this used to be the case, it is now more generally true that they come expecting to remain. And if they could be assured of a profitable business, more would come to stay. It will be said too that the poverty of our immigrants would prevent them from engaging in farm work. But it is true, I believe, that on arriving in America Italians usually have a small sum of money. If they could reach a farm before falling into the hands of the various swindlers who make their living by taking advantage of the ignorance and inexperience of their victims, there would probably be capital enough to begin with.

One other objection from men who have given some thought to the question, may be noticed, and that is that Italians are not likely to succeed as farmers. In this country most farming is extensive, whereas Italians are accustomed to intensive farming. Without carrying on the work on a large scale, and after American methods, some doubt their success.

To this objection the answer is, *they have succeeded.* Colonization is already a fact. Seven or eight years ago a settlement of Italians was located near Daphne in Baldwin County, Alabama. It has thrived and prospered. Land has been cleared for cultivation, grape cuttings and fruit trees have been put out and various agricultural products have been raised. According to a recent observer the settlers are "intelligent, industrious, orderly and law-abiding, and they are so polite and cheery in their manners and demeanor that it is a pleasure to meet them. Their hope is soon to sit under their own vine and fig tree in a land truly flowing with milk and honey, and to make their lives bright with the light-hearted gaiety and peaceful content that made existence pleasant even amidst the exactions and privations of sunny, but over-taxed and over-crowded Italy. Already the sounds of music are borne on the evening air as these pioneers in a great movement of their race rest at the close of day from their labors, and rejoice over their freedom from heavy burdens, and in that feeling of independence that the ownership of land gives to foreigners of small or moderate means." Other instances of successful colonization could be mentioned.

Colonization is strongly advocated by intelligent Italians interested in the welfare of their countrymen. The editor of *L'America* has urged it in a series of strong and earnest articles in his journal. *L'Italia,* is no less enthusiastic in its favor. It seems to be the natural solution of the problem of Italian concentration in the slums. Its reasonableness together with the successful attempts already made, and the quarter from which it is advocated insure the truth of the statement formerly made, that henceforth the tendency of Italians to congregate in large cities will decrease.

Of course colonization cannot do everything. It cannot relieve us of our personal obligations, nor our municipalities of their duties. We may regret the necessity for altruistic effort which embraces our so-called "pauper immigration", but in this case altruism is the most sensible form of egoism. Let us once do our duty toward our Italian immigrants and we shall hear much less about them as a "Dangerous Class".

Italian grandmother at Ellis Island, 1926.

# 26

# The Italian Emigration Department in 1904:
# The Possibility of its Co-Operation with the Immigration Department of the U.S.[1]

GINO C. SPERANZA[2]

The report recently made by Signor Egisto Rossi, acting commissioner-general of emigration, to the Italian Parliament on the work of his department contains matters of interest to the American observer of Italian immigration to our country.

The Italian Emigration Department was founded to look after the interests of the half million yearly exodus from Italy. The report shows that this vast and important work is being ably and intelligently carried on.

It may surprise some to learn that Italian emigration has been falling off in the last three years, the maximum of 533,245 reached in 1901 having gradually decreased to 506,731 in 1904. Of this last total, the largest number was furnished by the northern provinces of Piedmont and Venetia, with the southern provinces of Sicily and Campania following. Of the north Italian emigrants the majority, however, emigrated to European countries or to South America.

In relation to the population (*i.e.*, counting one emigrant for every 100,000 inhabitants), the highest figures are given by the southern provinces of Calabria (2,544 per 100,000) and Basilicata (2,416 per 100,000). Sicily and the Puglie showed a marked decrease during 1904. Of the total who emigrated from the kingdom, 82.31 per cent were males, of which 6.56 per cent were below the age of fifteen. The small percentage of women and children would seem to confirm the growing belief that Italian emigration all over the world is becoming more and more temporary in character.

1. *Charities and the Commons*, Vol. 15, 1906. Pp. 114-116.　　　　2. New York.

Of the total emigration to transoceanic countries, 67.29 per cent came to the United States. The actual decrease during 1904 of those coming here was about 70,000. This, the department ascribes to the industrial uncertainty of the "presidential year" and to the unusually long and severe winter here. While these causes will also explain the very large number of Italians who returned to the mother country during 1904 (129,231), such large repatriation is further evidence of the temporary character of such emigration.

The report does not mince matters regarding the attitude of Americans towards Italian emigration. It plainly says:

Despite the admittedly progressive improvement in our emigrants, they are still considered in some respects by Americans as little desirable. They are mostly day-laborers and peasants, an active and useful element, but considered unstable and not susceptible of being assimilated. The proportion of those unable to read and write among our emigrants is still high... The Italians, moreover, tend to crowd in the great urban centers, where they live a life apart, with habits of possibly too great economy, in contrast with the habits of Americans.

We are glad to see the advice given repeatedly and unconditionally in this official document that the Italian should go to the agricultural states, such as Virginia, Georgia, Louisiana and Texas. Such distribution is stated to be "one of the most pressing problems" of the department. Towards its solution the department will probably endeavor to establish labor-bureaus here, and to co-operate in any of the various plans for distribution which are being discussed in this country.

This would seem to offer a splendid opportunity to our government to call an international conference on immigration.

## The Schools for Immigrants

Of special interest is that part of the report which treats of the schools which have been opened for intending emigrants in those parts of the kingdom from which the emigration is heaviest. In 1903 the minister of public instruction proposed to the Emigration Department to contribute financially towards the support of such schools. Thereupon, the department appropriated 50,000 lire for the purpose. This increased the total of 3,000 schools opened for the instruction of the illiterates in the evening and on Sundays by 450. Of these 450 schools for the special instruction of emigrants, the largest number was opened at Avellino (70), where the percentage of illiteracy is 73.9, and 62 at Teramo, where the percentage is 74.9.

The department also prepared a mural chart of the United States, especially for the use of such schools. The chart gives the number of Italians living in each state of the Union, and the proportion of Italians to the total population of each state, while special marks are used to indicate those cities having the largest Italian population, and where an Italian consular officer resides. At the bottom of the chart are printed data and suggestions which may be of profit and use to the emigrant coming to this country.

The department calls attention to the difficulty of controlling clandestine emigration. As a possible basis for arriving at the number of such emigrants to the Americas, the report cites the difference between the number of those who sail, as given by the emigration statistics of the department, and the number of those who land on the other side, according to the statistics of immigration. This difference amounts to over 25,000 yearly. Such discrepancies are especially marked as regards the statistics for the United States. Thus, the excess of tabulated arrivals of Italians here over tabulated departures from Italy, was +13,180 in 1902, +27,806 in 1903 and +14,437 in 1904. These large differences do not represent clandestine emigration (which the department, however, believes to be several thousand a year) but are mostly made up of Italian emigrants sailing from foreign ports over which the department can exercise no jurisdiction.

Obviously this is another matter for international control.

The department justly complains of the increasing number of emigrants sailing on what are known as "prepaids", that is, on tickets bought, for example, in the United States and sent to Italy. The financial advantages which we may gain by having the tickets bought here cannot be offset against the obvious abuses of such a system. In 1904 the number of such prepaids was 57,754, while during the first five months of 1905 the number rose to 45,881.

## Enforcement of the Emigration Law

The activity of the department in enforcing the strict provisions of the Italian Emigration Law is shown by the number of proceedings brought against authorized agents of steamship companies, sub-agents and other persons, which in three years amounted to 1,254. The department complains, however, that the courts have been too lenient in emigration proceedings and urges greater severity. To the above total of penal proceedings should be added 637 civil actions brought on behalf of emigrants against steamship companies, upon which (1902-1904) judgments aggregating 58,000 lire were secured.

As regards the work of societies founded outside the kingdom for the protection of Italian immigrants, and which are subsidized by the department, the report is somewhat non-committal. It recognizes the importance of such societies, especially in the United States, and of increasing their number and strengthening those already in existence. It appears that the largest subsidy (35,000 lire) is paid to the Society for Italian Immigrants of New York, founded by Americans, while the Italian Benevolent Institute, of the same place, and the Immigrants' Aid Society of Buenos Aires, come as close seconds (25,000 lire each). The Italian Benevolent Institute appears to have the largest outlay (94,458 lire) as well as the largest income (102,112 lire) of any such society.

The part of the report relative to the money carried by emigrants and the amounts sent by immigrants is instructive. The Bank of Naples is the authorized financial agent of the department for the transmission of the money of emigrants. Yet it is doubtful whether it handles even one-half of the total business. Hence, the figures cited can represent at most only one-half of the amounts going from and coming to Italy. The bank now issues at its Naples office drafts payable in the United States in dollars. The number of such drafts during 1904 was 25,868 for a total of $366,030.85.

During the same year there were sent from the United States to Italy through the Bank of Naples 125,133 drafts, totaling over twenty-two millions of lire. It is safe to say that at least thirty million lire were sent through other channels.

*An International Solution Needed*

The reading of the entire report shows not only that the Italian Emigration Department is engaged in a great, useful and beneficient work, but also (and this is of special importance to us) that it appreciates the American viewpoint regarding Italian immigration and is willing to meet us half way.

The problem of the immigrant, as I have recently insisted, is an international one. Italy is as much interested as we are that her peasant-emigrants shall settle in our agricultural sections rather than crowd in unhealthy city quarters. She is aware that it is in her interests as well as in ours that the character and condition of her emigrants here shall be acceptable to us. She has repeatedly and officially advised her subjects here to become American citizens and to take part in our political life.

On our part, we must change the often trying attitude of suspicion, doubt and even discourtesy towards a friendly power such as Italy, with whom we are at peace.

Let us call an international conference and come to an international understanding of benefit to all concerned.

# 27

# Political Representation of Italo-American Colonies in the Italian Parliament [1]

GINO C. SPERANZA [2]

During the past discussion has been renewed in Italy on the suggestion made by some parliamentarians that the Italian colonies, outside of the Kingdom be allowed political representation at home.

This proposition is not devoid of interest for us, because by "colonies" in this case are included what we are in the habit of calling our "Little Italys".

The importance of New York, for instance, as an Italian colony, is growing every day. There are more Italians in this city than in any city of Italy except Naples, Milan and Rome. Nor is its importance merely a question of population. Its commercial and financial interests are actively on the increase. The irresponsible "bankers" who victimized the ingenuous immigrant are being supplanted by solid banks like Perera's on Wall Street and Conti's on Broadway, and by well-financed institutions such as the Italian Savings Bank, the Italo-American Trust Company and the American branches of the Banco di Napoli.

The Italian Chamber of Commerce is aiding in the commercial development between Italy and America. Italo-American trade is making yearly gains, and represents, both in exports and imports, a very respectable amount.

Add to these conditions the fact that many Italians here return to the mother country and that an even greater number hold real property there and invest yearly, relatively large sums in farm lands at home, and the grounds for giving such expatriated Italians political representation in the home parliament becomes apparent. Indeed, it is quite probable that "Little

1. *Charities and the Commons*, Vol. 15, 1906. Pp. 521-522.      2. New York.

Italy" in New York contributes more to the tax roll of Italy than some of the poorer provinces in Sicily or Calabria. That the financial importance of the Italian colony in New York is being recognized was brought out in the course of a debate in Parliament in Rome, in which a deputy urged that steps be taken for the listing of Italian *rentes* on the American exchanges, and the Minister of Foreign Affairs pledged the government's interest to such proposition.

From the Italian standpoint, therefore, the proposition of colonial representation would seem to deserve practical consideration. Nor would it seem impossible to overcome many difficulties which obviously would arise in putting such a plan into practice. Whether we could prevent such a scheme is a debatable question. But that we should favor it, is even more doubtful. At first sight such a plan would seem a most powerful factor against American assimilation. Its effect might be to isolate even more completely the foreign element from American life, to render our "Little Italys" more than ever out of harmony with their American environment, and make amalgamation more than ever difficult. Yet, on the other hand, it might be urged that the Italo-American "colonist" would, as other colonists before him, hold his allegiance to the motherland as a purely sentimental tie, or as binding only in direct ratio with the material interests held by the mother country.

The experiment, for such it would be, would, however, deserve general interest in that it would be evidence of those new conditions and relations between different countries which tend to destroy the ancient sharp lines of demarcation between nations. A universal brotherhood may remain a utopian dream, but commercial interests, the "annihilation of time and space" by improved methods of transportation and the ebb and flow of travel, will render the old distinctions of nationalities and the parochial character of present-day patriotism, more and more an anachronism. The conception of citizenship itself is rapidly changing and we may have to recognize a sort of world or international citizenship as more logical than the present peripatetic kind, which makes a man an American while here, and an Italian while in Italy. International conferences are not so rare nowadays. Health, the apprehension or exclusion of criminals, financial standards, postage, telegraphs and shipping are to-day, to a great extent, regulated by international action. Such action is bound to increase in scope and effectiveness. We have the Hague Tribunal and the Interparliamentary Union. The old barriers are everywhere breaking down. We may even bring ourselves to the point of recognizing foreign "colonies" in our midst, on our own soil, as entitled to partake in the parliamentary life of their mother country. Certainly it seems a suggestion worth studying.

# 28

# The Effect of Emigration Upon Italy: Threatened Depopulation of the South[1]

Antonio Magano

The story is told of a trip made by the late Prime Minister Zanardelli, through one of the Italian provinces where emigration had really begun to be a menace to the community. The mayor and chief men of one town met the minister at the station and escorted him in state to the central square, where, before a platform gorgeously decorated in the red, white and green of Italy, waited a motley throng. Looking down on those poor, half-starved, ill-clad peasants, the prime minister listened to an elaborately prepared address of welcome, read by the mayor: "I welcome you in the name of the five thousand inhabitants of this town, three thousand of whom are in America and the other two thousand preparing to go".

An extreme instance, do you say? Yes, yet this is the phase of our immigration question which strikes home to Italy, and vital as the question of Italian migration is to us, it concerns Italy vastly more. We have always asked ourselves hitherto: "How will the Italian affect us? How will he affect our social and political institutions if he continues to come? Does he contribute anything to our industrial welfare?" It is not my purpose to discuss in any way the desirability or undesirability of the Italian immigrant, but to give the facts as I found them. I have spent several months traveling through Italy, riding through the country and seeking out the villages and hamlets where tourists rarely go. It is from these villages that Italian emigration is largest, it is here that the effect of the enormous annual exodus of Italian workmen is most evident, and it was these peasant emigrants and the background of country which especially interested me on returning to my native land.

1. *Charities and the Commons*, Vol. 19, 1907-1908. Pp. 1329-1338.

In their official reports the Italians group their emigrants in two classes, temporary and permanent. To the first class belong all those who leave the country annually during the working season — from May to October — and those who leave for a definite period of time who, with few exceptions, return to Italy. In general the members of this temporary class go from the northern provinces — Piedmont, Lombardy, Venetia, Emilia, Tuscany. The north of Italy is a great plain containing the most fertile and productive land in the country. One may ride for miles past level fields of grain, past orchards of mulberry-trees, where the grapevines, planted half-way between the trees or at their feet, are trained in graceful festoons from one to another, making a beautiful lace-work of green over the whole field. The soil is so fertile that more than one crop a year can be raised and the systems of canals and irrigating ditches, perfected centuries ago, are so good that there never fails to be an abundant harvest no matter what the rainfall. The homes in this part of the country are larger and better than in many other parts of Italy, especially in the country near Florence, where houses are scattered over the fields and on the hillsides somewhat as they are in our own rural communities. For centuries Barbarians, French, Spaniards, Austrians have coveted and fought for this garden spot, but in spite of frequent wars and systematic pillaging, the country has always emerged, after a time, as prosperous as ever.

The northern peasants are taller, healthier and better fed and clothed than those of the southern provinces. The thousands, who leave their home each year, generally return when the working season is over, and spend their earnings in their native land. They are still loyal Italian citizens and their money adds to the prosperity of this region, which must strike even a casual observer as in strong contrast to the poverty and backwardness of the south. In many cases, the entire family emigrates so that the worker may be more comfortable during the period of absence which is generally not longer than three years.

While returning to Lucerne after a day's outing, our tram stopped just outside the town and about twenty-five rosy-cheeked girls and stalwart young men came clambering into the car, laughing and chattering gaily. On hearing them speak Italian, I entered into their conversation and asked what they were doing in Switzerland and if they intended to remain there. They told me that they were working in a silk mill; that their families were living in the town and that at the end of three years they hoped to return to their homes near Verona. Oh, no, they did not intend to remain in Switzerland, the country was pretty, yes, but not like "bella Italia", and then the people were different, and the language, ugh! so harsh. They were neatly dressed, so large and strong, and with such fresh complexions that one would almost think them Germans.

The same afternoon, we chanced to lunch in a hotel at a table near the orchestra. We paid no attention to the men, supposing them to be Germans, till suddenly the leader rose and sang, in their inimitable way, a rollicking Neapolitan song. There was no mistaking that. Later, I sought him out and learned that the entire orchestra was composed of Italians, one from Venice, another from Verona, others from Bologna, Florence and Milan. They played in the Swiss hotels during the tourist season and then returned to their homes in Italy.

In one Paris cafe we were surprised to be served by Italian waiters, and the same was true of a hotel in London. These people are all from the northern provinces and comparatively few of them come to America.

In the early days emigration was mainly limited to the provinces of the north. From the south there were but few who emigrated prior to 1885, unless the Basilicata be excepted. While a goodly number from the southern provinces may be found in South America and in Africa, there being a flourishing colony of 75,000 Italians in Tunis, by far the vast majority find their way to the United States. The following table taken from the annual report for 1906, as presented by the minister of agriculture, industry and commerce, shows the various districts which furnish the largest contingent of recent emigrants and, in a general way, gives an idea of their destination:

## Numbers by Departments

| Departments | 1906 | | | 1905 | | |
|---|---|---|---|---|---|---|
| | Europe and Africa | North and South America | Total | Europe and Africa | North and South America | Total |
| Piedmont | 38,305 | 33,885 | 72,190 | 37,409 | 30,987 | 63,396 |
| Liguria | 2,304 | 6,630 | 8,664 | 1,908 | 6,324 | 8,232 |
| Lombardy | 43,586 | 20,046 | 63,632 | 45,845 | 16,211 | 62,056 |
| Veneto | 88,547 | 16,338 | 104,885 | 95,453 | 12,571 | 108,024 |
| Emilia | 29,989 | 12,692 | 42,681 | 28,659 | 9,921 | 38,580 |
| Toscany | 23,151 | 13,960 | 37,111 | 21,123 | 10,497 | 31,620 |
| Marche | 10,690 | 23,811 | 34,501 | 10,788 | 21,131 | 31,919 |
| Umbria | 10,828 | 3,958 | 14,786 | 7,435 | 2,464 | 9,899 |
| Lazio | 2,181 | 16,326 | 18,507 | 1,586 | 13,116 | 14,702 |
| Abruzzi and Molise | 6,030 | 52,002 | 58,032 | 6,909 | 52,020 | 58,929 |
| Campania | 4,332 | 85,437 | 89,769 | 4,588 | 79,728 | 84,316 |
| Puglie | 3,963 | 29,799 | 33,762 | 4,809 | 16,541 | 21,350 |
| Basilicata | 310 | 17,788 | 18,098 | 534 | 16,475 | 17,009 |
| Calabria | 1,507 | 55,577 | 57,084 | 1,513 | 60,777 | 62,290 |
| Sicily | 5,934 | 121,669 | 127,603 | 8,329 | 97,879 | 106,208 |
| Sardenia | 4,655 | 2,017 | 6,672 | 2,360 | 441 | 2,801 |
| Total | 276,042 | 511,935 | 787,977 | 279,248 | 447,083 | 726,331 |

In this table, emigration is divided into two classes, those who cross the ocean and almost as a whole now come to the United States, and those who find their way to the countries of Europe and to countries bordering on the Mediterranean. During the year 1906, Piedmont furnished 72,190 emigrants, but only 33,885 crossed the ocean, and a large part of these were bound for South America, where the north Italians have been successful and are highly respected. Lombardy gave a total of 63,632 in the same year, but only 20,046 came to America, and of 104,885 emigrants from Venice, only the insignificant number of 16,000 crossed the ocean.

The southern districts tell a very different story. The Abruzzi and Molise give as the total number of emigrants, 58,032, only 6,030 of whom remained on the other side of the ocean; while Sicily shows 127,603 emigrants for the same year, 121,669 coming to our shores. The three provinces of Calabria, that is, Catanzaro, Cosenza, and Reggio, during the same period sent forth 57,084 emigrants, and all but 1,507 crossed the Atlantic. But it is the Basilicata which is to-day under greatest stress owing to the loss of nearly all its able-bodied men. From this province alone, in 1906, went 18,098 emigrants and all save 310 came to America.

Of more importance to the American are these foreigners who land at our ports and remain here permanently in the proportion of two out of three. The provinces from which they come are the Abruzzi, east of Rome; Bari, east, but farther south; Avellino and Basilicata, in the central and southern part; and Calabria, comprising the three provinces of Cosenza, Catanzaro and Reggio forming the extreme southern part of the peninsula and the Island of Sicily. To this second, or permanent, class of immigrants belongs those who absent themselves from their own country for a long period of time or settle permanently in foreign lands.

Nature has not been kind to man in these provinces; the lofty range of the Apennines is picturesque and magnificent in its snow-capped grandeur, but the barren, rocky sides are useless to the farmer and yield nothing even as herbage for flocks. The rest of the land is hilly, mountainous in some places, and full of stones. The Roman Campagna, the largest of the few plains in this region, has always been marshy and malarial and is used chiefly for grazing cattle and for flocks of sheep and goats. The Roman shepherd of the Campagna and his dog are familiar figures in art and literature. Recently, the government has taken measures to make the locality more healthful, and it is hoped that this beautiful plain may bear crops equal in value to those in the north. The Campo Felice, near Naples, enriched by lava deposits from Vesuvius, and the eastern coast of Sicily, under the shadow of Mt. Aetna, give large returns to the toiler. But vineyards are planted and tended there at risk of life and with the certainty of destruction of homes and harvests by occasional eruptions, while in Calabria and the Basilicata there are earthquakes and destructive land-slides. Most of the vineyards and orchards are on the hillsides, and where the slope is very steep the peasants have built platforms of earth, twelve or fifteen feet wide, supported by thick stone walls, six or eight feet high. Flights of stone steps lead from one terrace to another. Sometimes the hills and mountains are banded from base to summit by these walls. It is on these sunny hillsides, so glowingly described by travelers, that the grapes and olives flourish which produce the sweetest wine and finest oil in the world.

One of the charming features of the famous coast drive from La Cava to Sorrento, is this succession of terraced gardens. Pink almond blossoms fill the air with fragrance and in the distance are sturdy dark-leaved trees whose glossy verdure half conceals their golden burden of lemons and oranges. Here are fig trees, pomegranates and citron and entire hillsides covered with the silvery gray foliage of the olive, whose leaves rustle softly even in the fiercest gale. Where there are no orchards or vineyards, there are vegetables and these are often planted between rows of vines or trees so that every available inch of ground is used. The pitiful fact is, however, that even with so much hard work, so much intensive farming, the soil produces only food enough to scantily feed the increasing number of inhabitants, and wages are only thirty cents a day for a man, and less for women and boys.

An American is a marked man in southern Italy. Especially did I find this true in the out-of-the-way towns where tourists never go. The people quickly collect in a group and follow the stranger, eager to ask questions about America, which seems to them almost an enchanted country. Frequently on leaving the land of their birth, which could not furnish them the bread they needed, emigrants can be heard to exclaim as the train starts on its journey to Naples, "Viva l'America, viva il Paradiso". So with high hopes they start out, leaving the tragedy of the separation behind with the tearful women and the wondering children.

In the province of Bari, as I entered the town of Altamura, I saw a great throng of people. Upon inquiry I was told that they had been to the station to bid goodbye to one hundred and twenty of their townsmen who had just left for America. Three weeks later, in Gravina, a town of the same province only a few miles from Altamura, two hundred emigrants were accompanied to the station by nearly half the population of the town. These towns have only recently caught the migrating fever. In 1900 and 1901, Altamura sent us twenty-five and thirty-six and Gravina twenty-five and ninety-six respectively.

In Naples, I had been only a day at the hotel when the head-waiter, a very capable man who speaks fluent English, French and German, as well as Italian, introduced himself to me and asked if I thought he could find work in America. Since my return to this country, I have learned that a gentleman who needed an attendant while crossing the ocean, not only paid this man's passage over but paid him for his services besides. He is at present in New

York.

The concierge or head-clerk of this same hotel, a man speaking several languages, also told me he was planning to go to America. A week later, the little Calabrian elevator boy, prompt and faithful, met me in a tram and asked me if I would help him to get work in America.

Everywhere I went, I met with requests for letters of introduction for prospective emigrants. There was talk of America constantly in the trains, on the road, in the towns. I invariably met people who had been to America, or had friends or relatives there. Every train from the south which comes into Naples brings the familiar Italian emigrant. In the southern towns, it is no uncommon thing to hear English spoken. In Sale, a town of the Abruzzi, there were about twenty-five men who had been to America and settled in Astoria, Long Island, and who expected to return in the spring. In Toritto, I found young men, sons of emigrants, who could not speak Italian, but could speak excellent English. In a street car in Naples, I watched with curiosity a conductor who had a book in his hands and, between collecting fares, seemed to be studying. To my amazement I found that it was an Italian-English grammar and reading book. He was preparing himself to go to America.

While spending a few hours at the historic site of ancient Paestum, under the columns of the Greek Temple of Neptune, a peasant woman, young, though she looked old from overwork, came where a little group of us were eating our luncheon. She asked permission to pick up the pieces of white tissue paper in which the luncheon had been wrapped. I entered into conversation with her and found that she had a brother in America. I asked her if she ever thought of going across the ocean and with a sad, wistful expression on her face she raised her eyes toward heaven and said, "Would to God that I could go!"

Although Italian emigration is a new and remarkable phenomenon to us, the Italians through the centuries have become accustomed to constant movement among the ranks of their laboring population. Says Angelo Mosso, of the University of Turin:

Temporary Italian emigration began when the eagles of the Roman legions crossed the Alps and the Mediterranean to diffuse Latin civilization. The Italian artisan followed them into Gaul, Britain, Africa, and the East. The bridges, the aqueducts, the baths, the basilicas scattered over Europe, were reared by Italian workmen, and with their own blocks, as the stamp upon the bricks and the form of the tiles indicate. Even when Italy was under the dominion of the barbarians, the master-masons were always so highly esteemed that the Lombards exempted them from servile tribute, and the Magistri Comacini, who were master-builders from the vicinity of Lake Como, remained equal with the free citizens, with permission to unite into unions. When Charlemagne was building the cathedral at Aix-la-Chapelle, he sent to Italy for marbles, columns and workmen, and we remember late French kings did the same thing. After 1000 A.D., the Lombards are found in Sicily, building churches and palaces for the Norman, and during the Renaissance hundreds of workmen emigrated to different parts of Europe to assist in building cathedrals. To-day more than half a million Italians seek work every year in foreign countries. Of this number, nearly one-half scatters itself over Europe. The other half goes principally to America and of this latter half, for every three that depart, only one returns.[2]

While emigration has been going on in Italy for centuries, it was not till after the formation of the kingdom in 1870 that the movement assumed any noticeable proportions.

The following table, taken from official statistics of Italian emigration, shows the constant increase in the number of those who have emigrated from Italy since 1876. Accurate figures can be obtained only from that date. Beginning in 1876 with less than twenty thousand emigrants, in 1906 the total number for the year of those who emigrated reached three-quarters of a million.

### Emigration During the Years 1876-1906

| Years | Emigration North and South America | Europe and Africa | Total | Years | Emigration North and South America | Europe and Africa | Total |
|---|---|---|---|---|---|---|---|
| 1876 | 19,848 | 88,923 | 108,771 | 1892 | 114,246 | 109,421 | 223,667 |
| 1877 | 21,385 | 77,828 | 99,213 | 1893 | 138,982 | 107,769 | 246,751 |
| 1878 | 21,203 | 75,065 | 96,268 | 1894 | 111,898 | 113,425 | 225,323 |
| 1879 | 37,286 | 82,545 | 119,831 | 1895 | 184,518 | 108,663 | 293,181 |
| 1880 | 33,258 | 86,643 | 119,901 | 1896 | 194,247 | 113,235 | 307,482 |
| 1881 | 41,064 | 94,768 | 135,832 | 1897 | 172,078 | 127,777 | 299,855 |
| 1882 | 59,826 | 101,736 | 161,562 | 1898 | 135,912 | 147,803 | 283,715 |
| 1883 | 64,283 | 104,818 | 169,101 | 1899 | 140,767 | 167,572 | 308,339 |
| 1884 | 56,319 | 90,698 | 147,017 | 1900 | 166,503 | 186,279 | 352,782 |
| 1885 | 73,481 | 83,712 | 157,193 | 1901 | 279,674 | 253,571 | 533,245 |
| 1886 | 82,877 | 84,952 | 167,829 | 1902 | 284,654 | 246,855 | 531,509 |
| 1887 | 130,302 | 85,363 | 215,665 | 1903 | 282,435 | 225,541 | 507,976 |
| 1888 | 204,700 | 86,036 | 290,736 | 1904 | 252,366 | 218,825 | 471,191 |
| 1889 | 123,589 | 94,823 | 218,412 | 1905 | 447,083 | 279,248 | 726,331 |
| 1890 | 114,949 | 102,295 | 217,244 | 1906 | 511,935 | 276,042 | 787,997 |
| 1891 | 187,575 | 106,056 | 293,631 | | | | |

2. *La Vita Moderna degli Italiani* by Angelo Mosso, Professor of Biology at the University of Turin.

In 1887, emigration from Italy to transatlantic countries for the first time exceeded emigration to Mediterranean countries. This year marked, too, the crossing of 100,000 emigrants in one year. Since 1887 the emigration to other European and African countries has steadily increased, but the emigration to the American countries has outstripped it by leaps and bounds.

In spite of the vast numbers that have left the country during the last twenty years, four millions of whom have become a permanent element in foreign countries, the number of Victor Emmanuel's subjects has not diminished, but has on the contrary increased. Italy has an annual increase of births over deaths of 350,000, and in 1897 it rose to 406,000. This little peninsula with an area of 110,623 square miles, has a population of 32,449,754, or 293 people to a square mile as against France with 189 and the United States with only 21. Over population in districts difficult of cultivation, heavy taxation, fearfully low wages and proportionately high rents, have combined to keep the people poor and living conditions little better than during the Middle Ages, and at last, have compelled those who could not make even the poorest kind of a living at home to go elsewhere, usually to America. Emigrants, few in number at first, succeeded so well that others have followed until now the government, patriotic citizens and great land holders, are all deeply concerned about the departure of so many able-bodied workers.

To put it another way — considering the small area of the country, together with the fact that one-third of this consists of barren mountains which produce absolutely nothing, and large sections are virtually abandoned owing to the prevalence of malaria, it is quite evident that emigration must continue; otherwise the country will not be able to support its inhabitants. Indeed, unless hundreds of thousands of Italians expatriate themselves every year, they will increasingly have to build their homes on the sea shore and on the precipitous mountain sides. If the people who leave the country came in relatively equal numbers from all the provinces, and if the percentage of women were as large as the percentage of men, if the old and infirm would go as well as the young and strong, the government would not complain. The country can easily spare from three to four hundred thousand: or the same number as the annual increase of births over deaths last year. But it cannot with impunity be drained of four hundred thousand of its agricultural population, the food-producing class, especially when over three-fourths of this number are men from seventeen to thirty-five or forty years of age representing always the most vigorous and ambitious element in their home towns, and coming, as they do, from a limited section of the country.

While we, in America, are considering the restriction of immigration by means of an educational test, the Italian parliament has spent several sessions discussing the possibility of forbidding the emigration of those who cannot read and write. This would leave the educated classes free to emigrate, but would greatly restrict the emigration of the southern peasants who are needed to till the fields. Only last March one of the members of Parliament pointed out the fact that emigration, if it continued at the present rate, would surely prove a severe injury to the country. Mr. Celsea said:

The exodus of our people threatens to be in the near future far and beyond that which we believe, and threatens to absorb that gradual increment of population which for some years past had been our pride.

Allow me to remind you that our emigration from 88,000 in 1886, from 503,000 in 1903, enormously increased in 1905 to 726,000. During the first half of this year (up to March), the number is 458,000, a tremendous increase over 1905. Alongside of this fearful increase in emigration is the decrease in the number of those who return. For if in 1905, 78 per cent returned, in 1906, only 23 or 28 per cent.

In the southern provinces, we found an almost universal desire to emigrate. In every town that I visited the main question which I put either to the mayor or the secretary of the commune was: "Do you not think that emigration from these parts ought to be restricted in some way?" The answer was invariably, "Yes, the problem of emigration is a serious one for us. The people are crazy to go to America and nothing can be done to prevent their going. This is a free country and we cannot compel the people to stay here if they choose to go elsewhere. The only thing that can be done is to better conditions here, make the burdens lighter for the working classes and offer all the inducements possible so that the people will wish to remain at home instead of crossing the ocean."

In the course of a trip from La Cava to Sorrento, we passed through Positano, a quaint town perched on the hillside, that has been abandoned by its male inhabitants, all of whom are in America. We saw row after row of empty, desolate looking houses. In conversing at Amalfi, with the proprietor of the old Cappuccin Monastery Hotel, who has been on that beautiful spot for fifty years, he told me how twenty years ago Amalfi was a thriving town of ten thousand; by 1901 it was reduced to 6,681, and to-day it cannot contain more than 3,000 persons. America has all the rest. This explains why the factories cannot run and why the vineyards are going to decay. In fact, so serious has this depopulation become that an effort has been made to colonize the southern provinces with workmen from the north but, as the prefect of Reggio di Calabria told me, this cannot be carried out with success because the laborers from the north will not put up with the primitive conditions of life and work existing in the south.

When emigration had not assumed such enormous proportions as at the present time, the Italian government looked upon it with favor, for it served as a kind of balance wheel to the economic equilibrium of the country. The laborers would leave home when they had no work and return at the end of the season with money to spend. This kind of emigration is fostered by the Italian government notwithstanding what may be said to the contrary. But the great bulk of the emigration today is a very different sort. It is the permanent tendency in the tide of emigration which is occupying the attention of those most keenly interested in the welfare of the country as a whole. They are seeing before their very eyes the depopulation of entire provinces, and the soil which once was a veritable garden, maintained in a high state of cultivation by the labor of countless contadini eager to work for the mere possibility of existence for themselves and their families, to-day lies abandoned because men cannot be found to till it. In Potenza, the chief secretary of the city, while talking with me on this subject, opened the windows of his office and pointed out the barren mountain sides and said, "There is the result of emigration for us". This was repreated again and again in the southern provinces.

The most effective and lasting measures the government is slow to carry out, partly because they would require much money, and partly because the interests of the influential land holders would suffer directly at first. Of the situation as I found it, later articles in this series will tell in detail.

# 29

# The Italians in Congested Districts[1]

Gino C. Speranza

The great though unsuspected evil effect of congestion on Italians is psychological even more than physical. By this I mean that the suggestion of the worst or of the weakest is spread easily over the congested mass, whereas it would be sterile of results in a freer environment. Many an Italian who never would have thought of doing any other labor than that in the open air, some fine day hears that a neighbor of his is working in a cigar factory. Ninety-nine chances in one hundred that cigarmaker is a weakling who could not handle pick and shovel and, conscious of his physical deficiency, probably boasts what easy money factory work yields, where a man sits down all day and after work "goes home with the factory girls". The idea strikes the shoveller as novel and worth considering. The greater wage with the pick may for a while hold him, but if a day of temporary discontent or lassitude comes he digs up the factory ideal. I remember, a year ago, sending home a gang of strong, enduring Italian laborers from North Carolina, where they could perform hard work in the labor camps where I had found them, but one of them, just the one who was undersized and lazy, got a job in a factory on his return to the city. That entire gang is at the factory now.

I dwell on this psychological side of the influence of congested living, as we will see it especially active in influencing the civic relations of the Italian.

But so far, industrially, it is the Italian woman that has suffered most through congestion. The Italian wives or sisters, who in Italy used to work around the house or in the fields, never receiving compensation, see the "girl on the lower floor" go out every day and earn good money that gives her, what appears to the newcomer, not only splendid independence, but even the undreamed of joy of wearing Grand Street millinery. The home becomes

1. *Charities and the Commons*, Vol. 20, 1908. Pp. 55-57.

hateful, the traditional restraint which was considered a domestic virtue becomes a symbol of slavery, and the domestic woman will become a factory hand. Unused to such so-called freedom, she will misuse it as a starved man who overeats.

Congested living, working its evil spell on the morals of the Italians among us, in so far as it leads women to industrial work is, in my opinion, a greater evil, for it tends to destroy one of the finest of the Italian traditions, the unity of family life, and leads to the destruction of the Italian ideal of the home.

So likewise, in the civic relations of the Italians, our congested living works varied evils. One bad idea, one wrong notion, spreads by contagion over the mass, and it is the shrewd and often the dishonest that take advantage of this vehicle of contagion, which, under certain conditions, might be made a vehicle for good. The first to profit by it is the so-called Italian banker. I am not one of those who think all things bad of the Italian banker and of the Italian *padrone*. I think he has been and is an absolute necessity in the life of the expatriated Italian peasant. It will take years and years to obviate the economic necessity of the Italian *padrone*; we will have and we are having better and better *padroni*. The aim of those who wish to help Italians here should be to improve the quality of the *padroni* rather than to destroy them; to imitate their methods and use such methods to good end. It is against the abuse of the powers exercised by the banker that I appeal. Urban congestion is the very condition of life for the banker and the *padrone*; in exact ratio with the topographical nearness of his clients and *paesani* does he control them for good or bad. Each street has its particular region of Italy; Elizabeth Street is claimed by the Western Sicilian; Catharine and Monroe Streets by the Eastern Sicilian; Mulberry by the Neapolitans; Bleecker by the Genoese; MacDougal by the North Italians. The more crowded the street on which the bank is, the better for the banker; better yet, the more crowded is the block where the bank has its habitat, best of all, the more crowded with *paesani* the tenement in which operates the banker. Americans at times wonder how quickly a *padrone* can supply a large demand for laborers; it is simply that the *padrone* lives with them — and at his order the regiments of *paesani* turn out of the barracks of his tenement. Surely the *padrone* is not going to help you spread out his constituents.

Likewise the average Italian banker could not do the varied kind of business he does unless he had his clientele under close physical vigilance. He could not take the risk, even for a larger consideration than he gets now, to go bail for his clients who are in trouble; he could not, as he undoubtedly often does, make advance on wages and render services of value where the compensation is contingent on his client's work in the future.

This power to control a mass, which through its very congestion is more like a large family than a healthy community of independent units, is shrewdly used not only by the banker and the *padrone* but by the politician. The voter among this controllable and controlled mass is the easy prey of the political boss, an easily worked political machine.

The intimacy, I might say, gossipy nature of such congested districts massed according to the towns or villages in Italy, while it is a religiously closed book to the outsider, is too open a book for the insider; none of its members can do anything that it does not become the property of the entire community. If this stopped at harmless gossip — it would merit no attention. But the fact is, that it is taken advantage of in two important ways by the criminally inclined in the community. If Antonio puts $100 in the bank, if Giuseppe's barber shop shows evidence of prosperity, if Gaetano especially pampers his children and dresses them well, if Michele gets a little extra money from some unexpected source, all the *paesani* in the crowd know it. And very likely the day after Antonio has made his bank deposit or Michele has got his extra cash, each will receive what is picturesquely called a Black Hand demand. Or perhaps Gaetano, who has shown his fondness for his children too much and is also prosperous, one fine day will find that his little Beppino is missing.

Not only this, but the close knowledge of each other in these congested communities is not merely limited to the present status of its members but to their family histories. Therefore, if in the past Gaetano has had some trouble, big or little, with the police or otherwise, that fact is known to the community — he is vulnerable or invulnerable according to the willingness of the members of the community to let the past be dead. I am thoroughly convinced that with very few exceptions, so called Black Hand threats are never made against an irreproachable person — that is against one who either in the past or the present has not something, not necessarily criminal or immoral, but something in his life that he would prefer to keep hidden.

The other way in which this close intimacy is a culture bed for crime, is that differences between individual members lead to divisions into criminal feuds. If Antonio insults Giuseppe and it remained between them, they might often settle it if not forgive it. But everybody knows of the insult passed and it would seem cowardly to submit before such a large audience. This may lead to divisions into partisans for the offender and for the offended — and a quarrel between two becomes a war between two parties. That same communal spirit nourished into a spirit of intimate fellowship results into other dangerous principles; that if any member of the community commits a crime the community must protect him; above all will he be hid and sheltered from the outsider, from the police officer and the detective.

This congested living, this communal life is so intimately close that it might seem well nigh useless to hope that the breeze of American views will blow through its narrow ways and alleys. The tendency to congregate, especially in a strange land, is natural, neither this conference, nor any man or body of men can hope to find means of preventing it — it would be like fighting instinct or nature. But while it is in vain to fight such a tendency, we may hope to destroy or minimize its almost absolute segregation. Every city, even in Utopia, will have districts where the rich live apart from the poor, the scholars from the market men, the lovers of freedom from the lovers of comfort, there will be aggregations of tastes if not of conditions; but even these separate units must constitute one great whole; there must be one municipal spirit, its denizens must must constitute one people and not distinct clans. So the danger of our Little Italys, which in no way reflect the beauty and greatness of real Italy, lies not in their physical congestion, as much as in their spirit of aloofness, in the lack in their denizens of a sense of joint responsibility with all the people, not merely with some of them. These aliens must learn that they do not merely live their physical existence in New York, but constitute jointly with others the life of the city; that they must and can aid to make New York, not a bad copy of some ancient little Italian feudalism, but a great cosmopolitan city, different from other great centers in this essential regard — that its cosmopolitanism has its origin and life in the cosmopolitanism of the working classes.

# 30

# The Italian Immigrant on the Land[1]

EMILY FOGG MEADE[2]

Public opinion is generally unfavorable to the newcomers from southern Italy, but some observers of this people in their own country believe that it is because of their present settlement in the cities that the valuable qualities of these immigrants remain unrecognized and the probability of their Americanization and assimilation appears difficult, if not hopeless. Substantial confirmation of the truth of this opinion can be found in the Italian settlements of South Jersey.

Thirty years ago Southern New Jersey, now one of the garden spots of the Eastern states, was largely undeveloped. In particular the land included within the limits of the pine belt remained for the most part in its original condition. The "Pine Belt" is a wide strip of territory extending through the south central part of the state. Much of this country is covered even to-day with a thick growth of scrub pines and underbrush. This is not only hard to clear away, but until recent years the inducement to undertake the work was lacking because the sandy soil did not respond to the methods of agriculture formerly in vogue. The region, however, possesses one marked advantage — a dry, bracing climate, due to its position midway between the Atlantic Ocean and Delaware Bay, which gives it the benefit of salt air modified by its passage over the pines. Lakewood is the most famous of the resorts in this region, but the climate, beneficial for lung and throat diseases, is the same throughout the pine belt.

One of the oldest Italian settlements is Hammonton, in the eastern part of Atlantic county, from which the materials for this paper have mainly been

1. *Charities*, Vol. 13, 1905. Pp. 541-544.          2. Hammonton, N.J.

derived. This town was founded and settled largely by people from New England and New York, who chose Hammonton as a place of residence not because of the possibilities of its soil which they did not recognize, but to lengthen their lives. It was soon discovered, however, that although this sandy soil would not produce heavy crops, it was, when heavily fertilized, well adapted for fruits and vegetables. Peaches, pears, plums, apples, and grapes all grow well in the sand. The small fruits, however, raspberries, strawberries and blackberries, are especially satisfactory crops. The rapid growth of a demand for these products in the large cities of the Atlantic seaboard drew attention to the cheap land of New Jersey and a rapid development of agriculture was the result.

As the berry industry grew, the local labor force became insufficient to pick the berries. Italian labor was therefore brought in from Philadelphia. This annual invasion of Italian pickers has been repeated for more than twenty years. As many as 1,500 pickers have come to Hammonton in a good season. They are poorly lodged in barns and sheds, supplementing their bedding with the farmer's hay, using an old stove which he provides, and eating the simple food to which they have always been accustomed; but with their race love for outdoor life, they look upon the picking season as a gala time. They enjoy the freedom, the hot hours of the day passed in groups under the trees, and the evenings spent in dancing to the music of the accordion. They also make snug sums of money, since the entire family is employed at the work. A family of six has made $500 in four months when berries of all kinds were plentiful.

Many of these pickers who come to Hammonton year after year, drawn thither by the opportunity of these large earnings, become interested in the country life and remain to earn a home for themselves. Coming from a country where land is so heavily taxed that peasant proprietorship is almost impossible, the cheap land of Southern New Jersey is particularly attractive to the Italian immigrants and the settlement of Hammonton has grown also from direct immigration from southern Italy and Sicily. More then one-half the inhabitants of a town in the mountains of Sicily, a few miles from Messina, are now residents of the locality. The immigration has been constantly stimulated and aided by relatives in Hammonton. The father and, perhaps, an older son come first; then, the mother and children, to be followed later by uncles, aunts and cousins.

This Italian immigration has been of great benefit to the community. It has furnished a cheap labor force and it has brought in a large number of industrious peasant proprietors. The land has to be cleared, grubbed out with mattock and hoe and frequently drained — hard, patient labor, felling trees, digging ditches, tearing out roots, work extremely distasteful to the native Americans of this region. The Italian, however, knows how to do the work thoroughly and he is willing to do it for low wages. As a result, thousands of acres have been prepared for cultivation which, without his unremitting labor, would have been abandoned permanently to pine swamps and barrens.

The newcomer usually obtains work as a laborer on a farm, on the railroad, or in a neighboring brickyard. His living costs him little and he saves, as only frugal people robbed by tax collectors and landlords, know how to save. If his family is with him, they often live in one room in the house of some other Italian. When the immigrant has accumulated sufficient money he buys four to ten acres of uncleared land at twenty to thirty-five dollars an acre, according to its situation. Such hours as can be spared from his regular employment are spent in developing his new purchase.

When the land is brought under cultivation, the aid of one of the local building and loan associations is asked. The association takes the deed of the land and advances an amount large enough to build a small frame house. Settled in his home, the Italian may now continue his outside work, leaving the management of his farm to his wife and children; or his farm may be large enough to keep him occupied during the summer, while he still works at odd jobs during the winter. For the Italian, like the German truck farmer, has a useful working force in his large family of children.

In a number of cases, Italians have accumulated enough to buy out American farmers. From 1880 to 1895 many of the first American settlers sold to Italians, while the settlement of estates threw many farms into their hands. Some farms are purchased on contract, the Italian incumbent engaging to pay a certain amount each year.

The Italian immigrant of South Jersey lives well, according to his own ideas. His demands are few. He burns wood — often mere brushwood — instead of coal. His household goods include little besides beds, tables, a stove and a few chairs. Clothing is of the simplest character, the older women, for instance, clinging to the calico dresses, aprons, and native handkerchiefs for head and shoulders. For food, bread and salad are often sufficient, supplemented by garden produce, and meat when the family prospers. Chickens are generally kept and a large number of Italians own horses and wagons. A family of eight frequently makes a good living off five acres. Their frugality is shown by the gathering of brushwood for fuel and the collecting of fallen leaves from the trees to serve as bedding for stock. Most of the holdings are small and a striking feature is the patient thoroughness with which the farm resources are developed. Every foot of space is utilized. Small vegetables are planted among the large. The front yard is filled with woodpiles, grape vines, or vegetables.

The cash crop of the South Jersey Italians is berries; strawberries, raspberries, blackberries, and grapes following in order. In a good year a substantial sum of money can be made off an acre of berries. In 1902 an Italian cleared $160 on one quarter of an acre of strawberries; in 1903, $250 was made on an acre by another Italian. The time has been, it is claimed, when $1,000 was made on an acre of blackberries. Grapes are an Italian specialty. Every farm, no matter how small, has its vineyard, and it is said that an Italian can make grapes grow where anyone else would have no success. The grapes are used in making a sour wine for their food supply. Much of the wine is sent to Philadelphia and New York, where it sells for fifty cents a quart.

The living which the Italian makes off his small farm is better than that he can make in the city. Studies of the dietaries of Italians in Chicago and other large cities show that they buy the spoiled and withered vegetables. In Hammonton their vegetables and fruits are fresh. They have their own chickens, eggs and pork, and their own unadulterated wine, as well as good bread made of the best of flour in their outside brick ovens. They are not crowded into unsanitary tenements, but soon establish themselves in two and four-room dwellings. They live a healthful, outdoor life, often eating and cooking outdoors in the summer time. The Italian children born in Hammonton are large and strong. As the result of making a home, the Italians have become more generous in expenditures that make for comfort. The work they give the children is healthful in character, not sweat-shop labor, and the compulsory education law provides for their schooling. Their business relations require some knowledge of writing, arithmetic, and English and in consequence they value the information which is obtained by the children. Contact with Americans in the schools, and as neighbors, has a perceptible effect in the second generation, when their ways of living begin to conform more closely to those of the community. The progress of the second generation is such as to promise a speedy assimilation into our American life. The young people who have remained in Hammonton have identified themselves with the interests of the community. Those who have gone to the city have found themselves better equipped to cope with city conditions. The assessment list shows to what extent Italians are property owners. In the town of Hammonton, 237 Italians are assessed on 3,708.45 acres valued at $130,415 — 15 per cent of the total valuation of the town. The holdings represent variously: nine acres valued at $1,600; 14.1 at $4,000; 84 at $1,100, etc.; 232 Italians are assessed on $9,000 for personal property out of $89,525 for the whole town, an assessment which is, to be sure, probably out of proportion to the amount of property owned.

The savings of the Italians are partly shown by their bank and building and loan association accounts. Out of the $260,779 of deposits at the People's Bank of Hammonton, $56,614 (or 21.7 per cent) is owed to the Italians. In the savings department out of $88,768, $26,231 or 29.5 per cent belongs to Italians. In the Workingmen's Building and Loan Association there are 553 stockholders with holdings averaging 5½ shares; 129 shareholders, representing 23 per cent, are Italians. In the Hammonton Loan and Building Association 79 out of 460 stockholders, or 17 per cent, are Italians.

Of some interest is the amount of money sent to Italy. For the year ending December 31, 1903, there were 408 money orders sent, amounting to $8,774.39. While this amount undoubtedly includes the money of some of the pickers, it is offset by money sent from Philadelphia or in registered letters by Hammonton Italians. During the year 519 registered letters were sent.

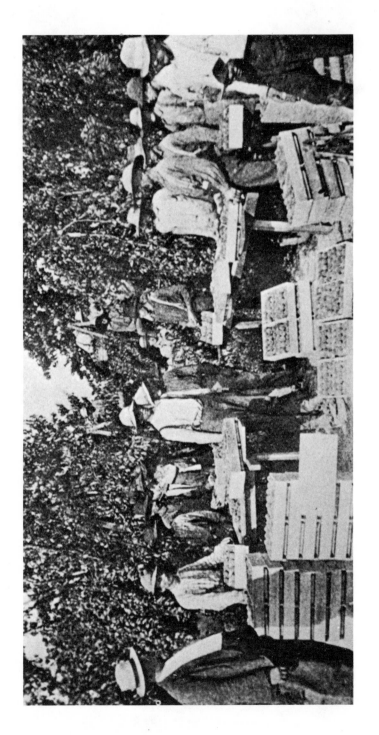

Peach orchard scene near Centralia, Illinois, an Italian settlement, ca. 1904.

# 31

# Italian-American Farmers[1]

ALICE BENNETT

In an interesting paper read recently before the New York Society for Italian Immigrants William Dean Howells stated that more than 500,000 Italians are living in Greater New York and drew a picture of the potential genius which might be lying dormant in this army of tenement people — suggesting a revival of those arts and crafts which have flourished to such perfection for centuries in Italy. We mentally applauded Mr. Howell's conclusion that these city dwellers should be distributed through country districts where they are bound to become an important factor in our national progress.

This article will deal only with the farmer or *contadino*. The first to cross off our list will be the black hander who is as far removed from our gentle *contadino* as the wolf is from the lamb. Here the Italian government assists by providing every subject leaving that country with a passport which answers also as a certificate for good or bad character. Every honest Italian treasures this passport as his most valuable possession. It should be carefully read by those contemplating business relations with him. The *mano nera* can find scope for his peculiar talents only in the crowded conditions incident to town life. He is a problem therefore for the police commissioners and courts to wrestle with.

The consensus of opinion gathered from the largest employers of Italian farm laborers throughout the United States is that, barring the Chinese, they rank all other nationalities coming to this country. Especially is this true of horticulture and intensive farming. One reason why the Italian farmer gets deflected to the city is owing to a lack of information in Italy pointing explicitly to where opportunity awaits the efficient farmer, the *contadino*

1. *The Survey*, Vol. 22, 1909. Pp. 172-175.

comes to friends in one of the overcrowded cities, and with only five or ten dollars capital, he must take the first job that's offered. Thus the man who would be invaluable as a farmer becomes a parasite and menace to the city. His health suffers from the overcrowding, lack of outdoor life, and change of diet. As sixty per cent of the Italians who come are *contadini*, some plan should be found to deflect them to the land.

Another reason why previous attempts to colonize Italians have failed is that men who had been trained to trades were sent to the country, while others who had all their lives lived on a farm remained in town. Neither have precautions been taken against mixing men from different provinces. The Italian's patriotism has its geographical limitations. With him *patria* means province. We must remember that United Italy is a matter of too recent date to have taken deep root in her peasant class. And while they are most catholic in their attitude towards the world in general, for an Italian belonging to another province they evince an antipathy amounting almost to aversion. Time doubtless will break these barriers down, but until it does this antagonism must be recognized in any plan of colonization.

About fifteen years ago Christenzo Seragosa, a Sicilian, drifted to Fredonia, Chautauqua county, New York, as a day laborer. He applied at a canning factory for work for himself and a friend from Buffalo. They were accepted, but owing to a prejudice against Italians they were unable to secure a house within two miles of the factory. Undaunted they moved in and by the end of a year had made themselves so well liked that the numerous Sicilian families which followed found no difficulty in securing houses. The factory attracted them only as a means to an end; what really drew them was the outlying land suited to grape culture. All that they could save from their wages was invested in land and planted out to vineyards. Now there are 1,200 Italians in Fredonia, many of them owning large vineyards. Nearly all have cottages with gardens attached. Their places are well kept, and they have raised the standard of farming in that vicinity — Americans have to hustle to keep up with them. Land which sold ten years ago for $50 and $75 an acre cannot now be bought for less than $250. Three hundred Italian children are in the grammar schools, ten in the Normal College and two have received diplomas in Buffalo, one is a lawyer, the other a physician. A Roman Catholic church valued at $25,000 has been built. The foundation was dug and the mason work done free by men of the colony. Fifteen years ago the only industry in Fredonia was one canning factory. Now there are two canneries, six wine cellars and a macaroni factory.

The most prosperous member of the colony is Pietro Elardo who owns 127 acres of vineyard, a large wine cellar and several houses. In a normal year his output is 15,000 gallons of wine, besides about ninety tons of grapes. His six children attend school and the eldest, a lad of sixteen, will soon graduate from the Normal College and become his father's assistant.

The class of Italians under consideration, the countrybred, are so far removed from mendicity that they will go without the commonest necessities in order to provide for a rainy day. A settlement worker told me of a man of this class, who died from pneumonia without calling in a physician because he had not money enough to pay the fees.

Last year, when so many were out of work, a valuable demonstration in temporary utilization of vacant lots was made by Italians. Little vegetable gardens sprang into existence all around the outskirts of New York City. Often a cabin was built from odds and ends gathered from rubbish heaps. I saw one such cottage which contained a kitchen, two bedrooms, a store-room and a stall for the horse. Where the boards would not join, pieces of tin and oil cloth had been utilized to make it weatherproof. The interior was plastered and painted red. Plants grew under the window. While there are exceptions, as a rule Italian farmhouses are clean and this little cottage was not one of the exceptions.

A group of seven men under the leadership of Dominico Condanti conducted such a garden at Sheepshead Bay, covering about two acres. They fenced it round with wire netting, dug a well, bought garden utensils, seeds and a horse and wagon; finally they built a stall from which to sell their product. At the end of seven months, after deducting all outlay including living expenses, they were about sixty-five dollars to the good. Residents at Sheepshead Bay became interested in watching their plucky effort to tide themselves over a season of unemployment, and offers of work were forthcoming sufficient to carry them through the winter while more vacant lots were placed at this disposal for the coming season.

It is unusual for such a settlement to ask for outside aid. Italians are most ambitious to give their children the advantage of good schools and will sacrifice a good deal to help any such enterprise. With some outside assistance the movement to the land could be greatly accelerated. The experiment at Vineland, N.J., became self-supporting in three years' time. A good method for any stock company undertaking such an enterprise would be to sell the immigrants alternate parcels of five acres, the company reserving the rest for appreciation in value. The immigrant could be given employment on the company's land until he had saved enough to start for himself. It would pay such a company to give a fair wage and good returns would be secured on the investment. Any plan for accelerating distribution of Italian *contadini* should be on strictly economic lines and should be put through by private enterprise. A government undertaking of this nature is handicapped in numbers of ways, one of the chief drawbacks being that a public bureau must place all who apply.

R. W. Vincent has given an interesting account of a colonization plan being carried on near Wilmington by the North Carolina Truck Garden

Company in which he states that the colonists are affable, hard working and contented with their lot.

Agriculture in Italy is chiefly arboreal — grapes, olives, fruit and vegetables. Nearly all the work is done by hand so that the *contadino* knows almost nothing of the use of live stock, especially horses and cows. It has been thought advisable by an Italian agriculture expert who has studied conditions in the United States for years, that a training school be established to teach Italians the use of machinery and the care of live stock. There should be associated with such a school a bureau of information which would co-operate with the authorities at Ellis Island. The duties of this bureau should be to select immigrants adapted to agriculture, gather information about desirable locations, and act as a clearing house and distributing station. Two classes should be received for training. Those of inferior intelligence could take a two months' course to fit them as farm hands; more capable men a six months' course to prepare them to take charge of large farms, estates and colonization schemes.

This school should become self-supporting at the end of three years. There should be a night school where the immigrant would be taught rudiments of English and civics. Recreation should be an important feature. This bureau should also supply information to employers, advising them how best to handle Italian workmen. The Italian farm hand is bound to become popular with the farmer's wife as he relieves her of all the drudgery she has been used to associate with the "hired man" — he prefers to cook his own food in his own way. His diet is largely spaghetti, fruit and vegetables.

Going back once more to Mr. Howells' happy suggestion, why could there not be one corner in such a training school sacred to some of the old arts and crafts, say those gorgeous brocades worn by the Florentine beauties at Lorenzo de Medici's court, or the Sicilian embroidery now being taught by Miss Amori in New York, or Venetian glass with its lovely Byzantine forms? Surely such an experiment would be well worth while in this crude, new world of ours.

# 32

# Italian Farmers in the South: An Interview with Adolfo Rossi[1]

GINO C. SPERANZA

Signor Adolfo Rossi, of the Italian Emigration Department, has returned among us at a time when the question of distribution seems to be uppermost in the minds of those interested in the problems of immigration. With the South badly in need of men, and with landowners and the railroads making special inducements to attract settlers, distribution, rather than wholesale restriction, is being more and more recognized as the real way out of the difficulties presented by our immense unassimilated immigration.

Closely associated with distribution is the question popularly and indefinitely called "colonization" which, generally, means the distribution of farm laborers and farm hands to agricultural sections, and their eventual conversion into farm owners. Can this be done, or rather can this be "forced" by inducements or legislation? It is on this point that we have interviewed Signor Rossi, who, with Chevalier Fara-Forni, the esteemed Consul of Italy at New Orleans, has been studying the problem of Southern immigrant distribution.

Signor Rossi insists that two conditions are absolutely necessary to the success of any such plan, which it may be remarked in passing is substantially what Bishop Broderick intends to meet through the Italian-American Agricultural Society. these two conditions are, first, that the utmost care be exercised in the selection of families who are used to farming, and second, that "colonization" be started with small nuclei and not on any large scale.

---

1. *Charities and the Commons*, Vol. 15, 1906. Pp. 307-308. Adolfo Rossi is the Inspector for the Royal Emigration Department of Italy.

These nuclei, if successful, will themselves develop into larger centers by attracting the families, friends and *paesani* from the villages from which the pioneers came.

Signor Rossi found that many colonization enterprises in South America have failed from the very fact of being too large ventures. To place a large number of peasants on a new and extensive territory, when they are unacquainted with and unprepared for the climate, the methods of farming, the habits and the seasons of the new country, is to invite failure.

## The Colony at Independence

On his last trip through the United States Signor Rossi found a number of very prosperous Italian villages, which owed their prosperity to small beginnings and to a slow development by a sort of "natural accretion", of newcomers whose advent coincided with a well-defined demand for them as fellow members of the agricultural community. A typical example cited by Signor Rossi is that of Independence, a town within two hours by rail of New Orleans. I shall give his own words: "I arrived at an early hour in May", he says, "and was met at the station by a number of Sicilian farmers who proudly took me to see their farms where they raise strawberries in the early spring, shipping them in refrigerator cars to the Northern markets, at good prices. Some years ago a few immigrants from Palazzo Adriano (Palermo) settled at Independence and, finding that a fertile soil yielded profitable crops, they wrote home, with the result that now there are three hundred families at Independence from that one Sicilian village. American farmers had abandoned their farms because they deemed them too wet and subject to becoming swampy. The Sicilians bought them up at nominal prices, dug ditches throughout and a three-mile drainage canal, converting the swampy lands into excellent soil. Each family lays aside several hundred dollars yearly which, except a small part sent to Italy, is deposited in the local American bank. A striking fact is that the Sicilians do not live in crowded quarters, but each family has its own house on its own separate farms."

## The Community of Bryan, Texas

Bryan, Texas, is even a more striking object lesson. There are in that township some 2,500 Sicilian *contadini* under the spiritual guidance of a young Sicilian priest, Father Giovanni Militello. They raise mostly grain and cotton, either on their own lands or on rented farms, which they get at five dollars per acre a year. They save from a hundred to a thousand dollars a year and live comfortably. Father Militello was able to collect in a few days eleven hundred dollars to cancel the debt on the local church. His parishioners embellished the church with a number of statues and presented their pastor with a safe and a buggy and team. Once a month he drives to the farthest point in the township where he celebrates mass under a tent. Nearly all the Sicilians there come from one place in Italy or from two or three centers — Poggioreale, Corleone and Cefalu. Living is cheap; flour, meat, sugar, coffee, and oil are at low prices. Meat sells at five cents a pound. State and county taxes are very light, and the climate is like that of Sicily. Land is so abundant that its use is given free for two years to those who will clear it of timber. The Italians cut the timber and sell it at $2 per eight cubic feet, raise grain the first year and get a crop of cotton during the second. Signor Rossi's description of the day he left Bryan deserves to be given in full: "It was encouraging to see along the road the vast cotton and grain plantations; those kept by Italians could be distinguished because of their freedom from weeds. As we drove past the priest would call out to some of the farmers by name and they would leave their spade or their plow, and come running to us, hat in hand. Behind the farmers came the farmers' wives and the children, and how many children! I found one mother with eleven of them!"

*An Elder and His People*

Twelve miles from Bryan some fifty *contadini* "some in wagons and some riding magnificent mules" met Signor Rossi and conducted him to the farm of their "elder" Francesco Tuiti, a "splendid type of *campagnuolo* and the father of strong healthy boys. His near-by neighbors, mostly from Cefalu, Corleon and Alia gather on his piazza to discuss 'current topics' ". Few are those among them who have not become landowners (from thirty to one hundred and sixty acre farms) in five or six years. Land is generally bought one-quarter of the sale price down and the balance on easy rates. But interest being at ten per cent the thrifty Italian loses no time in completing the payment of the purchase price, often doing so in two or three years. "Tuiti" said Signor Rossi, "invited us to lunch and told us about local conditions. The land is so fertile that several crops of cotton can be raised on the same land for several successive years. When cotton prices rise to 12 and 15 cents a pound, the profits are very large."

Five miles above Tuiti's is another small colony in Brazo County. About eighty Sicilians had gathered at Francesco Salvato's house to welcome Signor Rossi. They were a robust looking lot, some of them tall young fellows and splendid riders. One of them asked Signor Rossi what they should do in order to win the esteem of Americans. "Send your children to school", answered Signor Rossi, "and when you obtain your American citizenship, vote intelligently."

On his drive back to Bryan, Signor Rossi got into conversation with the driver who was a Negro. "How is it", he asked him, "that the Italians on these plantations save money and become landowners while you colored people never seem to lay aside anything?"

"Because", answered the driver candidly, "we don't like hard work and we love to drink and gamble, and some of us have three or even four wives! Your people, instead, work from morning till night and often on Sundays; they don't spend money at the plantation store because they get along with the chickens, hogs and goats they raise on their lands, and one wife is enough for them." And he laughed loudly.

Signor Rossi, in concluding, said "It would be a great mistake to attempt colonizing on a large plan through artificial immigration, when the natural inflow is already so large and is helped by the agents of the steamship companies. Experiments with more than fifty families will almost invariably result in failure; for large groups are subject to divisions and dissensions through the spirit of 'regionalismo', or the disintegrating influence of some malcontent who may join the *contadini*. Bishop Broderick, whose proposed work I have studied, agrees with me on this question of colonization, and I believe that if he sticks to his program, he will make a great success of it."

# 33

# The Italian Foreman as a Social Agent: Labor Abuses in West Virginia and Their Consequences to the Community[1]

GINO C. SPERANZA[2]

In answer to several complaints of alleged abuses suffered by Italian laborers in West Virginia, the Society for the Protection of Italian Immigrants, decided to make an independent investigation and sent its corresponding secretary to study the situation on the spot.

Four counties (Kanawha, Raleigh, Clay and Wirt) were covered, many camps being visited and much evidence obtained. The testimony secured established the truth of the acts complained of in almost every instance. These may be summed up as follows:

I. Resort to practices bordering on fraud to get men to go to West Virginia.

II. Resort to intimidation ranging from isolation to armed surveillance to prevent laborers from exercising their rights as free men.

III. Well-established cases of brutal, cruel and unlawful conduct by employers or their bosses against laborers.

IV. Abuses of the commissary or campstore through the indifference or neglect of contractors in letting out this privilege to improper persons.

I have elsewhere set forth in some detail examples coming under each of these heads, together with an explanation of certain geographic and economic conditions which to a certain extent explain, though they can by no means excuse, many and repeated acts of lawlessness, cruelty, and brutality.[3]

There are some aspects and consequences of such unfortunate conditions

1. *Charities*, Vol. 11, 1903. Pp. 26-28.
2. Corresponding Secretary of the Society for the Protection of Italian Immigrants.
3. "See Forced Labor in West Virginia", *The Outlook*, June 13, 1903; "Report on Labor Conditions in West Virginia", New York *Evening Post*, June 5, 1903.

as those existing in certain of these labor camps, which, irrespective of an appeal to our sympathies or our sense of justice, should be carefully considered. Men practically drafted from various centers of labor supply to strange localities, forced to work in many instances, not to save money, but to pay out their board and transportation, are very likely to become public charges. Dissatisfied, frightened, anxious to get away, these laborers, brought to West Virginia from distant places, will naturally scatter at the very first opportunity; they will not say, "We will remain till we have saved enough to go home" but, like all men who fear immediate danger, will take chances, in flight. Thus, I have seen a number of cases where Italian laborers, from lack of money for transportation (their savings all gone), walked long distances and became, temporarily at least, objects of charity.

The Italian in this country is seldom an applicant for charitable aid, yet conditions like those in West Virginia necessarily force him to mendicancy. Even in those cases it must have been an extreme necessity indeed, that drove Italians to become public charges. One group of about twenty walked from Charleston to Washington rather than beg transportation. Two that I found at the Washington workhouse were brought there because hunger and disease had driven them there.

Worse yet, the carelessness of some contractors as well as their brutality tends to increase the attendance at the public hospitals, which, in small towns, makes an appreciable difference in expense. Every workman assumes, of course, the risks and hazards of his employment, but the Italian laborers I visited in the hospitals were not there as the result of such risks and hazards, but of culpable negligence on the part of employers, if not of a brutal and inhuman treatment.

There is another important consideration which the abuses in the labor camps of West Virginia serve to clearly bring forth. It is not to be supposed that from even a business standpoint, contractors in that state wish to maltreat their workmen. If they do maltreat them, it is because they do not understand the men they handle. It can be said, for example, that to apply to Italian laborers, the methods of surveillance and direction applied to Irish laborers, is a vital mistake. It is fundamentally wrong because the Italian is essentially different from the Irish. The characteristic of the Italian is *personality*, he cannot be treated in masses but his characteristic views and feelings have to be considered individually. Courtesy is proverbial with him and he expects from others what he himself is ready to give. The cursing, the threats, and the blows of the foremen and bosses who cannot understand his nature will never get the best work from him.

Let us remember that thrifty and economical as these Italian workmen are, there are things that even the humblest of them hold dearer than money, and that no Italian laborer feels that he is fully paid by wages unaccompanied by the regard and consideration of his employer. This is the element — the new but hopeful element that is presenting itself in the immigration problem and in the labor situation, so far as these refer to the Italians who come to us. The Italian laborer is here to stay, nor can we do without him. He, himself, is becoming aware that his work has a distinct value on the labor market and its great demand adds to such value. Let us help in his endeavor to reach a new estate, and whatever we do in this regard, will be repaid in staunch and loyal citizenship.

There is one way in which we can help towards the solution of this problem of Italian labor in America. It is to turn our efforts towards developing and encouraging a class of Italian foremen as a distinct species from the purely American, or Irish boss, or middleman. These should be young men sufficiently well versed in American business methods, who understand primarily the characteristics of the men under their charge — men who in the present period of transition and unrest, while we await for the second generation of Italo-American laborer — will not merely get the best and steadiest work out of the employed, but establish good relations between employed and employers. As I said elsewhere: Wherever Italian labor is employed the Italian is at the mercy of the middleman, without any right of appeal. Whether it be the fraud of his own countryman, the banker-agent who sells his labor under false pretenses, or the extortion of his countryman, the camp-storekeeper to whom the contractor lets the commissary privileges; whether it be the "rake-off" of the foreman or the speculations of the paymaster; whether it be the brutality of the boss, or the unlawful order of the gang-foreman; no matter what the injustice may be, the laborer has no opportunity to appeal to his employer, either because the employer recognizes the decision of his middleman as final or because he will not bother with details.

Such a system is abhorrent to the finely adjusted character of even the humblest Italian, and the institution of middlemen that know the idiosyncracies and characteristics of this class of laborers will result in good all around. That there is plenty of good material for such middlemen is apparent to any one conversant with Italians in this country. There are among the younger laborers, honest fellows of remarkable intelligence who by a little help could become not merely foremen but spiritual leaders of their countrymen. They are men who will show their appreciation of any effort to help them to improve their conditions, not merely by gratitude, but by loyal service. The public mind has been so saturated with the journalistic idea that Italians are both frightfully ignorant and instinctively criminal, that it never stops to consider that out of these people came some of the greatest leaders of civilization and the foremost of the Humanists.

Possibly my judgment may be biased by my kinship with them, yet it is a permissible and reasonable belief that the Republic, by extending a helping hand to the members of this sturdy southern race, will gather in a worthy element for our composite Americanism.

# 34

# Behind the Yellow Fever in Little Palermo: Housing Conditions Which New Orleans Should Shake Itself Free From Along with the Summer's Scourge[1]

ELEANOR MCMAIN[2]

*Some Glimpses of the Italian Quarter*[3]

## I

He was a helper to a blacksmith, broad of chest and strong of limb, a picturesque young giant, the embodiment of physical strength and prowess.

I often stopped to watch him as he worked, and one day we began to talk together. He told me of his hopes and plans; how he was saving — saving — "and soon now — before many months" — he said one day, with a tender softening of his black eyes — "the little wife in far off Sicily is coming".

But while we talked together during those early summer days, an enemy had entered into the heart of "Little Palermo".

I was called on to do my part in fighting this enemy, and it had been more than a week since I had seen Tonio. Hurrying down St. Philip Street one day, I heard a voice calling, and turning saw a young Italian boy about twelve years old, running towards me.

"Come quick", he said, "to Tonio! He wants you!"

Down the street, up a narrow alley across the little court, I followed him. In a tiny, low-ceiled, windowless room, I found my poor young friend, with eyes suffused and cheeks red and burning. He was half sitting, half reclining,

---

1. *Charities and the Commons*, Vol. 15, 1905. Pp. 152-159.
2. Head-worker of Kingsley House and President of the Woman's League.
3. The four introductory sketches are set down as they were told to the writer by one of the Italian Relief Committee.

on his little cot. Naught else was in the room save one chair and a rude wash
bench which held a basin and pitcher. Jumping up at sight of me, he
grasped my hands in his fevered ones, and began excitedly — "I no sick — I
no sick! but I tell you something!"

"My poor friend!" I answered soothingly, "You are burning with fever.
Now lie quiet till I get you a doctor."

"No, no", he exclaimed wildly. "I go to my work! I no sick, but I tell you
something." Then sinking down on the little bed, he reached beneath the
mattress and drew forth a bag. With fever-palsied fingers he counted out his
treasure, one — two — ten— twenty — fifty — one hundred — two
hundred — three hundred — three hundred and seventy-five dollars.

"There", he said, with a look of confidence, "you, my friend — for my
wife in Sicily." Then he fell back exhausted upon his pillow.

While his comrade, a little lad who had called me, crouched whimpering
in the corner, I rushed out to find a doctor. After four hours I was again at
the entrance of the alley, and this time the doctor was with me. Tonio was
wildly excited when he saw us, and staggered to his feet, saying over and
over again. "I no sick, I no sick, I go to my work."

The doctor shook his head as he looked at Tonio; then round the stifling
little room. "No chance here", he said to me. "The Emergency Hospital is
our one hope, but", glancing at Tonio who was eyeing us suspiciously, "how
to get him there is the question."

"Tonio, my friend", I said to him, "let us take you to a place where you
can have nurses and medicine and get well. This is the doctor; come now
with him and me." As I laid my hand on his arm the young giant shook
himself free, and hurled himself at us with such fury that we beat a hasty
retreat; it was only with the help of two policemen that we finally got him
into the ambulance and to the hospital.

Late that night I got back to the hospital and to Tonio. Over him was
bending a nurse, gently urging him to take some cold water from a glass.
Tonio was glaring up at her, his teeth tightly clenched, all the suspicion and
hatred born of ignorance and superstition glowing in his fevered eyes. At
sight of my familiar face, there came a look of intense relief. Grasping my
hand as the nurse stepped aside, he began to mutter through cracked, parched
lips, "I no sick, I go to my work!" Then again — "You won't forget — the
money — for my wife in Sicily?"

Taking up the glass of water I held it to him saying, "Drink, Tonio, this is
water to cool your fever and ease your parched lips;" but he clenched his
teeth tightly and shook his head. "Look", I said, and lifting the glass to my
lips drank a part of the water. "Ah", he gasped, stretching forth both hands
eagerly for the glass which he drained greedily.[4]

4. The Sicilians, I am told, have a legend that when the cholera occurs in their country they

"Take some more, Tonio", I said, as the nurse quietly refilled the glass and handed it to me. Again the look of suspicion, the tightly clenched teeth, and he slowly shook his head. Once more I raised the glass to my lips and immediately his trembling hands reached out for it and again he eagerly drank. Then holding fast to my hand, he gradually sank into a fitful sleep.

"What are his chances, doctor?" I asked. "Too late, I am afraid", said the physician, "he must have been ill two days before you found him."

Just at sunset the next day, I went again to see Tonio. He had been wildly delirious for hours, the nurse said, but now he seemed perfectly conscious and quiet.

"Well, Tonio", I said, "don't you like this bed, and is not your nurse all right?" He nodded approvingly, and a faint smile hovered about his lips.

In a little while he began to mutter and we saw a shadowy pallor creeping over his face. Bending over him I heard — "I no sick — I go to my work" — then in a little while he began groping feebly for my hand — whispering — "I — I — not see — you — my — friend — hold — my — hand — so — it makes — me — feel — stronger. — The — money — for my wife — at — home — you — won't — forget?"


## II


"Do you know", said a fellow-worker to me, "that Joe Orlando has the fever? There he is in that one room with his wife and his five little ones. Can't you get him out of there? You know him and can talk to him. He has just taken ill, and if we can get him out at once, he may get well and the others may escape the fever."

"No, no; I stay right here", said Joe, vehemently, a few hours later. "Look here", said I, "this bed is hard; you have to sleep with the others. At the hospital you have a bed to yourself, clean and soft, plenty of nice air, nurses, doctors, medicine, come!"

Reluctantly, after much persuasion, he consented. But my first visit to him found him restless, dissatisfied, begging to be taken away, back to the one bed in the one room with the dirt, the discomfort, the bad air. That was home to him, the one place where he longed to be.

"If he does not stop exciting himself and let us do what is necessary for him he cannot expect to get well", said the doctor and nurse. "Now look here, Joe", I said to him, "don't be a fool. You know Mary and Francesca came here, and they got well, didn't they? But how about Tony and

---

are poisoned to death by the authorities, if they are considered hopelessly ill. The yellow fever coming suddenly upon them, for they know not whence has been regarded by them as the same thing, or something similar, and they have been distrustful and suspicious of the many efforts that have been made to help them.

Antoinette and the others in your block that didn't come here. Did they get well?"

A thin, sallow, but very happy Joe met me a few days ago, and embracing me after the manner of our country, said, "Ah, a grand-a place — the hospital — grand-a-place-a!"

## III

He was a stranger from the country, and was taken at once from the lodging-house to the Emergency Hospital. "Write to my father", he said to me, "I have a father, mother and five sisters; get me what I need; I can pay. We have a strawberry farm at Independence, Louisiana. Do what you can for me, doctor, I don't want to die."

He was making a brave fight, but the chances seemed against him. Higher and higher went the fever. Word came from the father, "Save him, we will pay, do all you can". The dread black vomit came, and doctor and nurse looked grave. "You had better telegraph", they said to me. I sent the message that was to prepare them for the worst.

The next evening as my wife and I sat at dinner we heard a strange sound issuing from our front hall — a sound of sobbing and wailing. Rushing out we found an old man and with him six women (his wife and daughters), all clad in the deepest mourning.

"Oh! take us to him", they cried. "Take us to the place where his body lies. We have come from Independence to look upon his tomb."

"Why, my good people", I said, "sit down and stop crying, and hear the good news I have for you; there has been a change; the doctor has great hopes. He thinks that your son may live."

About three weeks afterwards a happy family party took the train for Independence. They were no longer garbed in mourning robes and they were willing to brave quarantine and to dwell in detention camps, for their son whom they had mourned as dead, had come back to them from the brink of the grave.

## IV

In a clean, white bed, in the Emergency Hospital lay Salvadore, weak and very ill, but perfectly conscious and filled with suspicion of *everything* — doctors, nurses, medicines and all. He would have none of them. But he did not protest violently; he lay quiet, and when anything was brought him he would say, "Wait! my wife-a come-a give-a me". She had been sitting beside him a little while when he said in a whisper, handing to her a box of capsules: "Look-a Mary, they say I take-a this-a", picking up one capsule. "Now", (still more softly, lest any one should hear) "You give-a this-a one to the goat — if the goat-a die then they want-a poison me-a." Hiding the small parcel under a fold of her dress, Mary slipped quietly away. After four hours had passed back she came, and her cries could be heard before she reached the hospital door. With hands clasped over her head and eyes wildly staring she rushed to her husband's bedside, and falling on her knees, she cried: "Oh! Holy Mother save us! The goat is dead! The goat is dead!"

## Relief Work Among the Italians

In the back part of the offices of Mr. Del Orto, on Decatur Street, the Italian Relief Committee has assembled each morning at ten o'clock since early summer. Sometimes before that hour on the day of my visit, on invitation of Mr. Patorno, the chairman, a group began to gather in the outer office and on the sidewalk. Black-robed women, each one with a child, either in their arms or clinging to their skirts, men and boys, some pale, weak and haggard looking; others strong and healthy, bearing no marks of their recent illness in their outward appearance, — about fifty in all, I suppose. Just a few minutes before ten two of the Italian Sisters of the Sacred Heart entered.

"Let the widows come first", said the president. One by one the black-robed women were admitted to this inner office and courteously invited to sit down at the table with the committee. Here their stories were listened to, the secretary the while consulting records and making entries. The sisters were occasionally referred to when some fact needed verification, and each one was helped according to her neeed and dismissed with kindly and cheering words.

Next came weak, haggard-looking men and boys. "These are the convalescents", explained one of the committee. They were given tickets to the kitchen, where proper food for the convalescents had been regularly prepared and served. Then the other men were brought in — sixteen of them — strong, well, perfectly able to work, but with nothing to do. They had been helped back to health and strength by the committee; now the committee was considering how to help them to help themselves. All of them were bound for the plantations when the fever caught them and stranded them here. They could not now possibly be a source of danger to any uninfected locality, for they were all immunes. "But who will let them in?" asked one of the committee. The writer was asked to interview the Marine Hospital authorities and see what could be done. The authorities assured me that while they were perfectly willing to furnish the would-be travelers with clean bills of health, these would not be accepted in the country parishes, and the only thing to do was to send the sixteen men to a detention camp to stay the required time before attempting to get to the plantations. This meant an expenditure of money that the committee naturally wished to avoid, but it was the only thing to do — one of the many instances of unnecessary hardship that has been worked through the operation of senseless quarantines. Since then plans have been perfected for the handling of the laborers for the plantations by means of detention camps maintained by the planters and the railroads. The secretary of the Louisiana Immigration Association estimated that 10,000 Italians would be handled through New Orleans this fall enroute to the plantations.

After the visit to the meeting of the committee, I went down to the kitchen maintained to furnish food to such fever sufferers as have had no means of procuring it. Here I saw 379 women and children receive food; meat stew, macaroni and bread for the well; milk, broth, crackers, for the sick and convalescent. In a room adjoining the kitchen were a number of tables, and here the unemployed men and boys were served with what was left after the women and children had been waited on. The women and children bring buckets, and take the food home.

The Italian Missionary Sisters have co-operated with the relief committee throughout and have been able to give valuable assistance in the way of accurate information. For since the beginning of the trouble in Little Palermo they have been tireless in their gentle ministrations to the sick and unfortunate ones, coming from family to family with both spiritual and material comfort, gathering up the orphans and taking them home with them, when, as in some cases, there was no one left to befriend them.

*An Old-Time French Dwelling and Its Occupants*

In visiting the Italian quarter,[5] I found it very difficult to get full or accurate information in any instance. The people were suspicious, and in some cases refused to admit us to their premises. They spoke no English and understood but little. I could have found out nothing had not my companion spoken Italian, smoothing the way for me.

The first house visited was one of the old-time French dwellings, handsome in its time, well-built, with solid brick walls, wide windows and doors, and beautiful, fan-shaped transoms. To-day the place has a dilapidated, forlorn air. The ground floor of the main building is now used as a shop. The passageway at the side of this is broad and high, and like the court to which

5. In September Miss McMain went into one of the worst fever districts, to see what sort of quarters were to be found in blocks where the records of the Marine Hospital Service showed the disease had been especially prevalent. The neighborhood chosen lay between Chartres and Decatur Streets, where they are crossed by Barrack Hospital, Ursuline, St. Philip and Dumaine — four blocks which then had tallied 77, 89, 50 and 53 cases or one-twelfth of the entire number of cases for the city.

it leads, is paved with wide flagstones. The walls are very thick and it takes a long time for the heat of the sun to penetrate, and as we entered from the street the air seemed singularly cool.

Going to the courtyard, we found a row of six small rooms (possibly 10 feet by 12 by 10) three above and three below, arranged as a wing to the main building. This wing is evidently a modern addition to the old house. It is built of wood; the thin walls are unplastered; there are no windows, but one door in each room, opening upon the court on the ground floor, and upon a narrow gallery above. A tiny fireplace with its chimney is the only ventilator when the door of a room is closed.

In these little rooms the heat was intense. In each one of these rooms we found an entire Italian family. The first room on the ground floor housed a father, mother and four little children. The father died of yellow fever some weeks ago. All had it in that one room and one bed. They seemed dazed and miserable. We found the mother cooking macaroni on a charcoal furnace. They were being helped regularly by the Italian Relief Society (a condition true of all the Italian fever sufferers).

In the next room to this one lived a family of five children older than those in the family just described. One had died of the fever. In the other rooms were families of three, four, two and five. Most of them had but one bed, for the rooms would not permit two double beds. In one room only we found a small cot in addition. When we asked the landlady to let us go up the quaint, winding stairway that led from the ground floor to the upper stories of the main building, she vehemently protested. Why, we could not imagine, for conditions could hardly have been as bad there as in the wing (because of the great size of the rooms, the thick walls and the large openings) unless the large rooms had been partitioned off into a number of small compartments as is sometimes the case. The landlady further informed us that the house contained eleven rooms in all, bringing her usually $40 a month. At the time of our visit the tenants she had could not pay, and she was allowing them to remain for the present, rent free.

Just across from the wing I have tried to describe, parallel with it and about eight feet away from it, is a row of rough sheds or stalls, used to stable horses.

### Typical of an Entire Block

This building is typical of the entire block, I was told; large houses, closely built, small courts covered over in any part by added buildings and now used as dwellings and stables; in almost every room a family and rarely more than two rooms to a family. Every house had the ghastly white strips of paper about the openings, showing where the Marine Hospital Fumigating Corps had been at work. For every house and almost every family has yielded up its victims to the fever.

In the next two blocks the appearance from the outside was the same, but we could not gain admission. One woman who would not let us in volunteered this information. "I got-a ten-a room-a — thirty-two people-a — twelve-a sick — three die."

On another street are houses with six large rooms, three up stairs and three down, and a wing with rooms upstairs and down. The downstairs rooms have no side openings. The front has a door and window opening to the street; the second room opens by a door into the front room and by a door into the room in the rear, which in turn opens into the courtyard only by a door. The rooms above these are similar, but seem dryer and less musty. The rooms in the wing face the courtyard and are well lighted and ventilated, having a door and window to each room. They were evidently built at the same time as the main portion of the house and have high ceilings and thick walls. The courtyard is large, sunny at midday, but poorly drained, a leaking hydrant making little pools of water in the uneven places. The odor that hung over it was stifling. There is but one closet for the whole building.

The three rooms on the ground floor of the main building, housed a family of six. All had the fever. Two died. In the ground floor rooms of the wing (two rooms) lived a family of five. Two had the fever. Both recovered. Upstairs the front room housed a family of eight. Five had the fever. Two died. In the upstairs middle room a family of four lived. They were not yet stricken with the fever. And in the two upstairs wing rooms a family of eight lived, two of whom had been ill, but recovered.

Another house of similar type on the same street had:

One room, large, ground floor, no windows, large front door; occupants 9; 6 had the fever; 2 died.

Two upstairs rooms; occupants 7; 3 ill; husband died.

One upstairs room; occupants 5; 2 ill; both recovered.

One room; occupants 2; no sickness.

Three rooms; occupants 5; no sickness.

A house on another street showed:

| Number of Rooms to a Family | Number in the Family |
|---|---|
| 1 | 6 |
| 1 | 2 |
| 2 | 7 |
| 3 | 6 |
| 1 | 2 |
| 2 very small | 3 |
| 1 very small | 2 |
| 1 very small | 1 |

One tenant was very ill with fever the day of our visit, a young woman, only six months in this country. Neither she nor her husband could speak a word of English. Three others in the house were convalescent. Two had died. In these three last houses then (and there were several unoccupied rooms) the number of families admitted to was ten, eleven and twelve in thirty-one, twenty-seven and twenty-nine rooms.

## A Lodging-House for Plantation Hands

A lodging-house was next visited. We were not admitted, but were told that as many transients as 10, 20, or even 30 odd are frequently accommodated in one room over night. "But just for the night", said the woman — "they go off to the plantations right away." That they do not all get away at once, is proved by the number in these lodging-houses, who suffered from the fever and to whom the Emergency Hospital was a blessing. One of the Missionary Sisters of the Sacred Heart said to me "Why, what could be done for them? They had no room — no air — nothing."

That this situation is common among the lodging-houses is testified to by the Missionary Sisters, by Mr. Patorno, head of the Italian Relief Committee, and by the secretary of the Louisiana Immigration Association, all of whom are most anxious that some measures be adopted that will serve to protect the Italians when they come to us from these deplorable conditions.

## Types of Houses in Other Quarters of New Orleans

Some of the facts gathered by Mr. Towles, a student of Tulare University, who investigated housing conditions in the neighborhood of Kingsley House, show how far the situation in "Little Palermo" is duplicated in other districts.

The following are conditions found in one square block which in the 493 rooms of its 71 houses, housed 144 families comprising 517 people. Three types of houses were found:

1. Two-story brick buildings divided into tenements; two rooms each; rooms large; no side windows. First floor tenements have one window to each room — really a door, and is so used; ventilation, especially in winter, bad. Upper tenements far superior to those on the ground floor; dryer and better lighted.

2. Three-story (usually corner) buildings; first floor used as bar-room or shop; second and third stories rented out to families in suites of one, two and three rooms; courtyard and rear buildings once used to store goods, now rented to families; rear buildings are double-sided, two rooms on each floor. The worst one of this type, not a corner building, had once been a store. All three stories are now rented to families, the ground floor having only the two front openings, and a small side door leading into an alley that is never dry and into which the sun never shines; the house is a death-trap.

The upper stories are well lighted, but fearfully dilapidated and sanitary arrangements past belief.

3. Old French style; two or three stories high; vaulted passage; small paved court; courts damp, usually darksome, mere niches at the backs of the houses; no openings in middle rooms upon light or air.

The general features of all houses visited in this block were these: The houses are closely built, jammed together; with no side openings. Twenty-five per cent of the yard space is damp and gloomy. Entrance to second stories is only by vaulted passages, or through back alleys. Where the houses are three or more rooms in depth, the middle ones are dark, without outside ventilator. There are no genuine rear tenements; the yards being generally too small, but shed-rooms and outhouses are used as such. There is no fire protection whatever.

The toilet conveniences are the worst feature of the section; vaults are in fearful condition; 70 per cent of them are bad. Of the 144 families, only 35 have separate vaults. The rest share water supply, yard, and toilet conveniences with their neighbors — sometimes two families, three, four, five, and in a few instances even six and seven families. The floors in many of the tenements on the street level are wet and rotten. Not a single bath-tub was found in the district visited. One family of eight lives in one room with one window; one bed and trundle-bed accommodating them at night; a family of six and another of five, each in one room; a third of eight in two rooms, unventilated. The majority of the families live in two rooms. Reliance for water supply in nine-tenths of the houses is upon cisterns, so inadequate that many run dry in time of drought. Some of these were found to be in poor condition, the tops rotten and broken. (The fixing of these cisterns was one of the first tasks in fighting the fever.)

The population of the block was made up of 145 men, 187 women, 85 boys, 100 girls — a total of 517. Twenty-nine per cent were foreign born — mostly Italians.

The average rent paid was $6.30, 54.4 per cent paying over 15 per cent of their income for rent; 14.4 per cent over 30 per cent — figures which must be compared with 14 2/3 per cent as given by United States Department of Labor as a fair share for rent. Fifteen of the families own their homes. The average income was found to be from $5 to $10 per week, 47.7 per cent getting less than $5, and 76.7 per cent getting less than $10. The disposition of this income is seriously affected by certain parasitical agencies of a questionable sort in the neighborhood — an installment house, an insurance company and a lottery shop.

The streets surrounding the block are unpaved in part and appear never to have been cleaned — not within the memory of the present residents. The drainage is of the worst; gutters are cleaned once or twice a year. Yet certain good points can be noted — the streets are wide and sunny and river breezes sweep through and purify. The neighboring breweries and mills flush the gutters occasionally; the land is high; the water runs off well; and the banquettes are in good condition.

The needs which stand out pressingly are better tenements, sanitation, public baths, more schools and playgrounds. (We have *one* now.)

Italian family picking cranberries in New Jersey, 1938.

# 35

# In Berry Field and Bog:
## The Seasonal Migration of Italian Pickers to New Jersey — Its Profits — Its Cost in Illiteracy and Disease[1]

MINA C. GINGER[2]

During the last few years there has occurred annually a migration of people into one of the old eastern states which by reason of its character and rapid growth seems well worth social study. As the acreage for the cultivation of fruits and berries has increased in southern and central New Jersey the demand for large forces of unskilled workers to pick the berries has become acute. The result is a yearly exodus of Italian families from Philadelphia, so large in certain districts that the lower grades of the public and parochial schools were almost depopulated during the past season. Upon the request of the Philadelphia and the New Jersey Consumers' Leagues, the writer has made an investigation of these migrating harvesters.

In the early spring the farmers go to Philadelphia to make their contracts with the padroni. These men agree to provide the working force, to transport the various parties, to "boss" them during the season and to be responsible for their good conduct. For this service the padroni receive from $1.50 to $2 a day, and the privilege of bringing their families to work with the rest of the party. The bosses then make a house to house canvass of the Italian districts picturing to everyone the astonishing sums which can be gained so easily and pleasantly, in return for a small outlay. Each worker is promised free shelter, straw to fill his bed tick, cheap fruit and vegetables. The padroni assure each one that the season will afford him a net profit of from $150 to $400, and that a large and industrious family will readily clear from $400 to $600. With such promises borne out by testimony of those who have gone

1. *Charities and the Commons*, Vol. 15, 1905. Pp. 162-169.
2. Newark Bureau of Associated Charities.

to New Jersey in past years, there is no difficulty in securing workers. As each family binds itself to labor under a particular boss, he exacts a fee of from fifty cents to one dollar per member, which he considers a fit charge for his trouble in securing summer employment for them.

When the numbers of people specified in the contracts with the farmers have been filled, the bosses of the various gangs call upon two of the shrewdest Italians in Philadelphia. These two men are said to control all the means of transportation necessary for the distribution of thousands of pickers over the fruit-growing sections of the neighboring state. Under their supervision, schedules of dates are arranged and trains of from ten to fourteen cars are despatched to New Jersey. In return these two men receive ten per cent from the railroad company for every ticket sold to their countrymen. In addition to that, they sell the tickets to ignorant travelers for fifty per cent in excess of the regular passenger rate.

The preparation for this annual migration becomes apparent early in May when the children begin to drop out of school. The actual moving begins about the twentieth of the month when the strawberries are ripening.

### The Pickers Arrive

Imagine groups of Italians — men, women and children — from thirty to sixty strong, scrambling out of one of these trains at some small country station. Children from two weeks upward are in the party. Every one is loaded with bundles as big as himself; fathers carrying cook-stoves on their heads; mothers clutching babies and cooking utensils; grandmothers balancing their share of the luggage and holding the rest of the babies; youngsters following with the remainder of the equipment, while the self-important padrone, with a club in his hand, brings up the rear. Most of the parties are met by farmers who bring wagons to help them to their destination.

Immediately upon their arrival they take possession of the "Fresh Air Home" supplied by the farmer. In the strawberry sections this is usually a shed built for the purpose, an old barn, or the loft of a stable. Here they remain as long as their work in the region lasts. Their mattresses are laid on the floor in solid rows. Trunks and boxes are opened, and the odorous contents of cheese, bologna, wreathes of bread, strings of onions and toasted bread are suspended from rafters. Packages of rice, macaroni, sardines and tomato paste are in evidence everywhere among the clothing and bedding, and later these stores are supplemented with heaps of fresh vegetables, fruits and various weeds used as vegetables.

This beginning of an outdoor life for a tenement people, which insures fresh air and plenty of sunshine for the children during five or six months, may seem an alluring picture to students of social conditions. Unfortunately, however, the housing conditions are so wretched on a majority of the fruit farms that the resultant overcrowding is often worse than in the congested city districts from which the people come.

## How the Workers Are Housed

Many lofts visited in the strawberry sections averaged not more than 14 by 25 feet, with a tiny window at one end and a door at the other. Men, women and children herd together in these partitionless buildings. One unusually large shack measures 40 by 36 feet, contains sixteen windows on the first floor and eight on the second floor. There were sixteen thin partitions in this shack and it housed 130 people.

In the cranberry sections a step in advance has been made by the growers who provide wooden bunks ranged in tiers, but the overcrowding is just as bad as elsewhere. One building, which contained 200 bunks for pickers, was built around a central enclosure used for stabling horses. The accumulation of dirt left by the last season's occupants had not been removed when this year's party arrived. Some shacks were better and some worse than those cited above. Very few were seen in which, or around which, the conditions were anything but filthy and improper. One exceptional shelter is owned by an Italian farmer who refused to let his workers live as squalidly as savages. That some of the Italians are not content with the makeshift shelters provided for them was shown by a padrone who exclaimed to the visitor, "What! Do you wish to see how the pigs live?" Most of the farmers do not hold themselves responsible for the quick development of unsanitary quarters. They argue that the shacks are clean when the Philadelphians arrive, and if a state of filth and indecency is created, it is obviously a continuation of their mode of living in the city tenements. No matter whose the responsibility, the fact remains that throughout the berry counties, some thousands of Italians live for months each season in shacks and barns which invite disease and immorality.

A glance inside these sheds on a rainy afternoon reveals a promiscuous horde of men, women and children, unpleasantly suggestive of cattle in a freight car. Even in the field filth accumulates, which must be a menace to the health of the farming community. Typhoid fever broke out this year in the Little Italy of Cumberland County among a people as ignorant as the Italians in the villages of Louisiana, who have trebled the danger of the spread of yellow fever throughout the whole South. In both cases the absence of health ordinances, coupled with unsanitary quarters and overcrowding by a stranger-folk, has multiplied the danger, as well as the actual suffering. An instance? — the woman berry picker who has managed to keep at work, in spite of the fact that she has cancer of the jaw. She herself dresses the diseased spot.

## The Children of the Berry Fields

A second consideration in weighing the advantage of fresh air for the children as against the manner of life of the berry pickers, is the gross neglect of the little ones. While the mothers are far out in the fields, swarms of flies and mosquitoes hover over and feed upon the helpless babies and toddling youngsters. Their husbands and children may be earning a fair wage, but spurred on by their earnings, as well as the insistent padroni, they, too, often ignore the cries that reach them. It is a pathetic sight to see these groups of restless babes forced to remain in the care of a few little mothers, six or seven years of age, in the tiny space alotted to them by the padroni. All the children over seven are working in the fields, not consecutively from sunrise to sunset, as are the older children in the long June days, but as diligently as their parents and the boss can force them to do. When not working, these younger children constitute a lawless and destructive element. They are too young and untrained to have any judgment in selecting the berries, they destroy trees, rob orchards, and make themselves a general nuisance, besides causing a considerable yearly loss to the farmer. In the cranberry bogs, they trample upon the fallen fruit. One large grower says he would be thankful if no child under nine years of age, were permitted upon the bogs. But from the standpoint of the parents, the more children one has at this time, the greater the income.

Undoubtedly, on many accounts, these months spent in the country are better for the children than the summer in the city. Yet to offset this advantage, one must place the long hours of stooping required in picking most berries. "Look at that child playing over there", called a farmer's daughter to a padrone, while the visitor stood by. "Why don't you make her work?" "You think it's fun to pick, because you are doing it for a few minutes", said a young girl in the bogs, "But just come and do it steadily and see what a backache you'll have." Perhaps none of the younger children work more than ten hours a day, but ten hours would seem to be quite enough for any child under fourteen years of age, even in the fields.

The farmers make a good profit on the berries. One who had 20 acres of strawberries under cultivation, employs and houses 45 people during the season. His profit from these berries alone amounted this year to $4,000. The average farmer, who owns a farm of about 35 acres and raises a fair crop of strawberries and raspberries, makes from $400 to $1,000.

## In the Canneries

Not all of the time of the Italians is spent in berry picking. At intervals during the season they work in the canneries hulling berries, which are preserved and sold in the city for table use. It is stated that half of the strawberry syrup used in the United States is made in New Jersey. One canner who has experimented with the Italian labor, says he prefers to make syrup from unhulled berries rather than have them thus handled. He did not relish putting whole families to work, and allowing the little babies to play at their own sweet will in the bowls of berries just hulled by their parents.

At the close of the strawberry season the laborers migrate to the adjoining counties of Gloucester and Atlantic to pick blackberries, raspberries, huckleberries and other kinds of fruit. The Italians seem to consider that they have the right to pick huckleberries wherever they can find them. During the huckleberry season many of them become veritable gypsies, roaming over all the woodland sections. They market the fruit through the nearest freight agent, and often make three dollars a day. When this work is finished, some pickers move into Cape May County to skin tomatoes and peel sweet potatoes and pumpkins for canning.

## The Cranberry Bogs

Cranberry picking occupies the greater number of the laborers during the close of the season. Cranberry culture is very profitable and has had a steady growth in New Jersey during the last few years. In the West, the Cape Cod cranberry, long considered the finest in the country, is no more in demand than the New Jersey product. Last year 1,000 pickers were employed by a single grower. Most of the cranberry bogs are bleak and desolate and miles away from any habitation. When properly drained, they are as dry as any field, but a heavy rain turns the thick and tangled mass of vines into a vast sponge, which quickly saturates the clothing of the pickers. Cranberries are picked both by hand and by scoops. The handpickers receive from 40 to 50 cents a bushel, and the scoopers, who must be more intelligent, receive $1.50 a day. The average wage for other small berries is 1½ cents a quart.

## The Cost to the Children in Education

From the beginning of October to the end of the month the parties are moving back to Philadelphia, where they enjoy the fruits of their labor during the winter months. The financial success of the trip is gained largely at the expense of the education of the children, most of whom lose from three to four months of schooling on account of this wandering gypsy life. They necessarily fall behind their classes, and there are always some who degenerate into chronic truants, whom the truant officers find it almost impossible to keep track of. Teachers and principals in Philadelphia, when questioned in regard to these children, have been emphatic in their condemnation of the summer expeditions. They say the little berry pickers are generally the most depraved children in the schools.

The name, age, address and school last attended were obtained from children working in various parts of the strawberry sections, and on October 5 an effort was made to learn how many of them had returned to school. Out of 50 children, ranging from 6 to 14 years of age, 26 had not returned, 3 returned on October 8, 2 on October 9, 9 returned to school at various times up to October 10, and 12 who gave addresses in Philadelphia could not be traced in any way.

### The Permanent Settlements in New Jersey

A brighter side to the berry picking industry can be found near Vineland and Hammonton, where many pickers who originally came to work in the fruit-growing districts under the padroni system, have bought their own little farms and have settled permanently. Frequent additions to their farms have placed the Italians among the prosperous farmers of the state. Friends and relatives have joined these settlers, so that at present they are independent of outside labor, and their crops of small fruits and berries are gathered under very fair conditions. Their children have educational advantages, and their homes are among the comfortable dwellings in both towns. Other successful foreign farmers are found among the Jews of Woodbine, Rosenhayn, Carmel, Alliance and Norma. The only Christian in Rosenhayn is the postmaster. The village shows that its people are intelligent and progressive, and at the same time they preserve all their Russian characteristics. The bearded patriarch in his long frock coat is seen on the roads of the settlement, and Tolstoi's picture is everywhere in evidence. While the young men preserve all their Jewish customs still, they are genuine Americans at heart, and are rapidly developing into prosperous farmers. The berries of one young Russian Jew are called the finest and largest crop in the section. He is proud of the fact that he owes no man anything, and that the family can use their first American home as a storehouse and live in a comfortable modern dwelling. His profit on berries was $400 this season.

To sum up, what are the advantages and disadvantages of this annual migration of a city district to the New Jersey berry counties? The most evident advantage is that the berries and fruits which ripen rapidly and for which there is an eager demand are now being picked as quickly as need be, and the farmers and the Italian families each consider that they are making a handsome profit out of the arrangement. Six thousand dollars was expanded for four weeks' labor on one bog last year; the owner of this bog estimates that $250,000 is taken back to Philadelphia each year by the cranberry pickers alone. The farmers do not care greatly that this large aggregate sum is spent among Philadelphia rather than New Jersey merchants, and only a minority of the Italians object to the filthy manner of life which is necessary under the present arrangement.

*The Problems Involved for New Jersey's Citizenship*

Is there anything to deplore, then, in this apparently smooth and prosperous method of industry? Is it not time for the farmers, having partially solved the labor problem, to consider their responsibility to the community, to insure common decency by providing separate quarters for each family, and enforcing rules of cleanliness? Is it not time for the local and the state boards of health to consider the possibilities of contagion under the present lack of careful and disinterested inspection? After a study of what the Hebrew Immigration Societies have accomplished in the New Jersey settlements, one wonders why the Italian Immigration Society cannot make a similar effort in helping to establish winter industries in the berry regions. Such a step would meet with the approval of many berry growers. In Cape May and Ocean counties tracts of ground are offered free as sites for factories.

If the berry pickers were recruited from the New Jersey cities, it would help to solve the present difficulty in enforcing the compulsory education law. As children of school age of residents of the state, they would be legally obliged to attend the nearest school, so long as it is in session. The school authorities could be held responsible for their non-attendance, both at the beginning and end of the school year — possibly through a state truant system, such as is in force in Connecticut and Indiana. Depriving the Italian child of so large a share of his schooling — short at best — cuts off the chances of his Americanization along right lines. How to protect the smaller children from the necessity of working is not an easy problem. Its solution at present must rest on the consciences of the farmers, in whose power it lies to prevent and prohibit such labor.

A humane interest on the part of the citizens and farmers of New Jersey should arouse them to a serious consideration of their responsibility in the protection and proper care of the Italian children, and self-interest should inspire them to formulate plans for the permanent settling of these wanderers in their own communities.

Market Day at Independence, Louisiana, a thriving Italian Settlement, ca. 1905.

# 36

# Piedmontese on the Mississippi[1]

ALEXANDER E. CANCE[2]

Rural settlements of Italians are comparatively numerous in the eastern and southern states and some of their communities are large and flourishing. Perhaps the most progressive communities are those at Vineland and Hammonton, New Jersey, where hundreds of Italians, most of them from Sicily and Northern Italy, are living on farms. Several rural groups of truck growers are to be found in the coast states; one prosperous settlement of North Italians is settled at Valdese, North Carolina, and other larger or smaller groups are farming in Arkansas, Missouri, and Tennessee. In Wisconsin two settlements were investigated by the immigration commission — one of South Italians in Cumberland county, the other of North Italians in Vernon county.

Concerning Italian immigrants in agriculture, two notions are rather firmly fixed: first, that they have only recently engaged in farming, and, second, that they are small farmers who depend on hand and hoe cultivation to mature their small crops of fruit or of garden truck. Italian cotton planters, dairymen, wheat farmers, or raisers of live stock are not common either in Italy or the United States, and the opinion prevails that the Italian is incapable or disinclined to undertake farming on a large scale. True as this is in the large, perhaps, a few notable and gratifying exceptions appear. One of these is the North Italian agricultural community at Genoa, Wisconsin,

1. *The Survey*, Vol. 26, 1911. Pp. 779-785. This is the first of a series of three articles by Alexander E. Cance on agricultural immigrant groups in the United States.
2. Expert in charge of the report of the Immigration Commission on recent immigrants in agriculture.

about eighteen miles south of Lacrosse, on the Mississippi River.

Southward from St. Paul, the Mississippi winds its way between banks that frequently rise abruptly, almost perpendicularly, from the water's edge to a height of several hundred feet. The traveler over the Burlington Railroad, which closely hugs the east brink of the river, has noticed numerous coves or pockets, a few acres in extent, marking the place where some small tributary creek has cut its way down through the rocky barrier to reach the level of the great river. Through these narrow defiles or coulées, the woodsmen and farmers living back on the uplands were accustomed to bring their produce to the river for barter or shipment. In time, little villages grew up in these narrow openings, huddled, disorderly hamlets, poorly laid out, depending for their existence on the traffic between the back country farmers and the rivermen. One of these hamlets is Genoa. About 200 persons live in the village, 1,000 in the township; 207 families, of whom forty-four are of Italian descent.

The first building that catches the eye as one climbs the rocky street from the river is the Catholic chapel, built of grey quarried stone; somewhat resembling a little Swiss chalet. The chapel was built in 1863 by eight newly settled Italian families, who quarried, hauled, shaped, laid the stone, and constructed the church with their own hands. The eight families constituted the entire "colony" at that time.

The present Italian settlement is 90 per cent rural, but the precipitous, rocky steps towering above the village give no hint of the agricultural population or of the possibilities lying beyond them. But follow for perhaps two miles upward and eastward the narrow winding roads that ascend the hills along the course of the steep, rough stream valleys, and one reaches a broad plateau 200 to 300 feet above the river — a "rapidly rolling" expanse laid out in well-tilled, well-fenced fields, in harvest time a picture of agricultural wealth and rural prosperity. From a superior elevation the region presents the appearance of an upland plain cut up by old ravines twenty to fifty or a hundred feet deep, branching out in every direction. Cultivation has worn down and rounded off the summits of the hills, and broadened the narrow ridges into fields easily tillable.

Over considerable areas 80 per cent of the land is in cultivation, and the succession of neat farmsteads, with their conspicuous windmills, big red barns trimmed with white, white farmhouses, and numerous outbuildings, are almost all owned by Italian farmers.

The first arrivals came immediately from Galena, Ill., whither, fifty years ago, they had somehow come together from various parts of the globe — one from South America, another from the California mines, a third from a picturesque career in Africa. Genoa was selected for settlement because one of their number, who had gone on an exploring trip up the river, brought back news that he had found the duplicate of his Piedmont home. They chose the site because it looked like Switzerland, and renamed it Genoa. The colony grew slowly; there was no colonization and no considerable influx of immigrants at any one time. The settlers are all from Piedmont or Lombardy, Italy, and practically all the foreign-born arrived before 1890.

Land was cheap in the sixties, and the steep hillsides covered with hardwood were considered almost worthless by the ordinary pioneer. Many filed on homesteads, settling first in the coulées and ravines; but later the more fertile areas on the uplands farther from the river began to be occupied. Having selected and purchased a timbered tract the colonists began to clear the land; and they have continued the clearing until they now own several thousand acres of fine farms, some of them 200 acres in extent, well stocked and highly improved. The greater number purchased land immediately on arrival because of the easy terms offered, and the opportunity afforded for making an independent home. Later on, some of the newcomers worked for a few years as farm laborers or as sawmill hands during the summer, or chopped wood in the winter until they had saved enough to buy a team and make a first payment on an uncleared "eighty".

The first crops were wheat, oats, infrequently barley, rye, and corn; wheat was the principal and the money crop. No one of the Italians knew much about grain raising, or about the care of the horses or the oxen which they were obliged to keep to clear the land, to haul the wood to the steamboat landing, and to break the virgin sod. But they learned rapidly, and gradually log-houses appeared; clearings ate into the woodland, and bountiful harvests rewarded the transplanted husbandmen. No one sold much grain. They were — like most pioneers — self-sufficing farmers, content to consume the products of their small holdings. After 1870, wheat growing began to decline, and corn and live stock were raised in increasing quantities. At one time, the hop craze struck the settlement and several Italians went rather timorously into hop growing; but the hop industry was short-lived. Tobacco growing began in Vernon county in the early eighties, and about 1887 some of the Italians became interested. Since then, nearly every Italian has made money and lost money, raised tobacco, and stopped raising this precarious crop. About one-half of them now plant a few acres every year, and care for it with their own households.

Dairying is perhaps the most important present industry. The impetus came with the introduction of the creamery between 1885 and 1890. The dairy region of Vernon county is practically included in the tract of rough, hilly territory, some twelve miles wide, lying along the river and including Genoa township. This section is well adapted to grass, despite the insufficient supply of running water, and some cattle have been raised since the inception of the settlement. But dairymen did not enter largely into the pioneer farming system; it was confined chiefly to the few pounds of butter which the farmer's wife had difficulty in exchanging for groceries at the village store. Cows were seldom milked in winter either by Italians or Americans, and in summer butter was frequently a drug on the market at eight to ten cents a pound.

The dairy industry was developed in the Italian settlement exactly as it developed elsewhere in Wisconsin. The creamery made the Wisconsin farmer a dairyman after the opening of the Minnesota wheat lands and the ravages of the chinch bug had wrought havoc with his wheat growing. The central feature is a farmers' co-operative creamery, really a joint stock company in which the patrons, Italian, German, and American diarymen, are share-holders. The cream is separated from the milk by hand or power separators before it leaves the farm; a cream collector hauls it to the creamery, where a hired butter-maker determines by test and weight the amount of butter-fat in each farmer's cream, and churns it. Cream is paid for on a butter-fat basis, the patron receiving his check every two weeks. The butter is sold by the co-operative company, and any surplus is returned as dividends to the stockholders in proportion to the shares held. Last year the dividends were 11 per cent on the par value of the outstanding stock. Since the patrons hold shares roughly corresponding to the quantity of cream delivered, the division of surplus is fairly equable.

The Italians have been fairly successful dairymen and stock raisers. Their dairy herds range from three to sixteen milk cows and about the same number of young cattle. In addition to an average of 200 pounds of butter made and consumed yearly at home, the income from dairy cows runs from fifty to nearly five hundred dollars for each farm. Not a large average, surely, for there are no pure bred or high grade herds, but comparing well with the income of other patrons in the vicinity. While the principles of breeding are not well understood, the Italian farmer takes great pride in his herd.

Italians, by reputation, are notoriously bad horsemen; they are quite the contrary in Genoa, where the horses are the finest animals on the farms. The Italian farmer may well be proud of his horseflesh, large, well-bred, well-broken animals, chiefly of the Percheron strain. Three-horse teams are the rule, for steep hill-sides, clay soils, and heavy modern machinery require more than the ordinary amount of horse power. Each farmer raises his own horses, and six or eight horses may be kept on a farm.

It is a significant fact that these Italians are buying and operating modern farm implements of the most approved models with as great efficiency as their neighbors, the Scandanavians and Germans. Two and three-horse plows, drills, corn cultivators, and disc harrows are employed; mowing machines, hay tedders, and horse forks are used in haying; every farmer has a self-binder, and no field is so steep or uneven that the grain must be cut or bound by hand. The ordinary outlay for farm machinery on a 120-acre farm is between four and five hundred dollars. Hay loaders and gang plows cannot be operated successfully on the hillsides, and manure spreaders have not yet been introduced.

The farmsteads of the Piedmontese in Wisconsin present a better appearance and represent a larger outlay of capital than those of any group of Italians known to the writer. The houses, even on the small farms, are neat, well-constructed, and comfortable. On the larger farms, many of them are of brick or of stone, some of them erected years ago. Most of them are surrounded with well-cared-for lawns, ornamented with shrubbery and native trees. The big basement barns, the granaries, the tobacco sheds, the corn cribs, the tool sheds, and the milk houses on the greater number of farms give a picture of thrift and prosperity that one seldom associates with an Italian farmstead. The Italian has made sure, if slow, progress. The log granary or the hog house, he tells you, was his dwelling house for twenty years. He built his new barn out of stone which he and his son quarried, and every timber and rafter he hewed out of trees that grew in his wood lot; it was put up the year following a very profitable tobacco crop, and paid for as soon as the cupola was in place. Not one of the forty farmers brought any large amount of material wealth with him to the community. Every one endured many discomforts and inconveniences in order to become independent. And with the majority economic independence is a religion. An Italian rarely goes into debt for anything less than an economic necessity. For example, one rarely finds a top buggy or a bicycle that is not fully paid for. The American frequently contracts debt for luxuries, very often for comforts; the Italians, as a rule, never.

In matters of saving, thrift, careful attention to small economies, prevention of waste, and care of capital goods, the Italians at Genoa closely resemble German farmers. The women gather up anything that may be left in the fields — hay, scattered stalks of grain, small potatoes, and the like; they cut out the fence corners and mow closely around the stumps, even when the labor amounts to more than the produce saved. It is of interest that the husbands are inclined to laugh at their "rakings and pickings".

Measured by the ordinary standards of material wealth, none of these Italians is rich; most of them are well-to-do or comfortable, none is in want. Some have debts for recent purchases, but none are tenants. These are no married farm laborers. Their holdings vary in size and value, the medium farm being about 120 to 130 acres, valued from $3,000 to $4,500. Of fifteen farmers interviewed, eight reported real and personal property valued between $3,000 and $5,000, four between $5,000 and $10,000, and three less than $3,000. The estimated values are conservative, but approximate the truth.

But what of standards of living, and progress in American ideals and ideas? How about assimilation or even fusion of races?

"Yes, Henry married a German girl; they are living on the other side of the hill."

"Also Rosa. She has an Irish man. Pretty soon will be all mixed, yes, but all American."

Examine the list of marriage licenses and one is impressed at once with the number of inter-racial marriages. There is little race consciousness. The second generation have grown up together and mingle with great freedom. Here, of all the colonies visited by agents of the Immigration Commission, the Italian is not an Italian foreigner, but an individual citizen, a member of the community.

On the whole, very few foreign customs or standards survive. The trim, snug, well-painted, comfortable little homes tucked away in the nooks and hollows of the hills have a cheerful, prepossessing aspect. Both within and without, the dwellings present a better appearance than those of the ordinary Italian or Polish farmer. The interiors are nearly all clean, with ceiled and plastered walls, uncarpeted pine floors, and comparatively low ceilings. There is a parlor or best room, with center table, lace-curtained windows, and white-washed or papered walls, decorated with mottoes and texts of Scripture. Usually a separate bedroom is found on the ground floor, but in any case there is a fine bed, piled high with feather mattresses and covered with an ornamental bedspread. In addition to these two rooms, there is on the first floor a kitchen, frequently a fourth room that serves as dining and living room. A telephone, on a farmer's line, is in nearly every home, giving long distance connections with the surrounding cities. Those who can read English take local, often daily and agricultural, newspapers. Books are not numerous, but one notices a few, and in some homes of the second generation an organ or a piano.

Few Italian foods or dishes are used, although the diet continues chiefly vegetable. The distinctive foods are macaroni, occasionally peppers, and polenta. Polenta remains, in fact a favorite dish. Cheap, wholesome, readily prepared — and when well cooked said to be very palatable and nutritious — it makes a most excellent food. As elsewhere, the Italians consume less meat than the Poles or North European immigrants, although each farm provides some beef, pork, and poultry for its own use. Speaking in general terms, the food standard is perceptibly higher than among most farm families from Southern Europe.

The position and treatment of the women is a rather accurate index of the degree of advancement in civilization and enlightenment. In most foreign communities the labor of wives and children is one great economic advantage that accrues to the farmer. In Genoa, women's work out of doors has been growing less and less for many years, and except among the older people in cases of special need the ordinary field labor is left to the men. Old settlers relate that in pioneer days the wife worked side by side with her husband, grubbing, splitting rails, clearing land, binding grain, pitching hay — in short, performed the same tasks as a man, and in addition cared for the cows, pigs, and poultry, looked after the house and reared a large family. Women still help in haying, frequently gather potatoes, husk corn, and milk cows. The children all are brought up to work, but the adult girl and younger married women have learned American ideals, and confine their activities chiefly to the household. The change in the duties exacted of women which a generation has brought about are very significant and much lamented by some of the older men. Bare-footed women and men are very seldom seen in the fields of this American Piedmont, and the children, with few exceptions, are allowed to continue in school during the school year.

The education of the children is practically limited to the required period in the country school, of which the directors are usually Italians. Very few farmers' children attend high school, occasionally a young man goes to a business college, but ordinarily the girls who do not remain at home become housemaids or hotel girls, or go into Lacrosse factories. The young men find work as farm hands in the neighborhood or migrate to newer lands farther west, where more than one "New Genoa" colony has sprung up; a few get employment in the skilled industries in the cities, and a number have engaged in farming in the neighborhood.

Socially, most of the community enterprises center in the Catholic church, whose broadminded, progressive pastor ministers to a congregation of Italians, Germans, and Americans. The services are conducted alternately in Italian, German, and English, but the mingling of races at church and at the various church gatherings has done much to break up the spirit of clannishness and to remove the social restraints brought about by racial characteristics. Except between North Italians and Sicilians there is no race friction. The former consider themselves superior to the Sicilians, and have nothing to do with the few South Italian railroad laborers who at times live in the village. In fact, they rightly declare they do not belong to the same race. At the informal meetings, dances, private parties, and church "sociables", Germans, Americans, and Italians meet on equal terms — as Americans. As might be expected, the percentage of intermarriage is high, particularly with the Germans and American Catholics.

Other than the national and ecclesiastical feast-days the Genoa Piedmontese celebrate very few strictly Italian holidays. The Italian customs, indeed, seem to be falling into disuse and one finds less of old Italy here than in most Sicilian communities. One delightful custom that still survives grows out of their love of music. On summer evenings young and old will gather on their porches and sing the melodious old Italian airs. At weddings, too, this custom still prevails. As usual the customs clustering about the home and the church seem to have more vitality than those adhering to other institutions.

More than 90 per cent of the foreign-born have taken out first papers, and half of these are full citizens. Until recently an alien with first papers who had lived one year in the state was invested with practically all the privileges and the prerogatives of citizenship; now the law permits only citizens to hold office or to sit on juries, and since a number of Italians have never felt the need of second papers, some have been disqualified by the new law. They are not indifferent to political affairs, however, and for many years some of the township officers and members of the County Board have been Italians. They are said to be excellent officials, but they believe in strict economy and are not likely to support any project calling for large expenditures. The older men vote as a unit, ordinarily, on state and national issues; the second generation are more independent. All are reputed politically honest.

This Wisconsin settlement is one of the very few Italian communities where the Italian and the Italian-American are not regarded nor spoken of as Italians, but as fellow citizens. Most of them speak fluent English, the young people all do, and converse intelligently, frankly, and without suspicion, on agriculture, politics, or topics of current interest. They attend strictly to their farming, and display more intelligence and real knowledge of diversified agriculture than any group of Italians investigated. They remind one of the German and German-Swiss farmers who have proved so successful both as farmers and as citizens. They have confidence in themselves, and the community feels that they can and do take their places and assume the responsibilities of citizenship shoulder to shoulder with the non-Italians in the neighborhood.

It may be that the environing conditions — natural and social — have molded this community differently from others where the opportunity for race isolation was afforded and conformity to the traditional type of agriculture was the line of least resistance. At any rate, Genoa exemplifies the adaptability of the North Italian, and illustrates his capacity for diversified agriculture and for American rural life as it has developed in our mid-western states. The community has not yet begun to live abundantly, or to enjoy fully its evident prosperity. On the other hand, who shall say that the great rank and file of American farmers has advanced farther or more rapidly in rural wealth, welfare, or well-rounded citizenship than this small group of Italian fellow citizens?

# 37

# The Italian Workmen of America to Americans[1]

EDITH WALLER[2]

Give us a chance! We are men!
Not "wops and dagoes" base;
Cease with your names
    that would disgrace. —/
The blood in our veins
    of an ancient race/
Flows proud and fiery free;
Your scorn does ye debase.

Give us a chance! We are men!
Know ye the past whence we come?
Back of us Rome, the glory of Rome!
St. Peter's embracing dome,
The law and art of the world.
Have ye a name like Rome?

Give us a chance! We are men!
Forth our Columbus bold,
Braving defeats untold,
Out of the seas of darkness old,
Brought light to your continent new
For ye to have and hold.

Give us a chance! We are men!
To-day Marconi stands
And weaves the nations' strands,
Annihilates seas and lands,
Holds elements in thrall
To make the worlds join hands.

Give us a chance! We are men!
Not earthworms born of the soil.
We would upbuild not despoil,
Faithful and earnest we toil;
But music and beauty,
    life's pulsing joy./
Are ours above the moil.

Americans! We are men!
Strong bodies with souls of flame;
Where ye can progress claim
Help us to win the same,
Give us a chance, but a chance —
Forget not Italy's name!

1. *The Survey*, Vol. 29, 1912-1913. P. 47.   2. Miss Waller is the author of *English for Italians*.

Left to right: Joseph Caruso, Joe Ettor and Arturo Giovannitti, Lawrence, Massachusetts, 1912.

# 38

# Arturo Giovannitti [1]

MARY BROWN SUMNER

Half England came to echo the protestantism of an imprisoned tinker. We in America today are quick to respond to the poet of a Russian dungeon who sings of the wrongs of Russian peasants. But what of a lyric singer in a New England jail, whose arraignment of American democracy would put it on a par with Russian despotism?

Some of us may not follow him all the way because, though we acknowledge substantial justice in his criticism, we believe that the structure of democracy can be restored by other means than by destroying to rebuild on new foundations. But we are forced to recognize in the work of the Italian, Arturo Giovannitti, on trial in Salem for complicity in the murder of Anna Lopizzo in Lawrence, the first American poems in a world-wide outpouring of working class verse that is giving literary expression to that revolt against our present day institutions, industrial and political, which has expressed itself in action in the last three years in the mass strikes all over Europe, from Barcelona anti-militarists to disenfranchised Belgian workers.

More particularly Giovannitti represents the polyglot internationalism of the industrial workers of Lawrence, for he is an Italian immigrant, only twelve years in this country, who has turned his hand to any kind of work, from that of the mine to teaching languages and editing the organ of the Italian-American industrial-socialists. He had written not only Italian prose and verse, but some English verse before his arrest. Among others is a poem called "Blind Men", addressed to orthodox Christians, which is interesting

---

1. *The Survey*, Vol. 29, 1912-1913. Pp. 163-166. The poems are quoted from the *International Socialist Review* and the *New York Call*.

in view of the fact that soon after he came to America he entered a Protestant
theological seminary intending to prepare for the ministry.

It was as he sat with Joe Ettor on the Prisoner's Bench in Lawrence Court
House that Giovannitti wrote the first of five English prison poems which
give an idea of his poetic message and of his adequacy to express that
message in a language which to an Italian poet whose message was not true
for all nations would be exotic:

Passed here, all wrecks
    from the tempestuous main/
    Of life have washed
    the tides of time;/
Rags of bodies and souls,
    furies and pains,/
    Horrors and passions
    awful yet sublime,/
All passed here to their doom.
    Nothing remains/
    Of all the tasteless dregs of sin
    and crime/
But stains of tears,
    and stains of blood, and stains/

Of the inn's vomit
    and the brothel's grime./
And now we too must sit here, Joe.
    Don't dust/
    These boards on which
    our wretched brothers fell./
They're still clean;
    there's no reason for disgust;/
    For the fat millionaire's
    disgusting stench/
Is not here,
    nor the preacher's saintly smell./
And the judge—
    he never sat upon this bench./

From Lawrence jail, soon after, he wrote his indictment of the republic,
which he inscribes "July 4-July 14":

A Goddess of the common weal.
. . . . . . . . . . . . . . . . . . . . . . . . . . . . . .
Not hers the wisdom which decrees
    That time alone can wrongs allay.
    Not hers the craven heart to pray
And barter Liberty for peace.

Not hers the fear to hesitate
    When shame and misery cry out:
    "Love has no patience,
    Truth no doubt/
And Right and Justice cannot wait."

She called. . . . . . . . . . . . . . . . . . . . .

The Mob, the mightiest judge of all,
    To hear the Rights of Man
    came out./
    And every word became a shout,
And every shout a cannon ball.
. . . . . . . . . . . . . . . . . . . . . . . . . . . .

And when upon the great sunrise
    Flew her disheveled victories
    To all the land and all the seas,
Like angry eagles in the skies,

. . . . . . . . . . . . . . . . . . . . . . . . . . . .

To ring the call of Brotherhood
    And hail Mankind
    from shore to shore,/
    Wrapt in her splendid tricolor,
The People's virgin pride she stood.

This was the dawn. But when the day

    Wore out. . . . . . . . . . . . . . . . . . .

When night with velvet sandaled feet
    Stole in her chamber's solitude
    Behold! she lay there naked, lewd,
A drunken harlot of the street.

With withered breasts
   and shaggy hair/
   Soiled by each wanton, frothy kiss,

Between a sergeant of police
And an old dribbling millionaire.

But if our nineteenth century republic has to his mind been prostituted, the Mob has in the meantime become the Thinker. In the late spring two poems on Rodin's Thinker came out almost simultaneously; one by James Oppenheim, the other by Giovannitti. They form an interesting contrast; the one filled with all the graces of style, even to the rhythm of a refrain; the other irregular in meter and almost incoherent in parts, depending for its claim to poetic excellence on the strength and daring of the thought. In contrast with Giovannitti's Man, in whose hand lies the making of the future, Mr. Oppenheim's Thinker[2] is a musing Caliban. Here is the Oppenheim poem:

Thinks he: I come of a race of brutes,
   Tillers and killers and such:
Whose life was a feeding,
   a toiling and breeding,/
   And their joy was none too much.

  . . . . . . . . . . . . . . . . . . . . . . . . . . . .

Thinks he:
   our masters have given us light/
   Better their rule to obey:

Machines need brains
   to get good gains/
   And the brutes must pass away.

. . . . . . . . . . . . . . . . . . . . . . . . . . . .

Thinks he:
   we've paid in ages of sweat—/
   Must we pay again and again?
What if black ink
   shall set us to think./
   And thinking shall make us men?

Mr. Oppenheim is the reflective observer; Giovannitti is the apostle:

Think, think!
   Since time and life began/
   Your mind has only feared
   and slept;/
Of all the beasts
   they called you man/
   Only because you toiled and wept.

Of all the ages firmly set,
   Lone pillar of the world, you stood,
Beyond your hunger and your sweat,
   You never knew nor understood,

Till now. . . . . . . . . . . . . . . . . . . . .

Think, think!
   While breaks in you the dawn,/
   Crouched at your feet
   the world lies still./
It has no power but your brawn.
It has no wisdom but your will.

Beyond your flesh
   and mind and blood./
   Nothing there is to live and do.
There is no man, there is no God,
   There is not anything but you.

2. See *American Magazine* for June, 1912.

Think, think!
    What every age and land/
    Thought an eternal mystery.
What sages could not understand.
    And saints and poets could not see.

From you,
    the chained, reviled outcast,/
From you,
    the brute, inert and dumb,/

Shall,
    through your wakened thought,
    at last,/
    The message of tomorrow come.

It cometh like a flash of light,
    Of truth to save and to redeem,
And, whether Love or Dynamite,
    Shall blaze the pathway to
    your Dream./

"The Thinker" is not the only one of Giovannitti's poems which suffers from defects of style. All except the "Prisoner's Bench", the material defect in the last line of which may be intentional, have irregularities in meter as well as lapses into incoherency of expression; none is deficient in thought or the power to arouse "terror and pity".

Because it struggles with no metrical limitations, and because it expresses, as it has never been expressed in English, at once the psychology of the prisoner and the protest against the law that herds in a common jail the "apostle and the poet", together with the "hired assassin, the embezzler, the raper and the prostitute", "The Walker",[3] written after six months in jail, is the best of Giovannitti's poems.

### "The Walker"

I hear footsteps over my head all night.

They come and they go. Again they come and again they go all night.

They come one eternity in four paces and they go one eternity in four paces, and between the coming and the going there is Silence and the Night and the Infinite.

For infinite are the nine feet of a prison cell, and endless is the march of him who walks between the yellow brick wall and the red iron gate, thinking things that cannot be chained and cannot be locked, but that wander far away in the sunlit world, in their wild pilgrimage after destined goals.

Throughout the restless night I hear the footsteps over my head.

Who walks? I do not know. It is the phantom of the jail, the sleepless brain, a man, THE WALKER.

One—two—three—four: four paces and the wall.

One—two—three—four: four paces and the iron gate.

He has measured the space, he has measured it accurately, scrupulously, minutely, so many feet, so many inches, so many fractions of an inch for each of the four paces.

3. Copyright by the *International Socialist Review*.

One—two—three—four. Each step sounds heavy and hollow over my head, and the echo of each step sounds hollow within my head as I count them in suspense and in fear that once, perhaps, in the endless walk, there may be five steps instead of four between the yellow brick wall and the red iron gate.

But he has measured the space so accurately, so scrupulously, so minutely, that nothing breaks the grave rhythm of the slow phantastic march.

When all are asleep (and who knows but I when they all sleep?) three things are still awake in the night: the Walker, my heart, and the old clock which has the soul of a fiend, for never, since a coarse hand with red hair on its fingers swung the first time the pendulum in the jail, has the old clock tick-tocked a full hour of joy.

Yet the old clock which marks everything and records everything and to everything sounds the death knell, the wise old clock that knows every-thing, does not know the number of the footsteps of the Walker nor the throbs of my heart.

For neither for the Walker nor for my heart is there a second, a minute, an hour, or anything that is in the old clock; there is nothing but the night, the sleepless night, and footsteps, that go, and footsteps that come and the wild tumultuous beatings that trail after them forever.

● ● ●

All the sounds of the living beings and inanimate things, and all the voices and all the noises of the night, I have heard in my wistful vigil.

I have heard the moans of him who bewails a thing that is dead and the sighs of him who tries to smother a thing that will not die;

I have heard the stifled sobs of the one who prays with his head under the coarse blanket and the whisperings of the one who prays with his forehead on the hard cold stone of the floor;

I have heard him who laughs the shrill sinister laugh of folly at the horror rampant on the yellow wall and at the red eyes of the nightmare glaring through the iron bars;

I have heard in the sudden icy silence him who coughs a dry ringing metallic cough and wished madly that his throat would not rattle so and that he would not spit on the floor, for no sound was more atrocious than that of his sputum upon the floor;

I have heard him who swears fearsome oaths which I listen to in reverence and in awe, for they are holier than the virgin's prayer;

And I have heard, most terrible of all, the silence of two hundred brains all possessed by one single relentless unforgiving desperate thought.

All this I have heard in the watchful night,

And the murmur of the wind beyond the walls,

And the tolls of a distant bell,

And the remotest echoes of the accursed city,

And the terrible beatings, wild beatings, mad beatings of the one Heart which is nearest to my heart.

All this I have heard in the still night;

But nothing is louder, harder, drearier, mightier, more awful, than the footsteps I hear over my head all night.

Yet fearsome and terrible are all the footsteps of men upon the earth, for they either descend or climb.

They descend from little mounds and high peaks and lofty altitudes, through wide roads and narrow paths, down noble marble stairs and creaky stairs of wood, and some go down to the street, and some go down to the cellar, and some down to the pits of shame and infamy, and still some to the glory of an unfathomable abyss where there is nothing but the staring white stony eyeballs of Destiny.

And again other footsteps climb. They climb to life and to love, to fame, to power, to vanity, to truth, to glory, and to the gallows: to everything but Freedom and the Ideal.

And they all climb the same roads and the same stairs others go down; for never, since man began to think how to overcome and overpass man, have other roads and other stairs been found.

They descend and they climb, the fearful footsteps of men, and some drag, some speed, some trot, some run; the footsteps are quiet, slow noisy, brisk, quick, feverish, mad, and most awful is their cadence to hear for the one who stands still.

But of all the footsteps of men that either descend or climb, no footsteps are as fearsome and terrible as those that go straight on the dead level of a prison floor from a yellow stone wall to a red iron gate.

• • •

All through the night he walks and he thinks. Is it more frightful because he walks and his footsteps sound hollow over my head, or because he thinks and does not speak?

But does he think? Why should he think? Do I think? I only hear the footsteps and count them. Four steps and the wall. Four steps and the gate. But beyond? Beyond? Where does he go beyond?

He does not go beyond. His thought breaks there on the iron gate. Perhaps, it breaks like a wave of rage, perhaps like a sudden flow of hope, but it always returns to beat the wall like a billow of helplessness and despair.

He walks to and fro within the narrowness of this ever storming and furious thought. Only one thought, constant, fixed, immovable, sinister, without power and without voice.

A thought of madness, frenzy, agony, and despair, a hell-brewed thought for it is a natural thought. All things natural are things impossible so long as there are jails in the world — bread, work, happiness, peace, love.

But he does not think of this. As he walks he thinks of the most superhuman, the most unattainable, the most impossible things in the world.

He thinks of a small brass key that turns half around and throws open the iron gate.

• • •

That is all that the Walker thinks, as he walks throughout the night.

And that is what two hundred minds drowned in the darkness and the silence of the night think and that is what I think.

Wonderful is the holy wisdom of the jail that makes all think the same thought. Marvelous is the providence of the law that equalizes all even in mind and sentiment. Fallen is the last barrier of privilege, the aristocracy of the intellect. The democracy of reason has levelled all the two hundred minds to the common surface of the same thought.

I, who have never killed, think like the murderer;

I, who have never stolen, reason like the thief;

I think, reason, wish, hope, doubt, wait like the hired assassin, the embezzler, the forger, the counterfeiter, the incestuous, the raper, the prostitute, the pimp, the drunkard,—I—I who used to think of love and life and the flowers and song and beauty and the ideal.

A little key, a little key as little as my little finger, a little key of shiny brass.

All my ideas, my thoughts, my dreams are congealed in a little key of shiny brass.

All my brains, all my soul, all the suddenly surging latent powers of my life are in the pocket of a whitehaired man dressed in blue.

He is powerful, great, formidable, the man with the white hair, for he has in his pocket the mighty talisman which makes one man cry and one man pray, and one laugh, and one walk, and all keep awake and think the same maddening thought.

Greater than all men is the man with the white hair and the little brass key, for no man in the world could compel two hundred men to think the same thought. Surely when the light breaks I shall write an ode, nay, a hymn, unto him, and shall hail him greater than Mohammed and Arbues and Torquemada and Mesmer, and all the other masters of other men's thoughts. I shall call him Almighty for he holds everything of all and of me in a little brass key in his pocket.

Everything of me he holds but the branding iron of contempt and the clamor of hatred for the most monstrous cabala that can make the apostle and the murderer, the poet and the procurer, think of the same key, the same gate and the same exit on the different sunlit highways of life.

• • •

My brother, do not walk any more.

It is wrong to walk on a grave. It is a sacrilege to walk four steps from the headstone to the foot and four steps from the foot to the headstone.

If you stop walking, my brother, this will be no longer a grave; for you will
   give me back my mind that is chained to your feet and the right to think
   my own thoughts.
I implore you, my brother, for I am weary of the long vigil, weary of
   counting your steps and heavy with sleep.
Stop, rest, sleep, my brother, for the dawn is well nigh and it is not the key
   alone that can throw open the door.

How do the best lines in "Reading Gaol", up to this time the best expression of
prison life in English poetry, stand comparison with "The Walker"? Says
Wilde's ballad:

But this I know, that every law.             With a most evil fan.
   That men have made for man,
Since first man took his brother's life,    And every prison that men build
   And the sad world began,                    Is built with bricks of shame.
But straws the wheat                        It's only what is good in man
   and saves the chaff/                        That wastes and withers there.


   Over against these last two lines, hear "The Walker", with a simplicity
and melancholy iteration suggestive of Ecclesiastes:

   All things natural are things impossible so long as there are jails in the
world — bread, work, happiness, peace, love.

We should stop perhaps with "The Walker" as the climax. And yet a much
inferior poem, "The Bench in Mulberry Park", which has come out recently,
has verses which show such a different and such an exquisite side of the poet
that it should not pass unnoticed:


   I dreamed and dreamed all night,        Aye, I was hungry—yet
   Young dreams and frail and bright,       Sometimes one can forget,
Like little buds that never grow         And empty stomachs
   to bloom;/                                 often find a dole,/
   Like silver clouds that pass,              Whilst the young days are fleet,
   Like crickets in the grass,                When one can fill with sweet,
Like yellow fireflies                    And moonlit dreams
   twinkling in the gloom./                   the hunger of the soul./


   For these dreams the poet had no bed but the park bench, a seat set not far
from that other seat of poverty, the prisoner's bench — for each night he
questioned:

Whether the dawn would hail
  Another thief in jail,
Or at the morgue another corpse unknown.

Surely we are not so rich in lyric poets that we can afford to send this one
to the chair or keep him longer in prison.

Strikers' children, Lawrence, Massachusetts, 1912.

# 39

# The Salem Trial[1]

JAMES P. HEATON

"Joseph J. Ettor, look upon the foreman. Mr. Foreman, look upon the prisoner." The two men gazed at each other — the buoyant Italian and the shrewd Yankee.

"What say you, Mr. Foreman, upon your oath — is the prisoner guilty as charged?"

"Not guilty."

Such was their verdict — four carpenters, a hair dresser, a sail maker, a leather dealer, a stock fitter, a morocco dresser, a grocer, a driver, a lamp worker — the men at whose hands the three chief labor cases[2] growing out of the Lawrence strike were brought to a conclusion November 26: cases which, more dramatically than any since the Haymarket riots sent four men to the hangman, hinged on the question of how far labor leaders can be held responsible for acts of violence committed in the midst of a strike.

After ten months in jail and fifty-eight days of trial, Ettor, Giovannitti and Caruso left the court house free men.[3] There were the joyous hugs and kisses of their fellow-countrymen, but the feeling of comity and good will, after the long months of controversy in the mill districts, was not limited to

1. *The Survey*, Vol. 29, 1912-1913. Pp. 301-304.

2. See "Legal Aftermath of the Lawrence Strike", by James P. Heaton, *The Survey*, July 6, 1912.

3. To the surprise of nearly everybody Caruso, though under a separate indictment for an assault to kill, was released on his own recognizance. As soon as he had given his oath to stand trial when summoned, he worked his way to the side of his wife, whose face lit up with a smile of content. Ettor and Giovannitti charged, along with Haywood and Giannini, with a conspiracy to intimidate Lawrence workers, were bailed by Helena S. Dudley, of Denison House, Boston, and Mary Kenny O'Sullivan, one of the old line labor leaders and an organizer of the Women's Trade Union League of America.

these. As the trial had drawn along, public opinion in Salem, despite the somewhat antagonistic attitude of the chief newspaper and occasional disquieting rumors of a plot for a jail delivery, had grown more and more favorable toward the defendants. One phase of it was reflected by Juror No. 6. "If a thousand Americans had been treated the way those fellows were treated, there wouldn't have been a mill left standing in Lawrence", he declared in recounting his sayings in the jury room. The friendly attitude, however, did not always mean a conviction that the accused men were innocent of all offense. It did represent a strong belief that the state had overshot the mark in getting full capital indictments against Ettor and Giovannitti, who were not present at the time of the shooting. The belief of the mill operatives in Lawrence that they were being held in prison "on a trumped-up charge of murder", originally brought as a piece of anti-strike tactics, has been shared by attorneys, newspapermen, ministers and students of public affairs, who have followed the proceedings.

"The best thing of all", to quote the dean of the newspaper correspondents, as he was congratulating Ettor and Giovannitti, "is that everybody seems happy. I enjoy a court trial assignment which ends like this. I have just been the rounds to say goodbye, and found everybody, including the judge, sheriff, court officers, and all the attorneys, in the best of good humor."

So it was that everywhere people sprang up to shake the hands of the three prisoners as they left the court, and on the sidewalk outside a battery of photographers, jostled by impatient and elated textile workers, waited for their game. The acquitted men started over to their lawyer's office, but the crowd fairly blocked the little one-track street of Old Salem into which they turned, until a friendly Salvation Army captain bade them come to his hall. Here an impromptu meeting followed, and soon out from its windows flanked by gospel mottoes gushed the rousing strains of the Marseillais.

The whole Lawrence struggle has been full of contrasts. There were the contrasts brought out by the strike itself. Here was a typical New England manufacturing city, with its "Dublin" of Irish, its French "Canucks" and Nova Scotian "Blue Noses" from across the Canadian line, suddenly overwhelmed by an influx of Latin and Slavic peoples; its hum-drum civil government bewildered, taxed to the breaking point by a tug-of-war between new and disruptive industrial forces. Here were the great textile interests, which had baffled tariff reformers and old-line craft unions, suddenly bearded by their unskilled day laborers.

In the trial at the sleepy county seat came more contrasts. There are three court houses in Salem, side by side, erected at different times in the past seventy-five years. And back of them range a dim succession of court rooms reaching in imagination to the trials of the Salem witches. It is in this town that the preachers of the new industrialism, of syndicalism, and the latest revolutionary doctrines of the world's labor movement, were before the bar for bedeviling workingmen in the minds of the grand jury. It was to the individualistic traditions of Puritan New England, to the principles of the revolutionary fathers which he believed are today threatened by foreign malcontents, that the district attorney made his plea when summing up the case. It was to the tidings of a world-wide working class rebellion in the name of industrial brotherhood that the prisoners made theirs.

But the contrast which reached furthest and deepest, perhaps, in its practical social significance lay in the new conception the trial has afforded the new wage-earners in the textile towns of what democracy stands for in America. The strikers at Lawrence had felt the force of government in the swinging clubs of police and in the prodding bayonets of the militia. They had chafed when that force barred parents from sending their children out of town, and had voiced their wrath when it was embodied in the unnecessary midnight arrests of young working girls. They had seen the government of the native-born in one day sentence a score of foreign rioters to serve a year's sentence in the House of Correction, and they had seen it falter in the case of Breen (school committeeman and son of a former mayor), who was convicted of planting dynamite to discredit the strikers, — falter and let the man off with a fine.

Now they had a new, potent embodiment of the old Bay State, not in the prosecution, but in the even tempered New England judge of the old school, and in the twelve "good men and true" who sat, listened and coolly made up their verdict.

There have been those who have felt that the fabric of the commonwealth of Massachusetts has been imperilled not only by new doctrines of social revolution, but also by the almost instantaneous recoil of the authorities against what they have deemed crime and sedition. It was recognized by all participating that the conduct of these cases could either win the respect of the mill workers of New England or plant and spread distrust. That the Superior Court of Essex County measured up to its responsibility for the maintenance of the reputation of Massachusetts tribunals for probity and judicial acumen was attested by Ettor himself in a statement at the conclusion of the trial. A former district attorney of the county, who is also a former judge, discussing the case in his office just after the trial was over, rejoiced because he felt the outcome answered completely those who feared lest public opinion in Essex County was so prejudiced against Ettor and Giovannitti as to make it difficult to secure for them a strictly fair hearing.

While there will be some in both camps who will claim that the three men got off because of the fear of what might have happened had they been sentenced to death, there has been borne in upon a great middle group, and with them upon thousands of alien workers, an abiding sense that American justice can weather times of industrial stress.

The trial opened on September 30 after a postponement which was requested last May by the defense. There has been misunderstanding about this delay. For this the defense committee of the strikers[4] is largely to blame, as in their appeals for funds they held up Ettor and Giovannitti as martyrs kept in jail through the dictation of the money powers. One appeal, issued while the trial was on, made necessary an awkward explanation to the court by the attorneys for the defense.

The trial itself went over much the same ground that was covered in the inquest before Police Magistrate Mahoney in Lawrence, February 9. In a clash between the police and a crowd of strikers on the evening of January 29, Anna Lopizzo was killed. Ettor and Giovannitti who, as Industrial Workers of the World leaders had come from New York to throw themselves into the strike and weld it into their movement for revolutionary industrial unionism, were charged with inflaming the actual murderer by a propaganda of violence.

The commonwealth obviously faced the task of proving two things. One was that strikers, or their sympathizers, fired the shot. The other was that a convincing connection existed between their acts and those of the strike leaders, a point involving far-reaching issues of strike leadership and responsibility.

The evidence on both points proved insufficient. The man who fired the shot was not surely identified. He was described by the state as Salvatore Scuito or a "person unknown". Scuito was never apprehended and it was not for weeks that Joseph Caruso, an Italian workman who before the strike had been working in the Lawrence mills for a few dollars a week, was arrested as a principal. Witnesses for the state testified that a shot aimed at Policeman Benoit had missed its mark and killed a fellow striker. The defense produced witnesses who swore that Policeman Benoit himself fired

4. While the fund raised by unionists and Socialists throughout the country for the defense of Ettor, Giovannitti and Caruso did not approach in size that collected by the American Federation of Labor for the McNamara brothers, it did permit the engagement of five attorneys, whereas the state was represented by but two, District Attorney Attwill and his assistant.

The floor leader of the corps of lawyers for the prisoners was W. Scott Peters, a former district attorney, dubbed familiarly by his successor and pupils as "the old fox of Essex County". Caruso was represented by Joseph H. Sisk, an attorney who has figured in many Massachusetts murder cases. For his personal attorney Ettor had John P. S. Mahoney of Lawrence, who was the first lawyer of standing to be associated with the operatives and early in the strike became their counsel. The two other men in the legal force of the defense were George E. Roewer, Jr., a Socialist of Boston, and Fred H. Moore, a member of the Industrial Workers of the World, from Los Angeles.

The attorneys were aided in the selection of the jury by Robert Reid, a former Salemite who investigated the records of all the eligible jurors as he had done in several other big cases in New England. Practically a week, not counting a long intermission for enrolling a second panel of 350 jurors, was required for the selection of the twelve men who were to decide the fate of the three prisoners. The large representation of workingmen on the jury reflects the successful jockeying of the defense. Though the judge refused to allow the lawyers for the prisoners to examine the jurors about their financial investments in Lawrence woolen mills, the jury was satisfactory to the prisoners.

several shots toward Mrs. Lopizzo. The police denied this. To refute the imputation of the defense, the state showed that the bullet which killed the woman was of different caliber than the official police arm of the Lawrence force. The trial did not bring out strong evidence definitely connecting Caruso, charged as a principal, with the actual marksman. The most damaging testimony against him was that he stabbed Policeman Benoit, and an indictment for assault with intent to kill is pending against him. He claims an alibi; and it is to be noted that up to the time of his arrest he had made no effort to leave Massachusetts.

As evidence and proof of a propaganda of violence, the state introduced testimony concerning speeches made by Ettor and Giovannitti. The natural and intended consequence of these, the district attorney argued, was an organized attack upon the street cars to intimidate those going to work and the disturbance on the evening of January 29 when Anna Lopizzo lost her life.

Only one markedly inflammatory statement to the strikers was attributed to Giovannitti. Two detectives in the service of the Callahan agency declared that in a speech in Italian he told his listeners to sleep in the daytime and prowl around at night like wild animals. The witnesses admitted that they had destroyed their notes of the speech. One of the few other points which were seriously urged against him was his signature on a justly censured circular for which he and Ettor disclaimed responsibility.

Partly at least because Ettor's speeches were delivered in English, the brunt of the evidence was directed at him. The doctrines of direct action held by leading exponents of the Industrial Workers of the World were read into the record, and Ettor's position in the Anarchist wing of the industrial unionists was made clear. Stress was placed upon statements quoted from him that Lawrence would be an unhappy city and that the strikers would keep the gun shops busy. By the first of these, according to the defense, Ettor referred to an impending strike of the power-house employees which would have left Lawrence in darkness and without streetcar service. He contended that the second statement was his way of protesting against the issuance of revolver permits to special policemen and mill representatives. If the strikers asked for the same privilege, he argued, their wholesale applications would show how dangerous it was to allow private individuals on either side to carry deadly weapons in a time of industrial conflict. The plain advocacies of violence to be found in St. John's history of the Industrial Workers of the World were declared by Ettor to be personal views of the author, with which he did not agree and along with the Lawrence committee had not acted. The defense produced ministers, whose veracity the prosecution admitted, who testified to the innocent intent of Ettor's speeches. And finally the judge's charge removed the possibility of death for Ettor and Giovannitti because it limited the jury to a verdict of murder in the second degree.[5]

The great stength of the defense, proved to be the testimony of these two men themselves. Exact in details, Ettor gave a wonderful exhibition of memory. Day by day he recalled not only the events that had taken place, but recited the words of his speeches.

"Do you remember", Mr. Attwill would say, "that in the police court I asked you so and so, and you replied so and so?"

"I do not", Ettor would counter. "I did say in substance what you have just read, but it was in answer to another and a subsequent question, not the one with which you seek to connect it."

In a long and weary cross examination Ettor was master.

When the trial was all but over, the two Italian labor leaders, moved by what proved to be a true inspiration, disregarded the advice of their counsel and made the most dramatic plea for freedom or for death that has been heard in Massachusetts within the memory of lawyers and veteran newspapermen. In an impassioned speech of mingled defiance, persuasion and appeal, Ettor protested against being tried for his social ideals. He put it:

"If you believe that we should not go out with our views, I only ask that you will place the responsibility full on us, and say to the world that Joseph J. Ettor and Arthur Giovannitti, because of their social ideals, became murderers and murdered one of their own sister strikers, and you will by your verdict say plainly that we should die for it...I neither offer apology nor excuse; I ask no favors, I ask for nothing but justice in this matter."

But after all, Ettor's speech was not the one which carried away the hearers and left a spell over the court room till the trial was finished. Speaking publicly for the first time in English, Arturo Giovannitti, slender, pale, trembling, courteous always rather than assertive, showed himself truly the poet who lives, as well as writes with ink on paper.[6] His final sentences choked up some of the reporters, busy as they were trying to take them down:

"And if it be that these hearts of ours must be stilled on the same death chair and by the same current of fire that has destroyed the life of the wife murderer and the patricide and parricide, then I say that tomorrow we shall

5. From a legal standpoint, the prosecution, despite able personal work by the district attorney, did not make out a strong, compelling case. A number of close observers believe that the defense could have safely rested when the prosecution did and omitted all evidence in rebuttal. Some of the state's best witnesses were shown to have been convicted of various offenses so that their testimony was discounted.

The defense, however, partly offset this advantage by clumsy handling of their case. Perhaps this was due to lack of perfect team work between the five attorneys representing the prisoners. Some of their witnesses played into the hands of the state. One of the attorneys for the labor leaders, largely through overwork and worry, failed to take full advantage of his opportunities.

6. Excerpts from the verse Giovannitti wrote in prison were published in The Survey for November 2.

pass into a greater judgment, that tomorrow we shall go from your presence into a presence where history shall give its last word to us."

"In twenty years of reporting I have never heard the equal of that speech", said a veteran reporter, at the end of the trial. And, as a final bit of contrast, the old court crier, stocky of build as Joe Ettor himself, but clear-skinned, sharp-nosed and with the look of the fifer in the familiar prints of "The Spirit of '76", opened toothless gums and droned the formula which has closed the sittings of the Massachusetts courts of even handed justice since the founding of the state:

"Hear ye; hear ye; all persons having anything to do before the honorable, the justices of the Superior Court now sitting in Salem, draw near and give your attention. Know all ye that the September term of the Superior Court is now adjourned without day. God save the commonwealth of Massachusetts."

# Index